Learning Like a Girl

Praise for *Learning Like a Girl*

"There's no place like a girls' school to recognize ways to tap talent, engage intellect, inspire best effort, [and] revel in intellectual risk taking. The result? Girls who are competent, capable, courageous, and compassionate. Meehan, in *Learning Like a Girl*, walks the reader through her adventure of transforming a vision into a reality—founding a girls' school. Throughout that journey, she is driven by her belief that girls deserve classrooms of their own with teachers mindful of their possibilities, who prize education, and encourage their multi-dimensional success. We agree! A girl-centered education is indeed a transformative experience!"

—MEG MILNE MOULTON and WHITNEY RANSOME,
Executive Directors, National Coalition of Girls' Schools

"This is a book by a leader about leadership. It tells a story born of conviction and practical need. *Learning Like a Girl* is descriptive, concrete, personal, and undergirded with knowledge derived from useful research. Diana Meehan's narrative of how she and other women defied great odds and fought annoying demons in their quest to build a new community of learning and leadership for girls offers everyone a lesson in the dynamic power of a dream combined with a plan."

—RUTH B. MANDEL, Board of Governors Professor of Politics and
Director, Eagleton Institute of Politics Rutgers—The State University of New
Jersey

"This book presents one of the most compelling cases I have ever seen made for single-sex schools, but it is much more than that. Deeply thoughtful, full of wry humor, this is a wondrously well written account of how three women succeeded against all odds in creating a school to match their dreams. Describing her predecessors, Meehan writes that 'they were essentially adventurers with a noble agenda; they were steadfast, stubborn, dogged, indefatigable, obdurate, and indomitable. . . .' And so, indeed, was she. There will, I predict, be few readers of this book who will not wish their own daughters had been lucky enough to go to The Archer School."

—MARC TUCKER, President,
National Center on Education and the Economy

Learning Like a Girl

EDUCATING OUR DAUGHTERS
IN SCHOOLS OF THEIR OWN

DIANA MEEHAN

 PUBLICAFFAIRS
New York

Published in the United States by PublicAffairs™, a member of the Perseus Books Group.

Printed in the United States of America.

Book Design by Timm Bryson

Library of Congress Cataloging-in-Publication Data
Meehan, Diana M., 1943–
Learning like a girl : educating our daughters in schools of their own / Diana Meehan. — 1st ed.
        p. cm.
Includes bibliographical references.
ISBN-13: 978-1-58648-410-1 (hardcover)
ISBN-10: 1-58648-410-9 (hardcover)
1. Girls' schools—United States. 2. Girls—Education—United States. 3. Educational equalization—United States. I. Title.
LB3067.4.M434 2007
371.8220973—dc22

        2007002176

First Edition

10 9 8 7 6 5 4 3 2 1

For Gary, for our daughters and
for all daughters
and in memory of
Brenda Elizabeth McGourty Meehan
6/9/1919–9/6/1999

Contents

Note from a Dad

The creation of a school must be the same as the birth of a city-state, where human beings share common necessities—like shelter and water—at the same time each has individual needs—like prescription eyeglasses and relief from allergies. A school, particularly one made from scratch and meant to educate only girls, will need the familiar stuff like desks and restrooms. Much more than that, the school has to accept each girl as a quirky, one-of-a-kind human, then strive to transform her into the best of herself. Without that mission statement, all the school would be is desks and restrooms.

The city-state may start from random chaos and never recover. The school will have the same origins, but can somehow, perhaps miraculously, leapfrog the requirements of the brick-and-mortar needs, and, getting straight on into the nitty-gritty, turn a girl's high school years into a hair-raising adventure.

Diana Meehan, along with a team of allies that would give The Justice League of America a run for its money, did just that. She took that dream of an all-girls school and wrestled it through chaos that seemed, at times, insurmountable—juggling, fighting, begging, and negotiating all the way. And she succeeded.

The result is The Archer School for Girls, a place that lives up to the last line of its school song, sending their graduates out into a world where they will become "everything they can be."

From the perspective of a father of an Archer Grad, a single sex all girls' school may not be for every young woman. Just those who want to one day rule our city-state and the world.

Tom Hanks

Preface

Let me go back in time fifteen years ago to a turning point in our own lives, an incident that now seems almost trivial. It was at a screening of *The Rocketeer*; our daughters were eighteen and seven. It was a charity event, and we were in line to meet the lead, the young actor playing the Rocketeer, with what was apparently delightful allure for one of our party, our younger daughter.

Her sister and I stood with her as people waited to shake the Rocketeer's hand or congratulate him on his performance. Just before we got to him, we were startled to see her step slightly aside and flip her hair with her fingers, practicing a pouty smile.

Our eighteen-year-old, who a few years later would become a comedy writer, raised one eyebrow toward her sister and smiled ruefully as she turned to me. "Have a nice adolescence," she said.

I admit I panicked. This hair-flipping, pout-making, flirty-girl be-havior did *not* come from home. Home was heroes and gods of mythic Brooklyn (my husband's bedside stories) or heroes and goddesses of mythic Celts, Greeks, or some other ancient tribe (my contribution). This child and I enchanted ourselves with Inanna, Athena, Caileach, and Spider Woman; whispered wary tales of Pandora, Echo, and Deirdre of the Sorrows; and avoided the Furies and the cannibal kachinas.

And now this encounter with the Rocketeer. It seemed a portent she was opting for the wrong myth. Or singing the wrong siren song. And all of it too soon.

Does every parent look at his or her offspring and see painful possibilities emerging from everyday actions? Can the same child show a propensity to be Persephone, dancing around until she attracts the attention of some underlord who'll snatch her up and make her mother grieve, and also have in her Athena, the warrior-poet, the grey-eyed one who took guff from no one and had her own cities?

This daughter does. She wavers between extremes of Athena, commander in chief of the children of Santa Monica, and Persephone, too–cute coquette.

If you maddeningly have both characters in the selfsame child, how do you protect Persephone while she's dancing in the fields and encourage Athena to go ahead, take some risks, try to win some battles? What do girls need to thrive and prosper? What keeps them safe and helps them realize their potential to be great?

Every social scientist I've ever encountered argues it starts with family—the traditions, routines, guidelines, and rituals that provide context and meaning. In our family we had all of the above with a mixture of Irish-Jewish genes, Berkeley hippie sentiments, and Mexican and Italian recipes.

We urged playing team sports, honoring elders, and sharing Halloween candy, not necessarily in that order; TV watching was communal and clothing purchases, limited. We tried, we did, to do what parents can do; with three comics in this family of four, the dynamic was complicated but never boring.

Growing up, our older daughter had the strict parents firstborn often have: we sanctioned no TV other than shows with positive female role models (which at one point included only three protagonists, Nancy Drew, Wonder Woman, and the Bionic Woman, with urgent arguments made by that daughter on a weekly basis for the addition—this week only—of the Angels from *Charlie*). She also had a few piano lessons, American Youth Soccer Organization soccer games, and a single sex school.

Her sister, born eleven years later, has no girls' school; more distracted, permissive parents; and a more dangerously distracting, permissive society. She lives in what is virtually a different world than her sister did at her age. Everything we read says it's not a safer, sweeter place either.

Mary Pipher, a Nebraska therapist, wrote an important book, *Reviving Ophelia* (1994), arguing that even if we raised them to be dauntless and assertive, our daughters seem to be anxious and insecure "saplings in a hurricane." Two journalists, Peggy Orenstein in *School Girls* and Judy Mann in *The Difference* (1994), concluded, as Pipher had, that girls' adolescent "selves" were at risk in a culture that devalued them and undermined girls' abilities, achievements, and independence.

Nor was there any help from their schools. The social scientists, from Carol Gilligan challenging psychological theory about gender, to Myra and David Sadker observing our public schools and concluding that girls there were ignored and patronized, to researchers publishing findings in 1991, 1992, 1993, and 1996 that female students were being "shortchanged," all reported bad news for girls in the coeducational classroom.

A wide variety of social science studies seemed to make a strong argument for single sex schooling for girls, an option available in the late twentieth century to less than 9 percent of the population. Researchers for the U.S. Department of Education, as well as sociologists, psychologists, historians, and education policymakers, consistently concluded in one context or another:

Girls' schools are good for girls.

What's good about them is they are totally and exclusively dedicated to girls. The research about how girls learn urges us to find a place they can "own," which *only* occurs in single sex space; where their values, community, and connection are honored; and where their ways of knowing are respected and their hearts engaged.

In the best of these schools, girls make many of the rules. In all of them, girls play all the roles: girls are the clowns, the chemists, the classical scholars; girls play varsity sports (and they're not the Lady Eagles or the girls' team; they're *The Varsity*); play the leads in the drama productions; and hold all the leadership positions in every endeavor.

Free from the judgment of boys, girls are active, not reactive. They're not distracted, wondering, *What do the boys think of this?* They don't compete with each other for boys' favor. They remain little girls longer in those in-between years.

This kind of school provides an antidote to a female adolescent culture found to value cars, clothes, and boys, and it gives our daughters a little longer to be unadorned, plain ol' kids. Being spared a few years of the culture of consumption is a respite in which to develop talents, traits, relationships, understandings, and skills independent of *what's hot and what's not,* in other

words, a chance to evolve into the confident, caring, indepen-
dent-thinking members of society we'd like them to be.

Fortified with convictions about girls thriving in certain educational settings, prime among which are academic, innovative,
girl-valuing girls' schools, we set out to find a single sex school
that met our expectations. We were, at this point, two stay-at-
home writers, so the prospect of finding what we wanted in this
wide world was increased by what I thought of as geographic flex-
ibility. As it happened, however, there was resistance to reloca-
tion (from the one I hold closest to my heart), which meant we
went to Plan Two, which was to make the school we wanted.

This book is about the consequences of that decision: why we
made it, how we made it, what it means today. I wrote it not only
to share the journey but to encourage you to make your own
journey, in some way, to give our daughters, our biological and
spiritual descendents, the benefit of an educational environment
that is their own.

For us, starting a school would seem to be about who we wanted
to teach, what we wanted to teach, and where. Turns out, it isn't
that simple.

Our purpose was clear, sweet as a Girl Scout cookie: to educate girls: rich and poor and in-between, black and white and in-
between, ages eleven and eighteen and in-between. We
imagined a place where the best teachers could do their best
teaching and the girls would have the tools, the risks, the chances

to fail and to succeed—all they would need to become the leaders of their generation.

Mainly there were three of us who started this school: Vicky, Megan, and me. With the succor and life support from three husbands, especially mine. With help from our friends and interested bystanders. With luck. With money.

Innocently we thought the mission alone would carry the day. We expected the pure goodness of the dream (who could be against girls learning?) and our determination to see it realized would ensure success. We were ill-prepared for the breadth of the job, for the resentment and rage it would produce in the neighbors.

Founding a school turned out to be like the stages of becoming alcoholic. Initially it was fun. Then it became a series of late nights, long speeches, and arm-wrestling lawyers with false smiles who resembled the sad regulars in a neighborhood bar. It degenerated into crying in bathrobes in the middle of the night and eating vats of ice cream. Finally—if it turns out well—it will be about meetings and a mission and a relationship with a Higher Power, in this instance, First Republic Bank.

Like alcoholics, we weren't really prepared for the life we would lead. Vicky is a short story writer whose method of relaxation is reading Henry James. Megan is a documentary film producer who entertains herself by cooking the kinds of complicated dishes that require arcane tools and cream of tartar. I myself am a teacher.

We are parents—mothers of girls, five among us. We'd had personal experience in single sex institutions, high school or college, and like most alumnae of these schools, we cherished our time there. When challenged as threats to our community, we held fast to those memories.

None of us had been on a board of an independent school or started a business or been sued in court. We were not experts on children, although we all have them. We knew nothing of land use permits, employment law, or the city council.

We weren't totally dense. Vicky knew all that is currently known about Joan of Arc and spoke fluent Portuguese. Megan had interviewed the Unabomber. I myself in a modest way am good at research.

I'm addicted to social science research, especially studies which describe forty-four randomly chosen individuals agreeing to lose ten pounds by lunchtime or memorize the Social Security numbers of members of Congress. I like gender research — women and men and how we got that way. I know a theory which explains why a man would go to a baseball game, watch it, listen to the radio commentary on the way home, and then read about it in the newspaper the next day, as if he hadn't been in that very ballpark in person himself (Stephenson's Play Theory, for those who have wondered about this same phenomenon).

We knew things, the three of us, interesting things, but we knew little about schools.

We did not know, for example, that new schools are like magnets to the brave and the bold who seek new adventures but also attract the untried, the unfortunate, and the unstable, escaping unsavory pasts or unpleasant futures. New schools are models of chaos theory.

In the pages that follow is the story of founding a school, the protagonists, the parents, and the bit players, as well as the ogres under the bridge directing some of the fruitless, enervating battles that sapped our reserves and energies. Like a new country, we had financial insecurity, political opposition, betrayal, corruptions.

So, too, did the other young schools I visited—started after Archer but resembling us, inspired by similar aims, opposed by similar foes.

The Young Women's Leadership School, for example, a public institution in East Harlem, attracted the ire of the American Civil Liberties Union (ACLU) and the New York Chapter of the National Organization for Women (NOW), both objecting to the use of public funds for the benefit of girls only, even though they were exclusively poor and educationally disadvantaged. Public girls' schools in Chicago and Dallas, modeled after the East Harlem one, braced for similar battles, but first faced more immediate problems of providing places to teach. They were offered buildings without gyms or studios or even classrooms, where construction crews were unwilling to work overtime and unions wouldn't allow teachers to move chairs or hang banners from the ceiling.

Independent schools in Oakland, Atlanta, and Seattle encountered climates in their communities that ranged from cool to chilly: "You shouldn't be so activist," complained a prospective parent in Seattle. "We should be focused on boys," said a prospective donor in Oakland, alluding to a recent rush of boy-advocate books.

All of us had one additional obstacle: lack of resources, particularly caused by little money, big bills.

Against all odds, however, we continued to believe we were doing the right thing. Our mission was focused on girls: the social science research about female behavior, female values, female learning; what motivates girls to succeed; the importance of role models; ways of approaching technology. When we learned about the brain research that indicates males and females think differently, we were encouraged to incorporate it into the teaching methods. And as our understanding of the research and its applications to girls' education evolved, so too did our schools.

In "School in a (down-filled) Box" (Appendix A), you will discover ways and means to start a school of your own, and in "Mothers of Invention" (Appendix B), what sort of person has done that recently. In "Every Which Way but Here" (Appendix C) are resources for parents and activists who want to provide something of the all-girls' learning experience without giving up full-time jobs: programs in public schools, summer science camps, and Girls' Incorporated centers are among the options.

This is a journey I urge you to take, if you have daughters or nieces or granddaughters or students or girls in your neighborhood. We started thinking about this issue because we had daughters and we'd all read two books, *In a Different Voice* by Carol Gilligan and *Reviving Ophelia* by Mary Pipher, and we'd heard rumors of new research about girls' education. What makes us persevere is the girls themselves. So, too, will yours.

Although the story of our school and those of others included here are as true as memory allows, there are a few places where a name has been altered (two of Archer's heads, two students, and the Westside Alliance of Seminaries and Preparatory Schools). Pythia Lazarre is a composite. More detail can be found in Appendix D, Who Was Who.

Acknowledgments

Every teacher is inspired by her students and I'm grateful to those I've known at USC, UCLA, and Archer who've taught me that students will always surprise us and often surpass us. As they should.

I'm grateful, too, to those who read the manuscript early and made it better (but who are blameless in any errors, which are my own): Cailin (who helped with Appendix C), Shana and Scott Silveri, Marilyn Bergman, Kathy Bonk, Geoffrey Cowan, Arlene Hogan, Jeanne Forte Dube (agent provocateur), Heather Green (world-class assistant), Lisa Kaufman (editor nonpareil), and Gary Goldberg, whose love, humor, and jump shot are celebrated in these pages—but not nearly enough, he tells me.

I'm grateful to cofounders Vicky and Megan, to friends, godmothers, board members, and good-hearted people who supported Archer when she didn't have much of a chance. I'm grateful to those who went before me on the path and now are gone: Betty Friedan, Ann Richards, Lisa Goldberg, Brenda and Jack Meehan. To all of the above, your light shines like a beacon in my heart.

PART ONE

1

The Girl Pause

It's the early 1990s, I teach in UCLA's Communication Studies Program, and I know a little about the research on girls. Education isn't my field—media is—yet as a mother of daughters I've read Carol Gilligan's *In a Different Voice*. I've also seen some of the research that says girls and boys behave differently in the classroom.

In Gilligan's germinal, controversial book on moral development, she ascribes to women an ethic of care, empathy, and connection, wholly different values than those of achievement, autonomy, and independence typically esteemed by men. In subsequent work, Gilligan interviewed adolescent girls, exploring their attempts to hold on to relationship values in the face of a dominant (male) culture of autonomy and separation; she and other researchers working with her concluded that girls were silencing themselves in this environment, and as a result, they were "in danger of drowning or disappearing." Classroom research seems to corroborate this.

Adolescent girls in the classroom respond to their teachers with quiet compliance, whereas boys demand attention, commanding the floor for their ideas, comments, quips; in return, boys receive praise for participating, reinforcing their behavior. Communication scholar Deborah Tannen, for example, found that in the classroom and elsewhere males and females use language differently: that is, males talk, females listen.

Jean Bennett, a teacher I know from a local coed school, describes the boys in her class as dynamic, energetic, funny. "The girls," she says, "seem to be playing at school."

I offer two courses at UCLA, Political Communication and Mass Media and Society, with approximately ninety students in each, and I've seen in my own classroom what she describes. In a discussion of political symbols, Afghanistan arises as a topic and I say, "Uh, the capital is?" A male student in a middle row waves his arm actively, and I nod to him. With perfect timing he offers, "Denver?!!" and the class laughs. It happens again and again: the male students are pitching, coaxing, laughing, joking; the female students are largely quiet, polite, surprising me with top scores on the first test of the material.

Among educators this caution, this courtesy will become known as *the pause*. If a teacher asks a question, a boy blurts out an answer; a girl pauses, asking herself, *Do I know this?* Meanwhile the class has moved on.

The girl pause is not, I think, a bad thing in itself. If it means courtesy, not cowardice. If it springs from respect for others, not fear of risk, what one girl described in an email as the "sweaty-palm anxiety of getting figuratively smacked (if wrong)."

A friend describes the difference between eleven-year-olds at the class computers: "Boys jump in, start punching buttons, off on their searches like knights on a quest; girls sit before the screen as if before a Buddha and gather their energy before ever placing fingers on any part of the machine." She adds later, "There really is such a thing as *the girl pause*."

(Of course, my husband maintains something else. He says the girl pause is how long it takes me to get to the door, after I've said

I'm ready. That's because *ready* means I've decided what purse I'm taking and remembered where I left my lip gloss. It apparently means something different to guys.)

Girls have the advantage in grade school. From ages five to ten they have better social acumen, fine motor skills, and verbal ability. They are curious and engaged, exactly the sort of student that teachers like to teach.

Ask a nine-year-old girl how electricity works and she'll pause and think a moment. "Maybe the sun is attracted to . . . or fire is somehow captured. . . . Anyway, power gets in the wires and that's sort of where it starts."

It is always inventive. Offered with an optimistic doesn't-hurt-to-try shrug. Very different from the same girl at thirteen.

"I don't know."

"What do you think happens?"

"I don't know."

In the few years since this girl was curious and engaged, society intervened: in the classroom, where girls' questions were dismissed quickly so the teacher could engage the more active boys; outside the classroom, where peer pressure in middle school and high school worked to counter the impulse to be smart; and the media marketplace, where the message was to be cute and sexy, specifically by purchasing products. Because she's unaware that creative hypotheses, like she'd offered at age nine, are the basis of much of human knowledge, she just repeats, "I don't know."

To become the engineer who explains electricity or the surgeon or the scientist who uses it, she needs to be encouraged, challenged, directed to explore. She needs at the very least to be *heard* in the classroom, even if she pauses to collect her thoughts. Not likely to happen in the coed schools I read about in the Research.

THE RESEARCH

The Research is a fat body of studies which by 1994 concluded that in school boys are taught to be leaders, champions, and risk takers, but girls are taught to behave. I am severely impressed by these studies. One educator puts it this way: "Boys learn competence in school and girls lose it."

David and Myra Sadker, after looking at two decades' worth of research, concluded that in the coeducational classroom, girls got less attention, less encouragement to speak out, and fewer opportunities to achieve. I learned about their research before it was published when they came (coincidentally, to Westlake School, which was about to go coed) to talk to parents about their work. Their conclusions that coed schools were essentially hostile environs for girls' learning were indicated by the title of their book: *Failing at Fairness: How America's Schools Cheat Girls*.

How Schools Shortchange Girls was the title of another review commissioned by the American Association of University Women of more than 1,300 studies about education and female students. "We needed a comprehensive understanding of the educational experiences of America's girls and boys," explained AAUW president Alice Ann Leidel in March 1995. The AAUW concluded, like the Sadkers, that coed schools had a bias against girls and that the bias was widespread and damaging to their achievement and development as capable beings.

Our own capable being, our ten-year-old daughter, has not, in fact, been diminished by her coeducational experience. She has been in a FeelingCaring elementary school where everybody is unique, where there are no grades, only reports of how special she is, which evidently she has happily internalized. Moreover, on the first standardized test of her life, she scores in the highest echelons, and it is that, as much as anything, that inspires our search for a secondary school that won't extinguish her spark.

Gilligan has warned that girls are "confident at 11, confused at 16" and a school that understands and fights against the forces that cause that, in other words, a single sex school, might be the best chance for the confident eleven-year-old to realize her potential.

Books about girls being cheated of fair treatment in coed schools will be followed by books that argue that boys and boyhood are neglected, misunderstood, and "feminized" in the classroom and that boys have shorter attention spans and listen less acutely. Elementary school lessons favor girls, they will tell us.

Two books, *Raising Cain*, by therapists Dan Kindlon and Michael Thompson, and William Pollack's *Real Boys*, discuss the difficulties that active, impulsive young males have in elementary programs more suited to the developmental stages of girls. Boys are shown to have a reluctance to read, resulting in lower reading rates and lower literacy achievement for boys than for girls, lowering test scores overall and raising boys' suspension, expulsion, and dropout rates. There is new concern that coed schools are neglecting their students' needs, this time, boys' needs.

Choosing among coed schools which damp down the lights of their female students or lose their male students is like selecting chores in my childhood from the list my mother left on the refrigerator; it's not awful, but it's unappealing. Why isn't there something wonderful on the list that I want to do first? Some excellent choice?

Girls learn differently from boys. Not only do they hesitate before offering an answer, to ask, *Do I really know this?* but they take

turns in discussions, letting others speak. They have different motivations for striving.

One educator, Arlene Hogan, said girls hate to dissect frogs
(not startling, this), but if you tell them a dissected frog reassem-
bled in the right sequence in the right amount of time would
live, you'd see motivated girls. I suspect Hogan exaggerates, but
the example emphasizes the importance that empathy has for
girls, not only as a motivation to learn but even in shaping identity, in the stage of development where girls define themselves as
being wholly able to experience the vulnerability of another.

Girls in the pre-adolescent and adolescent years perceive the
world as interconnected, intertwined, and interdependent; they
learn in context (sometimes called *connected learning*), that is,
when subjects are integrated into and based on real world issues.
For example, some girls in a Chicago single sex school succeeded in combining scientific technique, chemistry, history,
and mathematics for the River Project, determining pollution
levels in a nearby body of water. Girls tend to connect feelings
and ideas, authenticating with their own experience what they
learn in the classroom.

Girls' social world is different from that of boys. Their development is different. Their sense of justice — not to mention their
sense of color — different. And competition is a wholly different
concept than it is for boys.

This is no surprise to my husband, the father of two girls. He
grew up in Brooklyn, where lunch money was a contact sport,
and fast wits and quick reflexes were required to protect food,
even at the family table. Now at fifty, he plays full-court basketball with twenty-two-year-olds, finessing them with something
called give-and-go.

I played every sport the boys played when I was young and
team sports in the Catholic all-girls' schools I attended, though

In the pre-teen and adolescent years, girls strive to be autonomous, independent, and individual yet paradoxically value and require strong relational ties. In considering important moral issues, Gilligan found, boys typically rely on abstract rules applied impartially, whereas girls tend to focus on caring and connection with others. It is a point demonstrated by the classroom experience of a seventh-grade girls' schoolteacher, Karen Pavliscak.

She talks about exploring the theme of social pressure in *The Outsiders*, a book she was discussing with seventh graders: Write about a time in class when you knew the answer but were hesitant to raise your hand out of fear of criticism, she tells them. The faces of the girls show they are perplexed by this. Karen expands on the idea, encouraging students to freewrite about a time when they censored themselves out of embarrassment. They continue to stare blankly.

With some dramatic flourishes, their teacher challenges her students to share a story about a time when they were bullied into thinking with the crowd rather than voicing their own opinions. "To ignite their imagination," Karen says, she tells them one of her own painful sixth-grade memories. Suddenly hands shoot up with what she assumes will be stories of similar social injury. "Instead," she says, "the girls offered me their sympathy—and reasons why they would never go to a school that would allow students to feel that way."

my favorite activities in boarding school were the unsanctioned games—marbles, poker, and cigarette bingo. We both like to compete and, whenever decently possible, to win. Our daughters seemingly do not.

Our older daughter played AYSO soccer from ages six to ten with a bunch of other girls with Title IX's hot breath on their necks and team names like Our Little Ponies, the Pink Team, and the Daisies. Once a week they ran down a grassy field with their arms fluttering before them like they'd all just had their nails done. She liked it when they won but she also liked the satin shorts.

The younger one played soccer, volleyball, and basketball, all with the conviction that a real win was a tie because, as she put it, "That way no one is sad." Her dad retrieved her from one basketball game wherein he cautiously inquired about the outcome. "Oh, it was the best game, Dad," she reported. "The girl who was guarding me was *sooo* nice."

Our older daughter went to an all girls' school. I remember her leaning over a library table working on a school project with four other high school girls, all in their uniform skirts, arguing, laughing, sharing confidences. But in their senior year, their school merged with a boys' school, so those who came after, including her sister, didn't have what she did.

We began our school adventure looking for the right school that could help this younger child of ours thrive and prosper. We thought she'd need a school that could nourish certain cerebral qualities and at the same time help her be safe and be brave.

The reason her school matters so much to us goes back a generation or two to what is known in both families—Jewish and Irish—as *the Old World*. At what was probably fifteen years of age—if they'd kept records of poor Jewish girls in that time and place—Gary's grandmother came to America by herself. Jennie came from a tradition that honored scholarship, especially the study of the written word. Young as she was, she was very, very able. But her abilities focused on survival, first her own and then the fate of her nephews and nieces.

I didn't meet Jennie until after our first child was a toddler (maybe Gary was nervous about the meeting between a long-haired hippie in tie-dye with macramé fringe and his formidable grandmother; our daughter was a definite change-the-subject). Jennie of sharp mind and keen understanding presided over the retired, mostly Jewish inhabitants of West Palm Beach's Century Village, a place where eons of close connection had created clear mores, careful morals—standards transplanted in Florida as a sort of Switzerland of manners, with Jennie as Captain of the Swiss Guard, the authority on everything acceptable.

Jennie was wonderful, a force to the end of her one hundred years. I imagine if she'd ever been taught to read English, she'd have offered briefs before the World Court in the Hague, simultaneously frying a dozen *kreplach* for the *kinder*.

Twenty-five years after Jennie, at age eleven, my own mother, Brenda, came over on the boat from Europe with her sister, Rosemary. The two of them were children (Rosemary, the older, was only twelve), and they trundled in with thousands in caps and kerchiefs and babushkas, carrying their belongings in cloth bags. Tucked inside a piece of linen were pictures of the relatives they'd never see again.

One of whom was their grandfather, a gentle, unsuccessful farmer, a poet descended from a revered "hedgemaster," one of the almost mythic teachers of old Ireland. That side of the family looked down upon their in-laws, the McGourtys, who were *in trade*. The McGourtys' very prosperity was to the Sheerans a satisfying indictment of their worthiness to mix with poets and teachers.

Fleeing from poverty and persecution effectively ended the childhoods of Jennie, Rosemary, and Brenda. Even in the new country, there'd be no time for the luxuries of bound volumes, syllogisms, or algorithms; the merit scholarship to Queens College could not be accepted. There was only yearning for it, respect for those who taught, who worked in libraries, who studied.

We are the inheritors of their dreams. In us their wary hopefulness is transformed into a core belief, the Freedom of Education. The Fifth Freedom of the New World.

Thus we begin the pursuit of an education for the youngest Irish-Jewish child of the line, investing in it the dreams and sacrifices of our immediate ancestors. We promise ourselves to be daring, open to change, even open to *moving* (Gary's a little shaky on this part), if we find the right place. We're writers, we can write anywhere, I say to myself. I begin searching.

In addition to the Research, I soon find the Brain Research, sophisticated studies like those at the University of Pennsylvania by the Gurs, Rachel and Ruben, or those at Yale by Bennett and Sally Shaywitz, which show sex differences in the way brains work. Although nobody yet knows what the differences mean, there is evidence that male brains are compartmentalized, dividing tasks between the left and right hemispheres, which may be what allows males to focus closely but makes them less adept at visually sorting through a variety of objects. There's a reason men can't see the butter in the fridge when it's right in front of them — it's not their fault, it's how their brains work.

Females, according to this research, use both hemispheres to solve problems, which could conceivably explain why they typically connect feelings and ideas, integrate diverse subjects, and perceive things differently from males.

There are implications for schools here. *If a train leaves Chicago and another leaves Baltimore, both going sixty miles an hour, when will they crash?* "WAIT. WAIT!" say the girl mathematicians. "Are there families on these trains? Are there animals? Why can't we stop the trains?"

Girls who are sympathetic to hypothetical train travelers can become compassionate political leaders who see statistics as people, like Golda Meir who, as prime minister of Israel during the Six-Day War, asked to be told, awakened if necessary, the names and ages of every single casualty in the conflict.

A school that understands girls could channel their natural sympathies and abilities to integrate information, values, and ethics. The girl who likes satin shorts may be the historian who documents the economic significance of sweatshops or the poet who protests the absence of beauty in the asphalt emptiness of the strip malls and parking lots.

But where to find a school like this?

There is a girls' school in our town, a hundred and something years old, some distance from where we live. We visit, our daughter visits, but we all feel it is wrong for us. Classes are static, lecture-style; nothing seems to have changed in fifty years except the new swimming pool. Courses are not integrated; there is no River Project, no real world connections.

We begin looking for a school that has incorporated the research, where girls' voices are heard, their values respected. We imagine moving to a town with a good bookstore, and in an optimistic mood one day we picture also an Italian restaurant, a convivial dog park, and a movie theater where the soundtrack can be heard above the popcorn machine.

Once we begin this endeavor, we do it methodically, earnestly, like a school project that counts for most of the term's grade. It is neither casual nor frivolous, but more like the last leg of the journey to America made by the young Europeans who are our ancestors.

We're looking for a school that's innovative enough to be aware of the research, inclusive enough to embrace today's young Brendas, Rosemarys, and Jennies—and also Yolanda, Jamaica, and Nilusha—with a program which encourages girls to be the kind of people who wouldn't mind beating their boyfriends at tennis, especially if it were a charity tournament to benefit children of the Chumash Indians.

We're a couple of parents, Gary and I, who are short on experience here, short on knowing, long on hoping. Since I have wrangled a semi-professional excursion to the East Coast, that's where the search will begin. I'll report to my family on my return.

2

The Odyssey

I've seen the ideal school, in upstate New York, in the town of Troy, which bills itself, slightly deceptively, as the home of Uncle Sam. It was once the site of cotton mills and factories for shirts and nails and soap, but today is a decrepit remnant of itself, across the Hudson River from Albany, the state capital. Many of Troy's wood-frame and brick buildings are crumbling, boarded, and closed, running to rural ruin a few blocks in any direction from downtown.

Industry is gone, but the lights are still on in the institutions of learning: Rensselaer Polytechnic Institute, Russell Sage College, and the oldest girls' school in the country, Emma Willard. The Emma Willard School is dedicated exclusively to serving one audience, the 319 girls who live and learn at the gothic-style, stone-walled campus on Mount Ida above Troy.

Founded in Middlebury, Vermont, in 1814, the female seminary which became Emma Willard School is a pioneer in women's education. From the beginning it was meant to foster a love of learning and intellectual habits in young women, an alarming notion at the time. It was, even then, a laboratory for pedagogical research, testing its own methods as it tested its students. It has a legacy of leadership as well, in educating women to be teachers and urging them to found schools of their own. And it was one of the first boarding schools in the country to accept minority students.

Emma Willard herself was radical for her idea that it was right and just to place "the sexes more nearly on an equality" at a time when some educators were complaining that young women would become infertile, feverish, or insane if they studied geometry. Furthermore, she believed that the public, in the form of the political "rulers," should pay for the education of its young female offspring; she moved her school from Middlebury when the city of Troy granted a $4,000 donation to establish the school within the town limits.

Emma Willard School (EWS or Emma) today leads by teaching itself, as it continues to investigate and apply techniques for teaching girls. In the 1980s EWS invited Carol Gilligan, then at Harvard University, to test developmental psychology theories at the school in collaboration with Nona Lyons and EWS's assistant head, Trudy Hamner. As a consequence of the three-year study, Gilligan described early adolescence as a critical period for girls, in which *the tyranny of niceness* may lead them to lose their confidence—to shut down, shut up, and smile.

Gilligan's work, describing a uniquely female psychological development, led teachers at EWS and elsewhere to consider their teaching methods in light of the girls' self-inspired silences. Teachers explored techniques of collaboration, student-centered investigations, and participatory interaction. Emma teachers collaborated on a project with students and alumnae, researching EWS's own history, including famous alumnae Elizabeth Cady Stanton and Jane Fonda. They collaborated with the city of Troy on a suitable memorial to their founder in the downtown district.

EWS recently installed state-of-the-art chemistry, biology, and physics labs; the young man in glasses who conducts me and another visitor through the new science labs tells us EWS didn't even try to get one computer per student in the labs because "girls want to work in teams anyway—that's shown in the research."

What makes EWS ideal is that it is small, daring, and safe. What makes it less than ideal for us is two realities: it's in Troy (we don't want to live there, and we don't want our daughter to board), and it goes from ninth grade to twelfth grade. We are ready for seventh grade. Next autumn.

I tend not to be reflective, but I sense that I may be veering toward motherhood run amok, like one of those parents on the sidelines of AYSO soccer games with a stopwatch, a lawn chair, and a mini-cooler of organic lemonade for one particular player. Having begun this quest, I've become single-minded, snatching frequent flyer miles and small blocks of free time to rush off and investigate any reasonable single sex school with a promising website. On the other hand, I tell myself and others this is a time in our lives when we are fifty, financially able, and relatively free from contracts and commitments, so if we're ever going to do it, it's now, when we know what we need.

We need a place like Emma Willard, only with a middle school. Eventually, we narrow the contenders to three: Winsor in Boston, Westridge in Pasadena, and Castilleja in Palo Alto. All three have exemplary programs, beautiful historic buildings, acres of playing fields, and, happily, middle schools.

I tour Winsor with the admissions director, a genial and hardy woman who is, she says, soon to retire and move out West to raise antelope or maybe mustangs. We move from classroom to lab to the new multilevel exercise facility, following briskly in the steps of the students. For their part, they are not my concept of Boston.

The girls are exuberant, dashing down stairs or sprinting across the green to field hockey or lacrosse. Dressed in pants and sweatshirts, civilian clothes, they renounce custom and fashion. They look like they can out-run, out-think, and out-sing anyone else in the Boston-Cambridge area.

"They don't seem very proper," I observe.

The admissions director laughs. "They're not."

I like the vigor. They do thirteen team sports, including crew and squash, which are unknown where I come from, other than as words for something else, like a neck sweater or a vegetable. Girls here can learn physical and mental discipline (an old Winsor motto is *sound mind in a sound body*), practice team playing and competitive behavior.

> Competitive behavior is not natural to some girls. A friend of ours, a former semi-pro player, coached his daughter's middle school basketball team. At a critical moment in the game, he called a timeout, and because he didn't see the whiteboard nearby, he began sketching a play for the team on his hand. One of the girls looked at his palm and interrupted, "Coach! Coach. Your hands are so *dry*." Before he could stop her, she'd run to the sideline and grabbed some hand cream from her athletic bag. He almost quit coaching.

On the plane going home I think about Boston—about living here. Our older daughter went to college here and loved it. Whenever we visited, we talked about how tidy, how lovely, and how manageable it was as a city, especially with the map and directions provided by the college. It seemed staid and skirted though, tradition-bound. Winsor is anything but. The energy of everyone there is exhausting. I sleep on the plane back to California, missing everything but the peanuts.

When Gary and I attend, the open house at Westridge in Pasadena has a carnival atmosphere. One of the parents, a man in a brown corduroy suit, promotes the school's attractions like a barker at the county fair: "The ceramics program! Ever see anything like it? Science! How 'bout photography? Those pictures will amaze you."

More quiet and constrained is the Fortune Teller, a woman in a long skirt, dangly earrings, and a colorful organdy flower which sits on her shoulder like a parrot. She sidesteps over to us and looks into her glass of white wine. "You'll meet some really nice families here," she says. "And your daughter will get a first-rate education."

Our daughter, meanwhile, is touring the campus and sitting in on classes. In one a girl passes her a note that says, "I hope you come here." She reports this to us as evidence that the girls are nice. "Nice" to a ten-year-old girl is laden with meanings, among which is "smells like fresh fruit," "likes creatures whose outsides are furry, fluffy, or feathery," and "shares her vegan chips." Westridge might be the place for our own vegan. The final contender in the education trials remains to be seen.

A very young Latin teacher takes me around Castilleja, the school in Palo Alto. She is pregnant and glowing with the self-possession of the high school cheerleader who also happens to be captain of the debate team. With me she has a didactic, patient manner like Aristotle training a dog. She points to a mass of backpacks on the cement ground near the lockers.

"What does that tell you?" she asks me.

"That they're teenagers," I say confidently, assessing the familiar mess.

"That they trust each other," she corrects gently.

I hadn't thought of that, but, in fact, it isn't the sort of thing one would see in a big city school. Those backpacks could be professionally disassembled and redistributed in seconds by a halfway competent urban gang.

We move to a pair of classroom doors, each with a little window at eye level. "Quick," she says, pointing at each door, "glance in these two rooms and tell me what you think is being taught."

I look in the first room, where students with colored pens and rulers are huddled over a table which has a large sheet of white butcher paper on it. In the second room all are in motion, a pair of students talking and gesturing at one end of the room and a handful of students at the other corner engaging a girl standing on a chair. I think I recognize the subjects.

"Art and drama," I offer.

"Math and science," she says with satisfaction.

At my look of mild disbelief, she explains. "You're thinking of math and science the way *we* were taught." I love that *we* since she is twenty or thirty years younger than I am and obviously never copied anybody's algebra.

"Girls don't learn math and science that way, sitting in their seats with an expert lecturing or shooting questions at them." It sounds both passive and aggressive, if not passive-aggressive, but that is the way I'd been taught those subjects; in fact, most subjects.

"Girls learn best in groups helping each other," she says. Picturing the charming tableau this conjures, I smile, an expression which she evidently mistakes for pandering, for she quickly adds, "Don't think we don't get results. We win the science awards for this area every year, beating all the coed schools."

The Latin teacher and I return to the admissions office, where I talk with the director. She is a sympathetic person, more my own age, who takes me out to the bench by the grassy courtyard. There we watch the girls in their school skirts and white shirts going to their classrooms, arms around each other, heads together, the occasional PowerBook the only sign that this is not a group of Victorian-era female friends.

"This is an amazing place," I say. "It's the only place in society, that is, a girls' school is, that's dedicated entirely to girls." I feel my throat closing over the words.

"I know," she says, her own voice catching. "I feel lucky to work here." We sit quietly.

"I love the fact that the head of the school is a woman," I say after awhile.

"Yes, she's great," the director says. "But you know what?" She leans in toward me and lowers her voice to the level of a color commentator at a PGA tournament. "For years we had a male head, Jim McManus, and he was very, very good. A lot of what we have here, we owe to him."

"I know him," I say. I picture his face, a smiling, bearded Scottish face in what may have been the *New York Times*. It is only about three days later that I realize I saw his picture and his written welcome on the materials the school sent in the admissions packet. My mistake. Still, if Jim McManus has given the school this atmosphere of confident camaraderie, he is something. It is nothing that *Inside Sports* would cover, but it is something.

Castilleja, which, according to the third sentence on the web-site, was started primarily to send girls to Stanford, is situated in a tree-filled neighborhood of quaint houses called "Professorville." When my husband, daughter, and I visit a few weeks later, we stay at an inn with clapboard siding, pink wallpaper, and little packets of instant coffee on the table next to the sink. There is no milk, so we don't open the packets, but I stick them in the pocket of my blazer, just in case I need a lick of caffeine during the day.

On Sunday we go to the open house, in which we are stirred by the student panel, the language demonstrations, and the weather, which is as brilliant as the color scenes in *The Wizard of Oz*. We eat that night at an Italian restaurant and then walk the streets, trying the ice cream, checking out the bookstores (of which there were several, one of which was apparently dedicated to books on pterodactyls). *Casablanca* is playing at the movie house, a refurbished, vintage showplace. The next day our daughter visits classes.

She is now wearing a version of Castilleja's uniform, having changed from the frippery she'd planned to wear, a pink miniskirt, white tank top, and a pair of pony-print sandals with red plastic laces and tiny, graceful little heels. As she leaves in the company of two seventh-grade escorts, she already looks intellectually superior to the girl who'd arrived the day before.

"See you," she says gaily.

I'm impressed with her daring. Some girls like to risk, despite conventional wisdom to the contrary. Our older daughter took social risks, reaching out to the oddball kid, for example, but not physical ones. This one takes both — ready to leap off cliffs, literally and figuratively. But she's eleven years old. If she's still daring at fifteen, if she's intellectually daring, too, this will have been worth it.

Gary and I look at houses. Our realtor in Palo Alto is a slim, smartly suited version of Glinda the Good Witch—the same blonde good humor and kindly advice. At every improbable selection, which we probably can't afford anyway, I expect her to say, "There's no place like home," but she only smiles and looks at us fondly.

There's a narrow, stucco, three-story fortress in which the second floor is one large room, perhaps a soldier's dormitory. She takes us to a small, two-house compound in which one has the bedrooms and the second, littler one has the den, kitchen, and garden; they can be purchased separately or together. She wants us to see a converted stable which has velvet curtains and a very large room smelling of fresh paint and old horses.

We find a house, an actual house, in Professorville. It has a tiny paneled study with a fireplace, an elevator for some reason, one bedroom, and a huge attic with beds and books and a closet bathroom. The yard is overgrown with ivy and bamboo and much of it is occupied by a flimsy, dilapidated shack, but the place has a run-down charm that reminds me of a beloved old dog who eases himself down on his haunches and looks at you with affection.

I make two more trips to Palo Alto and the school in the next few weeks. I see the house again and the backyard shack, which I can now discern needs only a desk, a lamp, and a rag rug to become a "Room of One's Own." On the second visit I'm to tell Glinda the real estate agent that we will make a bid on the house the next day.

This is the culmination of ten generations of two sets of families longing to be enlightened, of two years of research about schoolchildren and theories of teaching, of twelve month's travel and too many packets of instant coffee, and it comes down to such simple things: this one fit right. They knew we were going to choose them. We knew they were going to accept this girl (well, the wizardry she does on standardized tests may have improved the odds). All that remained was to do it.

At breakfast back in L.A. my husband and I sit at an outdoor café and talk about the move, while he barricades his plate of *huevos blancos* with salt and pepper shakers, toothpick holder, and assorted silverware. He looks like a man with multiple sports injuries who has swallowed half a dozen Advil and is waiting for them to take effect.

"This move is everything we wanted." He says it like he's taking his punishment.

"You don't sound convincing," I tell him.

"Well, we have a whole life here in L.A. A neighborhood. Friends. Our kids have friends here. I wish we knew if it is the right thing to do."

Somewhere in the background a dog howls, a forlorn wail as if maybe his people have left for work. Or moved.

After a period of time in which Gary carefully replaces the spoons with the knives, as in a prisoner exchange, he says, "Pete and Ben are here." (These are friends who were at his Bar Mitzvah.)

By this time in our relationship, I know what my role is in this sort of situation: I'm to embody wifely sympathy and understanding. However, I am distracted from my duty by my own imminent loss of women friends, relationships nurtured over twenty-four years of confidences, sympathy, and snaring the phone numbers of really good takeout food.

"What can we do?" I ask miserably.

"What about creating a school here?" my husband suggests in what, I do believe, is honest ignorance. It is, after all, November. It's getting late to be creating schools for girls who will be seventh graders in ten months. Even if we knew how.

"Well, there were these two women, Vicky Shorr and Megan Callaway, who were trying to open a girls' school . . . but I think they're several years away from actually opening and *we* need a school by September." I look around at the other tables and diners at this outdoor café. I think about our mutual friends, about the restaurants with hot bread on the table, the libraries and bookstores, all the theaters with Lucas Sound. I feel a foolish indulgence for the Air and Science Museum and the four hundred and forty-nine Starbucks.

"I could contact them," I say.

I have no idea what I am saying. I am in my middle years (I'm shooting for a hundred and oh, six or seven); I am happy; I am, as we say in California, following my path. I have a lot to learn.

3

In Their Footsteps

Everyone has an opinion about what school should be because, after all, everyone went to school once. The strict school with nuns and knuckle rapping has its advocates. (I was in third grade before I realized a yardstick could be used to measure, not just to smack people like me who made faces while Sister was talking.)

The permissive school with exercises in Sharing Feelings and Caring About Mother Earth attracts as parents ex-hippies and granola crunchers. (My husband, who will admit to fitting in both of these categories, once complained to our older daughter, who was then in a FeelingCaring school, that her writing assignment was substandard. She replied, "If I feel good about myself, that's all that matters." To which he replied, "Actually, it's not.")

There are schools with names like Country Day and the Oaks which evoke a bucolic world in which students stay after class to clap the erasers and then ride home on their ponies. There are schools named Seminary which are not the least bit religious and others with names like Presentation and Stephen S. Wise, which are. There are schools in Texas which are just football and urinals.

Our family wants a girls' school, thereby eliminating football and, probably, urinals but including *what* I'm not sure. Even the experts don't agree on what makes a good school, as is evident at any conference of educators.

The schools we like all resemble Emma Willard—small, daring, and safe—small enough to be a community, daring in mission, and safe for divergent views and different cultures. Like Castilleja, they make learning look like boisterous fun, fine-tuned for female sensibilities. Like Westridge, they're "grounded in emerging research." There are opportunities for leadership even, as Winsor says, "in the global community."

If we go ahead with this, at least we're not the first people ever to start a girls' school. There have been plenty of others, though maybe not all that recently.

I'm thinking of Mary McLeod Bethune. In 1904 she started a school in Daytona Beach for five African American girls and her five-year-old son. She had a financial cushion of $1.50. Years ago when I first read that, I thought it was a typographical error. It wasn't.

In the beginning, Bethune's school was in a four-room cottage. They borrowed books and used wooden crates for seats and desks. "We burned logs," she wrote, "and used the chopped splinters as pencils, and mashed elderberries for ink."

Mary McLeod Bethune walked the road between two worlds, penury and wealth, black and white. A fiery speaker and a fierce fundraiser, she was a black woman appealing to wealthy Southern whites, mostly men, to support an institution to teach black girls whose parents were common laborers only a generation or so from slavery.

Her vision of school as the antidote to the mental slavery which resulted from the poverty and oppression of Southern blacks—a vision in constant jeopardy financially—was nevertheless realized eventually. Today her school is Bethune-Cookman College.

Bethune's predecessor was Emma Hart, who lived up in New England before it was quaint inns and outlet stores, when it was farms and churches and ideas. Like Mary's, Emma's family encouraged her intellectual pursuits, even geometry, algebra, and physical science, which at the time were considered outrageously beyond the abilities of the female brain.

At seventeen years of age Emma became a teacher, struggling with the problems of student restlessness and discipline with which all teachers deal. She married at twenty-one, her groom Dr. John Willard, a much older widower with children, one of whom attended (the all-male) Middlebury College. Helping her stepson with his homework made her realize how fine a thing it was to have a boy's brain instead of a girl's brain because in the early 1800s, boys got to study real subjects like mathematics and history, whereas for *their* intellectual stimulation, girls had only threading needles and making samplers.

As luck would have it, Emma's husband suffered what she called "financial difficulties," and she talked him into letting her open a girls' school in their house. She would teach math and sciences, too, even though there were those who objected that academic studies for girls was clearly against the divine Order of Things. Emma Willard got support for her school by couching what she wanted to do in sanctioned terms. She described the objective in educating females as "the perfection of their moral, intellectual and physical nature," because women were "the companions, not the satellites, of men."

Emma Hart Willard, a bit of a radical in some ways, was committed to economic diversity, financial aid, and physical exercise as educational policy. She had the idea that girls were female people with minds which could be developed (the revolutionary impact of this idea would be shown in Emma Willard's students, among whom were abolitionists and suffragists of some renown), but in 1814 she rarely said that out loud. She was too much a lady.

Teresa de Cepeda y Ahumada was something of a lady also, who didn't live in this country but in Castile, Spain, in the sixteenth century. Her version of a girls' school was a convent. She had to deal with poverty, politics—both civil and ecclesiastical—and, since the Inquisition was on, the possibility of being burned at the stake.

For a saint (she is known as Teresa of Avila, the one who was *not* the Little Flower who I used to think of as the Wimpy Teresa), she was pretty cool. She liked good food: "There is a time for penance," she is known to have observed, "and a time for partridge." Still she had her troubles when she started her convent.

There was one man, Jorge de Vielo, who was a neighbor and a water maintenance authority of some sort who complained that her convent of thirteen women would use up all of the water for the city of Avila. Although he lost that argument, the forces of Not In My Back Yard (NIMBY) won a round when he said the shadow of the convent's hermitage would fall on the reservoir and freeze the water. The hermitage, a rough stone building used for meditation, was removed.

Teresa had powerful enemies, like the highborn, high-handed, and licentious Princess of Eboli, but she also had influential friends. Like Mary and Emma, she courted rich women and cajoled important men, among the latter the king of Spain and the pope.

Teresa was constantly being challenged by status quo people who resented her for her passion, her power (especially annoying to some because she was a *converso*, a Catholic descended from Jews), and her visits from God. Apparently God spoke to her a lot and also danced with her, which she found unsettling, literally, and she finally asked Him to stop so she could get some work done. He did, and she did. Teresa went on to found forty-three convents and although the Inquisition kept a close eye on her, they just couldn't catch her out in anything really damning.

The saints and rebels who faced formidable enemies and outrageous obstacles yet succeeded in founding schools cause me to conclude they were on the cusp, straddling two worlds; they were essentially adventurers with a noble agenda; they were steadfast, stubborn, dogged, indefatigable, obdurate, and indomitable: in a word, persevering.

Moreover, I note that their radical idea—that women had brains as well as souls, and both needed saving—is hardly the stuff of revolution today. At least not in Brentwood.

Thinking further to Maybe and Perhaps, I call Vicky and Megan to meet for coffee.

We convene on a November afternoon for coffee at a pseudo-rustic marketplace called the Country Mart. It's a collection of shops and eateries around a patio where a lava-rock fire improbably burns, wrapped by a link fence and surrounded by small picnic tables. Here patrons carry their broiled chicken and fries, their enchiladas, or, in our case, coffee, and sit staring at the fire or, in our case, talk about starting a school for girls. We are unreasonably casual at that first meeting, perhaps masking anxiety about success.

"We've been able to attract a consultant from a school up north," says Vicky. "His name is Jim McManus."

"I know him," I say once again, although of course I still do not—I just keep thinking I do. "He's impressive. Castilleja's one of the best schools in the country."

And then I tell them of our parent odyssey in which we were bedazzled ("they had these fields of light and green that went on and on all the way to town"), bedazed ("some of their ceramics were as sturdy and graceful as llamas and some were whimsical, like pottery humor"), and bemused ("we sat there, mute, crying in the courtyard").

Every journey has a destination, if not a purpose, and there at the Country Mart, I pull the Buick into the garage. "What would be good," I say levelly, "would be to create a school with the energy of Winsor, the joyful enthusiasm of Westridge, the academic excellence of Castilleja, and the solidarity and leadership of Emma Willard School." I say this without irony.

"That would be good," says Megan, also without irony.

Megan, invariably, is calmly optimistic, like a fairy-tale hero. She's the Miller's Daughter, conducting her daily affairs, spinning straw into gold. A documentary filmmaker by profession, she can do on-camera interviews with mobsters and derelicts without flinching, translating their world into parable or protest. Like Vicky, who does her craft with fiction, she is a storyteller.

She and Vicky do not know each other well, as I'd first surmised, having met only a year ago at a Barbara Boxer fundraiser. Both had lived for some years out of the country (Britain and

Brazil), both had gone to women's colleges (Vassar and Wellesley), and both had read Carol Gilligan and others' research on girls' education. Both wanted to do something about it.

"We need a site, a head, and money by February," says Vicky eventually, "in order to open our doors by September the following year. This can be done. It actually must be done because I," a pause to consider this, "am not thrilled by a project that lasts into infinity."

"Is there any way," I ask, "*any* way we could open this September?"

"Hmm. This September."

Megan looks at me. "Do *you* think it can be done?"

"Well!" I say, smartly. "I think. Well, what *I* think is this. . . "

Suddenly I am burdened by images of myself being foolish. Unfortunately, there are many such images, going back years and years. Most involve male companions, but one, in third grade, involved a spelling bee and the word *supercilious* (or *supersellious*, as I had it).

"I know it's a lot of work," I say wanly. "It'll probably be difficult."

I've known Vicky by fax for several months now, and I've even been to her house. She is a Yankee, principled and resolute, but with a blaze of Latin passion acquired in her ten years in Brazil, the very person whom Wellesley would elect to represent it, if for some reason mothers of three were required to defend our beaches from alien invasion, for which enterprise she would arrive in a pearl-button cardigan, carrying congas and a quart of tequila. I figure she knows indomitable. Indefatigable, too. Supercilious, probably not.

Megan, with fine, straight, honey-colored hair and blue eyes, is half-Irish—like Vicky, like me. In Megan's case the other half is something unflappable and extremely capable. Despite a severe budget, she dresses with an imaginative flair that owes nothing to negligees or appliqués or product names. She can make a four-course dinner from scratch, and once you have tasted Megan's chocolate *pot au crème*, you want to sleep in her kitchen.

Megan has two daughters, both way too young for this school, so her work on its behalf will be highly optimistic and future-oriented, like dieting in December for an event in June. Vicky has two boys and one girl. The latter, like ours, will be starting seventh grade in September.

Megan says now, "You know, Eleanor Roosevelt wrote, 'The future belongs to those who believe in the beauty of their dreams.'" (Personally I think this is the Irish side speaking.)

I nod. After a bit, Vicky nods, more firmly. Megan joins us, and, like Hasidic devotees at prayer, we bob our heads and stare into the middle distance. More or less by omission we are agreed to open a school in September, ten months away.

4

Bad Fairy at the Christening

Everyone who promotes social change, even revolutionaries, find the life consists of periods of thoughtful reflection on matters grave and foolish, from purpose to policy and procedure, followed by meetings, and then even more meetings. We are lucky, Vicky, Megan, and I, to agree wholly on the mission. Our meetings are about what it means and how to accomplish it.

At one meeting, looking for ideas and energies, we gather women leaders of our community, the wise women—lawyers and poets, therapists and grandmothers, mostly nice and unfailingly assertive.

They arrive fluttering, expectant, like bridesmaids at the back of the church. They accept glasses of wine or cranberry juice or sparkling water and greet friends and introduce themselves to those they do not know. Some of them address the dogs, Dreamer and Chelsea.

We have, at that point, two dogs, although they manage to seem like more. Dreamer is supposedly a lab-shepherd mix, but that doesn't explain his feathery flanks or why he catches and eats bees. Chelsea is a purebred Keeshond whose primary interest is food meant for humans, with an avocation of collecting candy wrappers and barking at men.

As guests arrive, Dreamer gives me a tolerant look and disappears, but Chelsea hesitates between various seated humans who have plates of food. Most avoid the look in Chelsea's moist, dark eyes as they deftly settle into cushioned chairs and couches and begin to eat and talk.

"We need a school that helps girls prepare to be leaders of the next century," says Susan, an attorney.

"Young women need sports," says another. "Athletics makes 'em tough. Tells 'em nobody can mess with their bodies."

"The Internet. They can learn everything we used to get in the library."

Susan, near my age, has the elegance of good manners and excellent perfume and the moral authority of someone with a strong set of feminist politics. She speaks passionately about poor children having computers. "They also need a fund like a bank account which they can draw on for special expenses. When wealthier kids go to their parents for money for the prom dress or sleeping bag or the science project, the poor student, the less affluent can come to the, uh. . . "

"Sliver money."

"Sliver money?" There are confused looks. "Huh?!" Susan stops mid-sentence and looks at me. I meant to say *pocket money* or *slush fund* or *living wage* or *something I-don't-know*, but it came out *sliver money*. I look to Keven the poet for help, but there's no need.

"Right," says Susan, "sliver money."

Diane, a former teacher, puts in, "And everyone should wear uniforms so there are no $400 sweaters."

"The name should have 'girls' in it. We've lost that respectable word," argues the poet. "It refers to female children, so it's quite appropriate."

~~

"*Adelphi* means 'sister' in Greek," says a woman reaching for a pita pocket. "How about Adelphi School for Girls?"

"Maybe we can name it for a great woman," says Vicky. "Like Eleanor Roosevelt."

"I can get her granddaughter to come talk to us."

"I like Adelphi."

"Maybe we should name it for a rich woman."

"I heard Stephen S. Wise changed their name to the Michael Milken School."

"Maybe it can be named for a pioneer like Amelia Earhart or Marie Curie or Julia Morgan."

"Who's Julia Morgan?"

"An architect. First female one in California. She designed Hearst Castle."

"Now there's a site for a school."

There is a commotion at the door as a woman enters, virtually flinging open the door. Chelsea glances away from the food briefly. The woman is Pythia Lazarre.

I didn't invite her. Perhaps Vicky did. Or Megan. She stands just inside the front door and, glancing warily at Chelsea, nods to me and climbs the two steps to the living room.

I know who she is. She is the director of the Westside Affiliation of Seminaries and Preparatory Schools. We had heard their acronym was applicable in both membership and manner. (Someday long in the future when we have an actual school, we will want to be, and in fact will be, accredited by them. Pythia's formal letter acknowledging this will be framed in the Head's office. And in my heart.)

Pythia smiles grimly at the offer of a drink and extends an anorexic arm toward the salad. "Is that dressed?" Weakly, I acknowledge that it is. She takes a seat on the only straight-backed chair in the room, her posture a reproach to us all.

"What about a site?" Susan turns to Vicky and Megan.

"We don't have one yet," says Vicky. "We've all, separately it seems, been thinking of the Eastern Star." She describes the old age home a few miles away, situated on Sunset Blvd amid several acres.

"Eastern Star?" Pythia scoffs. "Every school in the city has tried to get Eastern Star. You won't get it."

Her manner betrays very little: there isn't enough skin around Pythia's eyes to make expressions, certainly no wrinkles, yet around her mouth is a network of lines from constantly pursing her lips—it's a small mouth that resembles a hen's ass. She is dressed in raw silk the color of gun metal. Her hair is coiled in braids on top of her head like a yellow crown, which she pats tenderly as she repeats her prediction.

"You'll never get it."

I don't know what perverse pleasure there is in being a realist. Supposedly realists are honest, as in brutally, but maybe they're just malevolent, like Pythia.

The bad thing about Pythia's attitude, however petty, is that it is persuasive. She has a certain credibility within the world of school people and their wranglers. If she decides our efforts are futile, it will be considerably harder to convince parents and potential teachers that they're not.

People in the room tend mightily to their drinks and their eggplant sandwiches, repositioning the lettuce or suppressing an errant piece of cheese. Chelsea watches them intently. Cravenly, Vicky and I say nothing.

Megan, normally reticent, breaks the disquiet. "Actually, we don't know where we'll go just yet. We might rent," she says reasonably. "If you know of anything or hear of some place we should look. . ."

"What about school colors?" asks Patti, an artist.

"You know," Megan says smiling, "at Vassar our colors were pink and grey. I suppose they changed that when they began admitting men."

"There's red," says a woman wearing a red suit, red shoes, and a red and blue scarf. She indicates herself modestly and people laugh.

"Orange is good."

"Yeah, it repels sharks," observes Margie. Her warm smile takes the sting out of it.

"Green is the color of the ERA," says a political advisor.

"It's Westridge's color," I add.

"And it means life."

"But purple," says Susan, "is the color of the suffragists. They wore white when they marched, and they had purple banners and sashes."

"How about purple and green?"

"It goes with *Adelphi*. It's got history and a kind of seriousness of purpose." I glance at the room covertly, gauging the determination of these women. They are godmothers, the type of activists who founded schools, libraries, clinics in small Western towns a century ago, sometimes while running boarding houses or fending off marauders with a collie mutt and a Winchester.

When people are leaving, Dreamer sits beside me at the door, wagging his tail at some. As Pythia rises to go, Dreamer avoids contact in the indirect way by which dogs save face. He goes to the window and looks out into the yard as if there were something out there that had captured his attention.

⁓

A few days later Vicky calls. "I don't think I like the name Adelphi," she says.

"We have to have a name by tomorrow," I remind her. "Susan has to do the copyrighting by then."

"This is harder than naming the children."

Vicky is the only person I know who'd refer to two teenagers and a ten-year-old boy as *the children* (which to me conjures an image of a girl in a long, smocked nightgown and two boys in pajamas and a top hat, à la *Peter Pan*). She favors old-fashioned expressions and the conviction that words should be strictly governed by rules of form and order.

Vicky—who retained her surname when she married—is good with words and names, even if her speech sometimes sounds like the writings of Edith Wharton or Graham Greene. Vicky herself writes very good short stories, taking scenes and characters from her years in Brazil (where she gave birth to the aforementioned children) and endowing her literate description with the spare delicacy of sharp observation.

"If you don't like *Adelphi*," I say then, "you have to come up with something else. By ten o'clock tomorrow."

"Or you will."

I awake at three a.m. The sprinklers are on, but there is no living sound, no dogs circling the rug, no birds chirping yet. There is a sudden, distinct memory from a seminar I'd taken years ago from a classical scholar who described an event several thousand years old: young girls sent into the woods to build their own shelters, forage for food, and study history, poetry, and dance. No one would harm them, for they were under the aegis of the goddess, She who had various titles, including the Protector of Girls, the Archer.

Vicky calls early that morning. "I think I have the name."

"Me, too," I say. "What do you think of the Archer School for Girls?"

"Yes, that's it. That's my name," says Vicky.

"What do you mean?"

"I got a vision at three in the morning."

"What?!"

"Well, not a vision really. I was awake," she amends. "Look, we could name the school for someone fictional—someone balanced between two worlds, an independent young woman. At three in the morning I woke up and suddenly thought of Isabel Archer, from Henry James's *Portrait of a Lady*."

I tell her about my three a.m. images. "What I like about this classical story," I say, "is that in the forest the girls weren't cloistered in a convent-type way; they were taught to be self-sufficient and strong. When their forest time was over, they rejoined society and assumed roles as justices, scribes, wives."

"Perfect. But we can't tell people how we got the name."

"No." *Too California.*

5

Headstrong Puppets

With Vicky riding shotgun, Jim McManus drives us forward. Although it doesn't always seem to be forward. And it doesn't always seem like driving. More like riding around on motorcycles trying to erect a tent in a windstorm.

At least Jim knows what the tent should look like when it's up. He has served nineteen years administering girls' schools—five as headmaster at Castilleja, my favorite California school—and before that he was trained as a geologist. The two things seem to ground him, like tai chi does for some.

We're paying him from a gift made by an anonymous donor, an excellent person who wanted to provide seed money. I picture this donor as *The Millionaire,* a character from a 1950s TV series; sometimes I fantasize about the seed being augmented by a windfall. We've also passed the hat among ourselves with less impressive results.

As a consultant, Jim is consistently cheerful and reliable, like the male friend in a 1940s comedy. The one who tells the female lead that her new dress is very nice, that everyone gets drunk once in a while, that someone else whom she can love will come along eventually.

Just now he is preparing to interview candidates for Head of School (all of whom are long shots), candidates for Admissions Director (of whom there is one), and responders to a newspaper ad for administrative assistant (of whom there are two wildly inappropriate applicants and one who when offered the job says she didn't think she could do it; she only applied because her therapist said it would be good for her to go on an interview). Jim says we should not worry, someone we can love will come along eventually.

Despite the dearth of appropriate people to run the school, we make a start by recruiting an Admissions Director, or part of an Admissions Director, in Ruth Jenson.

Ruth looks as if she should be wiping flour from her hands onto her apron and opening the screen door with a broad smile. She was the former admissions director at neighboring Crossroads School, where she had mothered several classes of applicants, clucking over poor test results and encouraging parents to confide their fears and foibles.

She is now working in Arizona at a school with 300 acres and a stable, but she accepts a part-time (soon to be full-time) job with us. I'm not sure why she does this, applies for our job; perhaps she misses sashimi and long sleeves. It is clearly a huge professional risk.

We have no hard evidence there will be anyone to admit. We are aware in an anecdotal way of a market: soccer moms and sixth-grade teachers and sincere companions of our daughters have encouraged us. We will do a needs assessment study to survey the field of possible admitants before we get too far along.

We have no site. We are searching for a temporary home in Pacific Palisades. Nothing is a perfect fit.

There is the bank building which has a score of empty offices and a tae kwon do facility in the basement. The building has a manager who never returns our calls. Years later we will learn that he doesn't care for the idea of a girls' school, so he simply ignores our messages.

There is the Methodist Church which has some classrooms and a gym. The minister and the receptionist, Joy, are very helpful, but the real decisions are made by a board of deacons or aldermen or something, and *they* are painstakingly methodical. We go back and forth with them, and at one point they inform us that Methodists have never really been in the business of private schools.

"What does this imply?" asks Vicky of me and Megan. "That we're profiteers? Is this intended as a slur against private schools, or schools in general?"

There is Vilma's space. Vilma is the octogenarian dance teacher who reportedly taught Shirley MacLaine and is Buddy Ebsen's sister. In her office there is a picture of her and Buddy dancing as children; he looks like he's playing a game, and she appears to be counting toes on her right foot and multiplying the number by a figure with decimals in it.

Vilma is not offering her studio but the rooms above it, which are currently used for a specialty boutique selling painted pillows, woolen potholders, and a collection of wooden dolls with troll features and glued-on human hair. It's a little creepy.

If she decides to rent her rooms, which is appearing to be uncertain, they have the advantage of being two blocks from the Methodists' gym and two blocks from the library and the park. Unfortunately Vilma, too, is not really in the business of private schools. She is bankrupt, our lawyer discovers, and besieged by creditors trying to get some revenge or revenue to cover her debts.

We have no Head of School. We have courted a local educator sympathetic to our cause, who is, as we ourselves point out to her, respected and applauded in a school with its own site, not to mention its own books, teachers, and students. She sincerely and sweetly turns us down.

We don't get to interview our second head candidate, but Vicky has talked to her on the phone. She is supposed to fly in. Meetings have been scheduled with Jim and David Higgins, our lawyer, and the three of us. Then we get a call that a crisis has arisen in her school—a teacher caught with his pants down, so to speak—and she cannot leave just then. We never actually hear from her again.

The insubstantiality of this venture is difficult for Jim, I believe.

Jim McManus is a prudent man. This is confirmed by his wardrobe, which is invariably khaki trousers, Oxford shirt, and Irish tweed jacket with the narrow shoulders popular in the 1960s, and before that in the 1940s, and, I think,1920s. He wears this outfit irrespective of the temperature, which is often warm, as if clothes were meant to be all-terrain, all-weather garments in which one can climb Everest in the manner of Sir Edmund Hillary or take tea, also in the manner of Sir Edmund Hillary.

Our Sir Edmund is to advise, counsel, interview, administer, and act as business manager until we fill those positions with school personnel. He is called in this capacity "consulting head"; it sounds vaguely like one of those dashboard dolls bobbing in front of the driver on a Ford Fairlane, but it is really the conscience of the campaign. He is Jiminy Cricket to three headstrong puppets.

Jim is methodical and naturally cautious, a full stop away from our bright optimism. He is bemused by our reckless acceleration.

Once after several interviews, a potential head candidate suggests to him that the right thing to do is to build the board, interview educators, accrue assets, and open in eighteen months. To which Jim replies ruefully, "This car has no reverse."

My family is gathering for Thanksgiving in Vermont this year. It's our tradition that everyone, even children, makes a dish: roast turkey, my brother's mashed potatoes, our daughter's homemade cranberry relish, Gary's sweet potato pie (all of which are actually my mom's recipes, but never mind). Over the pies, apple and chocolate cream (by my other brother, but also my mother's recipe), I tell my family about the school.

My brothers, younger by six and eleven years, tell stories of their own and experiences they had when I was already gone from home, to boarding school and college.

My younger brother, Tom, talks about his school, which opened in his sophomore year and gave him three sociable years of high school and a pretty good education. He says the only disadvantage to a new school is the size. There were no schools in their league they could beat in sports, and dating among classmates seemed a little like marrying cousins.

This recalls something comedian Mary Sue Terry said about the town where she was raised, which "was so small that our school taught Driver's Ed and Sex Ed in the same car."

Then Terry, my middle brother, talks about a teacher he'd had twenty years before. He smiles slightly as he begins to talk quietly about this woman who sat with him day after day, ignoring the pile of essays she had to correct, guiding him through the maze of early adolescence. He taps his finger several times on his chest as if to say the problem was inside there, not in the head.

"We were dealing with subjects, you know, the Greeks and the Peloponnesian wars, but the subtext was my life," he remembers.

His teacher lived in nearby Boulder Creek, a little mountain town a few winding miles from the school. There is camaraderie and a connection to the elements there like a fishing village has to the sea. Every few years a forest fire threatens the town and the mountains around it, and people come running from the coffee shop and gas station, pulling on their jackets, to go fight the fire.

Terry was three thousand miles away in Syracuse, New York, living the penurious life of a graduate student, when he learned his old teacher had died. He and his girlfriend had only one car and little money, but he felt he had to return to California for the funeral.

"I have to honor this woman who was a crucial influence at a certain time of my life," he told his girlfriend. "She was pretty old when she died, and I don't think she had any family left; probably no one will be at her funeral."

He made the trip, driving through the night or sleeping in the car, and arrived on the outskirts of the town of Boulder Creek on the morning of the funeral.

He should have been able to drive right to the church. It's a little town, after all, but the road was blocked with pickup trucks and cars. Leaving his car by the side of the road, my brother walked into town.

The church was filled to overflowing, with people standing outside, respectfully, quietly, an atmosphere of suppressed energy and goodwill, like there is after they've successfully fought a forest fire. Townspeople and former students, unknown to each other, had come from all directions, some from great distances, for the funeral of an old teacher.

We have our first recruit. Katie is our daughter's best friend. Like a lot of future writers, she is caught in a cocoon of intellect and impending adolescence. She reads Latin and Virginia Woolf. In the grade school production of *Hamlet*, she was a convincing Gertrude. She is almost twelve.

When I see her next, she comes over to the car and gives me an envelope addressed in her handwriting. "Thank you for starting a school," she writes in the note. "You are saving my life."

Why does someone choose the unknown? Is it the known—the tedium of the familiar—or the unknown—the allure of the adventure—that makes the risk appealing? In this case there are other options.

In our neighborhood is Brentwood School, visible on the corner of Sunset Boulevard and Barrington Place as a stucco & bronze sign. Down the winding driveway is the school, several big buildings and acres and acres of grass and parking lots leased from the Veterans Administration. Brentwood, once a male military school, now coed, looks bland and affluent, the kind of place where students have Treos and Blackberrys in their book bags, not a sin in itself, but not appealing to us or to Katie.

There is Harvard-Westlake (H-W), massive, brawny, the former single sex schools now merged into something like a multinational corporation, IBM or Walmart: fifteen hundred students, two campuses of rigorous enterprise, one in Bel Air, close to Katie's house. The entrance to the other, H-W's twenty-three acres on Coldwater Canyon, looks like an embassy gate. One expects Harvard-Westlake to be negotiating treaties and making a bid for the Olympics.

Then there is coed Crossroads, a hip, urban environs, famous for its music program and its lifestyles. Students call the Head of School "Roger" and the teachers "Audrey" and "Rob," like favorite characters in a soap opera. There is rich drama to be had here, but Katie dismissively refers to its middle school campus as "the alley." It is no longer right for her.

In adolescence kids explore new definitions of self, striving to determine who they are as unique entities, separate from their families, with talents and skills and particular needs. They may reject their parents' conceptions of them, at least for a time, adopting images of themselves reflected back from friends or from key adults outside the family. If they're in coed school, they'll typically find that those images evolve around physical attractiveness in the social world of adolescence.

Some forty years ago, a sociologist named James Coleman found that typical coeducational high schools created a climate that was, in his words, "a rather strong deterrent to academic achievement"; as a culture, it devalued intellectual pursuits in favor of quests to be popular. Girls were expected to be pretty and not too smart; boys were supposed to be athletic, sexually competitive, and not too smart.

The anti-intellectual atmosphere of coed secondary schools today appears to be little changed from what Coleman called "a cruel jungle of rating and dating." According to educational authority and St. John's University law professor Rosemary Salomone, "A school climate in which teens suggestively display their bodies, engage in sexually explicit talk and freely touch each other, [creates] an environment . . . [in which] girls feel uncomfortable and powerless." Increasingly, this cultural climate that fosters being sexy, cute, and dumb is spreading even to middle school.

As Peggy Orenstein demonstrates in *School Girls*, the middle school years are troublesome for girls' self-image:

> For a girl, the passage into adolescence is not just marked by menarche or a few new curves. It is marked

by a loss of confidence in herself and her abilities, especially in math and science. It is marked by a scathingly critical attitude toward her body and a blossoming sense of personal inadequacy.

But maybe not in girls' schools. Away from the distraction of trying to attract the other sex, girls are free to define themselves as other than objects of male sexual fantasy. Encouraged by a school climate that urges them to be intellectually curious and disciplined, they can be smart. In choosing a single sex school, they or their families have committed to a course that is countercultural, and the rarity of that choice reinforces their purpose.

Girls will come to our school for various reasons. Some, like Katie, want a school that's new, where they will be the oldest, they will set the standards. Others will come because their parents want to keep them close or want to penalize them for bad grades or bad behavior. In those first classes, the students I'll follow most closely are ones who've been cloistered or exiled, as well as those who, seeking their own excellence, chose it for themselves. All will thrive.

We too are committing our eleven-year-old daughter and ourselves to a new school, one that is still in the idea stage of development. For me the risk, the chance we take, is justified by the research and the vision we have.

This is the vision I see clearly: the girls, white and brown and black, laughing, debating, creating, running on the fields, testing rockets, making friendships so strong they will hold each other when they are old and one of them wins a prize in mathematics or gets cancer or becomes ambassador to Chile.

6

At the Board Meeting

About start-up schools, Jim McManus says, "Most don't get past the excitement-in-the-living-room stage." Although Archer's living room stage was only a month or so ago, we have at least progressed to the excitement in the coffee shop, the encounters in the grocery, and the conversations in the street.

Our enterprise has attracted a lot of interested bystanders, not all of them helpful: At the health food store a yoga teacher with a cup of wheatgrass juice in her hand and purple mat rolled under her arm advises me to get Feng Shui for our new school; I'm not sure if this is something we buy or if we channel it with the right mantra. The clerk at the bookstore asks us to investigate why girls are going into puberty earlier than in the past: "It might be pesticides," he suggests.

We and Jim McManus field inquiries from local teachers, custodians, and gardeners—all job-seekers. There are, Jim says, "people coming from all over." He doesn't say "from out of the woodwork," but he calls the movement "human traffic." The spurious activity is unsettling.

Jim would prefer to have us go more slowly, plan the program, establish the educational philosophy, determine what kind of student we want. It sounds prudent and cautious and wise. It's not the advice we want.

This is a dream in a hurry. Our mission seems so obvious to us we hardly stop to write it down. An all girls' school for all kinds of caring, courageous, capable girls who will soon be learning in ways they love and leading everybody else into the next century. Opening in September in time for thirty or so students (our two daughters and Katie and others) to attend sixth and seventh grades, building up to twelfth year by year.

Jim believes in what we are doing. He says he "stumbled into single sex education" when he got his first job at Mayfield, a Catholic girls' school; his experience there, the friendships he saw among the girls, and the research studies completely convinced him of the value of the all-girls' school. He supports the mission, but not the pace at which we are trying to achieve it.

In January Jim resigns. He is gracious about it, praising the idea and the positive response it generates. He agrees to continue advising us and cheering for us, just not as consulting head.

Afterward he will conclude ruefully, "It was moving faster than I felt was good." He decides to "get out of the way." This makes us sound like bumper car drivers at the boardwalk.

We should have been worried at this point. Vicky, Megan, and I had worked with Jim McManus and knew his worth. We knew he knew his school stuff and that his caution was not misplaced. We weren't overly concerned about his resignation because we didn't realize we should have been.

Vicky, Megan, and I are outsiders, what is known in L.A., in the trade papers, as *non-pros*, which calls up our amateur status in the school business. We are three mothers, three writers, non-natives. As writers, none of us had school as an item on our résumés. Moreover, Vicky and Megan had recently arrived from outside the country; I'd come from graduate school, which is almost the same thing.

Outsiders, according to scholar Carolyn Heilbrun, are excluded from the heart of power in society and culture, a condition that insulates them from certain social expectations and may actually give them "a source of energy, even a sense of destiny." I think it is true in our cases.

We were outsiders in two societies, Westside L.A., where we'd arrived relatively recently, and school, where we'd entered a marathon without our running shoes. We were fortunate in our friends, who cheered and watered us and sometimes ran alongside.

The first person I meet at the first board meeting I attend is Charles. Charles hosts the board meetings of our new school at his house, offering cheese and wine and bottled water. He will make tea if anyone has a sore throat. Charles is dark, tall, and courtly like the Don Excellency in a Zorro movie, who absorbs himself in adjusting the lace at his wrists while you're spilling wine on his tapestry couch.

As the first order of business, Vicky informs everyone that Jim McManus will no longer be consulting head.

"That hurts our credibility," David says quietly.

"I don't think so," Vicky counters. "He's still involved. He'll advise us and represent us in the school community."

David sits in his dark attorney suit in an overstuffed chair in Charles's living room and takes a thoughtful sip of the Perrier Charles has provided. He drinks slowly and deeply, as if he were storing it for some time in the future when he might find himself alone in the desert.

David has the memory of Westlake School and the merger. Being a lawyer, he would never refer to it as a forced merger, but he regarded it as such when it happened. The Harvard School for Boys had combined with Westlake School for Girls by decision of the two boards in a lightning flash vote that left Westlake parents stunned, splintered, and charred like the desolate landscape after a forest fire. David was one of the parents.

Charles was on the Westlake Board, although he'd voted against the merger, and it was he who had brought David on the board of the school they both hoped would replace the one that had disappeared. Charles, too, is a lawyer, versed in the points of law that cover accidents and insurance and people suing you for no obvious reason that you could have predicted. This last specialty of his will prove to be significant at a later date.

I recently visited Harvard-Westlake at the smaller Bel Air campus where our older daughter had gone, a place that had seemed perfectly pristine, if a little privileged. I toured the rose garden, formerly the scene of Westlake's spring ring ceremonies, now resembling a sacked village recently visited by marauding hordes bent on destruction and violent sport, which, I suppose, is fairly much what middle school youth is about.

Westlake alumnae, our daughter tells me, return H-W appeals for money with *Never!* and *When Hell Freezes* and other less salutary responses across the requests. Perhaps they're sensitive about the rose garden.

"Do we really want a man as Head of School?" asks Charles, perhaps recalling that the former head of the former Westlake School is a man.

He looks to the other two men on the board, who furrow their brows. They shake their heads. *We don't.*

"Of course, we can't discriminate," says David the attorney.

In the corner, a clean-cut, square-jawed, quiet presence, introduced as Scott, clears his throat and says nothing.

I remember reading a book that describes school trustees as "respectful tourists" visiting overseas, as invariably they are dealing with a foreign culture. The school culture, so different from that of business (or architecture or law) is based on assumptions, values, and ways of thinking that are as alien to board members as Maori war chants or Navajo bonnets.

The school culture is based on an educational mission that is ambiguous and (unlike the bottom line in business) largely immeasurable. There in Charles's living room we face a further complication: the alien culture we are respectfully visiting is a feminist society, for underneath our mission is an essentially feminist value—that girls should achieve their potential. Can this goal be accomplished if the chief is a man? These men, clearly feminists themselves (or else they're FBI undercover agents), don't seem to think so.

"Well, I'd take Jim McManus in a minute," I assert to myself as much as anyone. "He's outstanding."

"He's a great source of knowledge and wisdom," offers Vicky. "I also like very much his fundamentally mild approach to life."

"Didn't he just resign?" asks Megan rhetorically.

"Well, he never really considered himself a head candidate anyway," Vicky gestures dismissively. "His commute would have been too long."

To defend our progress, to argue our case, and, if at all possible, to recruit students, we decide to hold Open Houses at a room we rent from the Palisades library.

The enormity of the task of convincing parents to choose our school over all others is daunting. We are asking them to trust us, yet can offer no physical evidence—no site, no head, no

teacher—that they should. Moreover, we want their most valuable resource—their daughters. The Open Houses will have to
be extraordinary.

We picture two Open Houses, each with thirty or forty parents
clamoring for information and an assortment of scrubbed and ea-
ger girls, some of whom can become, in the fall, the much-desired
students. Ruth Jenson will speak if her plane from Arizona arrives
in time; so will Jim McManus. Charles will talk about why he's
come on the board. I am, according to the board, to deliver a
solemn presentation on the relevant research findings, followed
by an oratory designed to, once and for all, wrest parents of their
daughters.

Betsy, who is taking notes for the minutes, wonders about a
brochure (I was working on it) or a video (Megan was working on
it). Betsy is the one who keeps track of our expenses. If this were a
Mission Impossible team, her task would be Details; she'd be the
one who would secure blueprints of the enemy stronghold, note
the blood types of team members, and ensure that the getaway
van had gas and a good battery.

In our operation she'll do the same kinds of things for the Open
Houses: conduct reconnaissance on the room at the library, have
a sign made that says "The Archer School for Girls" in forest
green with a deep purple lettering, and provide the cookies.

Betsy gives the financial report, informing us that—other than
the gift marked as seed money to pay Jim—we have $1,277.02 in
our Wells Fargo account. That amount will be stretched thin between the items needed for the Open Houses and a possible
down payment for wherever we land a lease.

Understand: if we come into a windfall, we'll know what to do
with it. We have a budget. Or if we become seriously deficient,
we'll go to some people we know and beg. (I'll start doing that
pretty soon now to raise scholarship monies.) However, we don't

want to peak too early. So we engage in the territory in the middle: Check our budget. Pass the hat. Wait.

Scott's report is brief. His job here does not require words as much as patience, as it is he who deals with the various site commandos. Scott is an architect, and on more than one occasion he has claimed to be inept with words. When he does use them, he can be quite descriptive, as when later he admits to "pre-game jitters" about the Open House, which conjures up for him "the adolescent hot flashes of high school parties in my Long Island basement, wringing my hands, thinking, 'Will anyone come?'"

To address that very concern, we issue invitations to about three hundred families of girls, some names harvested from troop leaders of the Girl Scouts; some, I confess, from class lists of the schools our daughters attend, the lists that say *Do Not Copy!* on top. We also have our own girls, daughters of Vicky, David and me, and Gary. We'll dress them in grey skirts, grey kneesocks, and green sweatshirts with Archer's name on them (our otherwise compliant daughters are appalled at the knee socks, so we have to abandon that part). The idea is not to fool anybody but rather to set the stage with realistic characters of our drama.

We feel we've thought of everything. Is there really anything to fear?

Megan, philosophical, reminds us: Humiliation. Failure. Bankruptcy.

Megan writes to me: "You know, the lines of Robert Louis Stevenson have been floating around in my head—'It is the mark of a good action that it appears inevitable in retrospect.'"

In my readings I find a quote from Amelia Earhart, "How can I resist this shining adventure?" It will become something of a motto for us and will be put on stationery, bookmarks, t-shirts, anything. At the time it is stirring.

We are rebel commanders reading Julius Caesar and Che Guevara, red bandannas tied at our necks and bandoliers of bullets across our chests. We are preparing both to engage the enemy (that would be the status quo) and to win the hearts of the peasants. Thus we produce our manifestos, our slogans, our stories with the help of other revolutionary forces, our sister schools.

Emma Willard School in New York has a pamphlet entitled, "There's only one problem with a girls' school: It's just not The Real World." It is a cogent argument that for girls, the best preparation for the real world is an education in an institution where girls are central to the curriculum, girls' strengths are developed, and girls' leadership is a given. Emma Willard School is willing to let us use this beautifully written piece for our brochure.

We crib their words; fashion photographer Leslie Sungail donates her time to photograph students from Westridge School who could have been an ad for enlisting in the WACs in World War II—girls in uniform laughing, scientists studying microbes, athletes scoring victories. My friend Marcia designs the juxtaposition of pictures and text.

Meanwhile, Megan is producing the video. She and Vicky tape a girls' soccer game and the all girls' math class at Crossroads School.

With erudite commentary by Fran Scoble, Head of Westridge, three cameras, two light meters, a sound recorder, four klieg lights, an editing room, and the help of twenty-one people over twenty-nine days, we have a good five-minute video.

Emma Willard School in Troy and Westridge, the girls' school in Pasadena, are too far away to be our competitors, but it is kind and sisterly of their administrators to be helpful in so many ways. For Crossroads, close to us in spirit and proximity, we really are competition: our daughters and some of their friends attend the Lower School and are candidates for our first two classes. The support of their administrators, therefore, is altruistic, if not actually worthy of beatification. It feels like we are a small part of an embracing political movement.

Like the League of Women Voters, we are ready to host the candidates.

7

Shortbread Cookies

On a shiny Sunday in January we hold our first Open House. The day is expectant, with just enough wind to unfurl the flag and snap it now and then with a cracking sound. The breeze billows the skirts of the girls standing at the sidewalk corner, giving them something to do while they wait for the invited families to ask for directions to the library room where the events will occur.

This Palisades neighborhood is quiet, tranquil, and as clear as a drop of Evian water. The library parking lot is empty. *Most schools don't get past the excitement-in-the-living-room stage,* I think. *Nor will we, if no one comes today. Or if things do not go well.*

I can tell that board member Betsy and our admissions guru, Ruth Jenson, have been here for awhile, for our sign is hung on the patio wall. Inside are plates of shortbread cookies in the shape of A's and the coffee machine emitting steamy sighs in the corner. The chairs are placed in rows as if for a town hall meeting, and a man making clicking noises with his tongue is setting up the video screen. The room is ready, Vicky and Megan are conferring with Jim, so I walk. I want to practice my speech.

When I return there are clusters of people with Ruth or one of our board members, in parties facing each other, arms crossed over the chest or hands on hips like members of a folk-dancing troupe. I go to meet some of the girls.

There is Katie and another Katie, both with brown fringed hair and the kind of crooked smiles that imply a sardonic view of the world. There is Neilah, tall and quick, who is a natural comic with furniture props. There is Fofy (who in August goes by Phophe, in October by Phofie, and whose given name is Frances), and there is Lizzie with golden hair, shy, thoughtful.

Except for the stately Helen and Cailey, who is quiet and composed, the sixth-grade applicants, unlike the seventh, are noisy and boisterous. There are six or seven of them standing in a circle drinking punch and eating handfuls of cookies with the crumbs falling on the library floor. With their bumping each other and giggling, they are the merriest group in the room.

At this age girls are like young dogs, specifically labradors or golden retrievers, who remain puppies long after they look grown. They are affectionate and indiscriminate; they'll play with anyone. They track in mud and eat their food with gusto. At swimming pools or seaside resorts they throw themselves into the water and then come out and sit on people's laps.

Then suddenly the girls turn into Russian wolfhounds, sleek and disdainful. They run with their own, they're so fast no one else can keep up with them. They're aloof. Inexplicably in an unguarded moment, however, they'll leap onto the couch next to you and give you a happy kiss on your ear.

The girls settle, some on the floor in front, and we begin. The program we have planned is more formal than might be expected. It's as if the insubstantial offering and open risk we pose can be offset by deliberate intention. Accordingly we carefully construct the presentations, addressing what we believe to be the primary concerns and worries.

Ruth Jenson's welcome and Jim McManus's reassuring words about girls' schools, old or new, lead the presentations. The audience members give them both the rapt attention the Cirque du Soleil crowd offers the high wire team. These two are risking their professional lives by this act of derring-do, and the audience seems to know it.

Then I speak on the theme of what makes a good school. In the rich diversity of great thinkers and creators and leaders in every endeavor over time, there is one constant—each had a teacher, mentor, or guide who inspired her or him. Good schools are good teaching in one place. It's nice to have a swimming pool and tennis courts, but the essence of the thing is not the site. It's more basic. (It's love. I think this, but I don't say it.)

I talk about the hedgemasters of Ireland (who also had no site) who taught the classics in the bushes by the roadside using slate and chalk from the riverbanks for the lessons. It was against English law for the Irish to educate their children, and the penalties for the hedgemaster who was caught began with fines and imprisonment and ended with death.

My great-great-something grandfather had been a hedgemaster, and the injustice of their treatment makes my face hot as I speak of it. I talk about creating a place where the best teachers can do their best teaching. I don't specify what this means, but people nod. I talk about a place where the lessons are designed for girls, where the captains of the teams, the class officers, *and* the class clowns are girls. Where girls of every race and religion can thrive.

At the close I invite all the girls to go out to the patio with me. We want to do an exercise with them that will give them a sense of what it's like to be in an all girls environment. For those who've never been in one in camp or sports, the experience will be liberating, quite literally. They'll feel free to be strong, smart, goofy, sentimental, whatever they want. It'll be a bonding experience, too, like Outward Bound without the stress of living without hairdryers.

The girls gather around us as I give them the assignment. Betters, a young friend, is helping me. (Betters, named by our younger daughter years ago, came to work for us part-time and stayed twenty-one years.)

Betters and I divide the girls into two groups, each to do a story—a folktale, an allegory, or fairy tale—enacting all the parts from animals to objects as in an animated cartoon.

One group of mostly fifth-grade girls decides to do an Uncle Remus's tale with girls portraying Brer Fox, Brer Rabbit, the briar patch, and several sticky but still cuddly Tar Babies. The second group does *Cinderella* and a plump, effervescent African-American girl plays Cinderella like a vaudeville actor doing Desdemona. It is not subtle, but it is lively.

While we are gone, Charles and the video have been featured, both successfully. Charles talked about being a single parent rearing two girls by himself until they discovered the Westlake School. Providing guides and role models from the mostly female faculty, it had been a haven in their lives. Then it merged and was no longer what they needed. We heard later that Charles had been fiery and vehement about the importance of a girls' school for girls. Scott described him as "Cotton Mather with a taffeta twist."

The girls and I return during the question-and-answer period. A blonde-ringletted woman wearing a pale blue suit and a startling amount of cleavage asks Jim McManus what kind of program we'll be offering. Jim McManus answers her kindly, his eyes focused on her face.

Someone lobs a question to Charles. Someone else, I think one of the two reporters who are there, asks about finances. David takes that one.

We have prepared answers to most of the questions we get— our commitment to the school, our courses, even our competition.

We've done a study assessing the need for another independent school in our area: the existing schools turn away 50 to 75 percent of their applicants. Answer by answer, we are building a structure like the human pyramid created by a family of acrobats—although in our case most of the family are just learning the handholds, and the two on the bottom are stunting part-time.

A woman on the aisle looks to Vicky. "What about tuition? What about uniforms?"

Vicky's pause is imperceptible. "We will have both." She smiles at the woman, and the audience laughs.

Tuition is something we've finally agreed to set by the old standard: how much *can* we charge? We ask our friends who are parents at competing schools what they pay, we make a chart, and we go for one hundred dollars less than the most expensive. It's not scientific, but it gets us past a quagmire.

Afterward, a couple approach and say with warm sincerity how much they appreciate what we are doing. They introduce me to their daughter, who had given a credible performance as a mouse-who-becomes-a-steed in the patio production of *Cinderella*. Her father, a dapper, urbane gentleman with impeccable enunciation, is speaking. "We were very touched," he said, taking my hand in two of his, "by your emotion. It is a good thing to be passionate about children and education." I could hardly disagree. I try to squeeze his hand firmly, but my hand is in an awkward position between two of his so I squeeze the first joint of his left thumb and let that be my answer.

Others are shaking hands with others of us or collecting their things, nodding their heads as if agreeing with themselves. One woman who stood at the back of the room throughout the program comes up to me. "OK, I get it," she says, and she leaves.

At the doorway my husband is standing with a screenwriter he knows, who has come with his daughter, a potential seventh grader.

They have their heads up and the expression that guys get when they're happy being guys together. They could be talking about sports, but I'm thinking it's about our school. They're both fathers.

The second Open House sixteen days later is on a gray, windy evening with dark clouds that provoke images of rain. People in our town become agitated and discomposed when threatened with water dropping on them. They dress in elaborate protective gear or even winter woolens, so if it does rain they end up smelling like wet sheep.

We thought the threat of rain might keep people away, and we may have been right.

The room fills slowly, people congregating near the coffee and talking in the hushed voices of a library reading room. Betsy's shortbread A's smelling of hot sugar and something distinctly forbidden, perhaps the pounds of butter, are disappearing at a disturbing rate. I hover over a plate of them, trying to decide how many I can hide in my suit pockets.

A girl joins me at the cookie table. She hesitates between the chocolate chip and the shortbread. "Are these good?" She indicates the cream-colored A's. She has soft brown eyes and a face that could charm the birds out of trees, as my grandmother would say. She doesn't look like the kind of girl who'd take all of them.

I answer truthfully. "They're great."

"My name is Dominique." She shakes my hand formally before taking a napkin and placing two shortbread A's on it.

Adults take seats, some with girls beside them, and a group of girls sit on the floor, as before, following the lead of our own girls. Those in front nestle themselves, adjusting their skirts, moving close together to fit another girl in their midst. One is trying to braid another girl's hair.

The program develops much as last time, with Ruth leading off and Jim and I and then Charles carrying the baton for our portions of the event. I take the girls out to the patio as Charles is about to speak.

When I was a recreation leader during the summers of my college years, one of our favorite activities on rainy days was to have the kids make paper fashions and put on a show. The fashions are created with a pile of newspapers and clothespins. Again Betters and I divide the girls into groups, give them the premise, and tell them to choose from among themselves designers, models, and announcers and to create original uniforms for the school.

They are as fantastic as I could have imagined: they invent skirts, shorts, hats, boots, vests, rain ponchos (it is beginning to drizzle), even bathing suits. The show they put on is so inventive and so funny, I am sorry the other adults are not there to see it.

We rejoin the program inside as Scott, our architect, is answering questions about the site, or rather the *possible* site or sites, in what sounds like honest forthrightness. I stand in the aisle by the wall and catch Gary's eye as he gives me a look that says, *It's going well. Don't worry.* Then from my feet where some of the girls have settled comes a raised hand.

I nod my head toward her. It is Dominique. What she might ask, I have no idea.

"Will we have cubbies?"

It is artless and sincere and exactly the note on which to end.

"Yes," I say. And the picture of cubicles filled with books and lunches and barrettes and nail polish, jelly beans, balls, and stuffed bears comes into my mind.

"Yes, we will," I promise.

When we are cleaning up, Betsy gives me a sealed plastic bag filled with shortbread A's.

8

The Wholeness of It

In the weeks following the Open Houses, we have seventy-three applicants to interview. With a frisson of anticipation, Ruth and I meet the girls and their families in two adjoining rooms the size of a double-sided waffle iron in the bank building. We still believe we will eventually be renting more space here (when the building manager can get back to us).

In the meantime we are pursuing the Vilma option, which should be a simple rental agreement. But nothing is simple with Vilma.

To begin with, she doesn't own the dance studio building outright. We learn, late in negotiations, from Vilma's lawyer, Rocky Wayne Dorsey, Esquire, that there is vagueness about who owns what of the property. Furthermore, in the background are creditors who are talking about a Cram Down. I don't know what a Cram Down is, but I wouldn't want to see it done to anyone.

Our greatest difficulty, David complains, is getting Vilma and Rocky Wayne to do anything in a timely fashion.

Vilma cannot be hurried. Initially we were talking about leasing the rooms above her studio and all the outside grounds, which consist of a front patio, a small back patio, and a terraced wall of gnarled poinsettia plants. In subsequent conversations Vilma's monthly fee grows. We balk. Vilma doesn't communicate with us for the next thirty-eight days.

While Ruth Jenson interviews the girls one at a time in the inner office, the parents, usually mothers, wait in the outer room, which is furnished with a loveseat, a hardback chair, and a table of reading material we have chosen: books on girls and girls' education, brochures, and a *Los Angeles* magazine open to a very favorable article about us.

One day I enter the outer office, and there is a woman in brilliant colors sitting on the loveseat, a very fair, blonde, blue-eyed person with a face like a kewpie doll.

"I hope this is right," she says. Her voice is a match for her face, a high, thin sound like the voice of the Gloria Lamont character who couldn't make talkies in *Singing in the Rain.* She makes a helpless gesture with her hands.

I smile at her fluttering ineffectualness.

She says to the space above the coffee table, "My first husband used to beat me."

"Ohhhh."

"No, it's OK. I mean, it's not OK. But it's not your fault. It's her father." She points with her chin at the room behind her where the buzz and laughter is like a party in someone else's apartment. "I don't want that for her."

Chastened by her revelation, I realize I was deceived by the voice and the circumstances. I was in banter mode, and I'm finding myself in a heartfelt, emotional exchange. She wipes the corner of her lips with a pink acrylic nail.

"Well," she says after a bit, "I think a girls' school could help her. Be more, you know, strong."

"I think so, too," I tell her.

Other parents and daughters come through that office seeking strength, autonomy, self-respect, and, for some, a sense of ease, that *ahhh* of finding the right place. Outside the office the hammers and backup bells of cement mixers like the twittering of birds announce the season. The girls with their bright animation echo the season's exuberance.

I have the same sense of enthusiastic optimism, but I try to temper it with the caution that we don't want to make a mistake here. If we choose a girl who cannot succeed or a girl who is wholly unsuited for this inventive unknown, it will be bad for her and bad for us. But at this point, I can only see a girl as a pathbreaker, pioneer, pillar in a school designed with her in mind.

There is a reason we need a site, even if it's just a mismatched collection of rooms and a patio. There's a reason we aren't satisfied with just signing our kids up for the all girls math class at Crossroads, although we sincerely cheer them for offering one. The reason has to do with M. Elizabeth Tidball, whom I imagine our applicant families have never heard of and we don't even know. It is, however, Tidball who convinced us that, like individuals, schools, too, can have integrity.

One of the most referenced studies ever done in education is M. Elizabeth Tidball's 1973 report on successful women, comparing graduates from women's and coeducational colleges. Tidball found a decided advantage to single sex schooling at the postsecondary level. Advocates for girls' schools may applaud, but we can't really take results from women's colleges and substitute secondary schools that involve a different level of psychological and educational development. We may, however, learn something.

Tidball studied a random selection of women cited in *Who's Who*, investigating, among other things, what contributed to their successes. Many of her subjects, a disproportionate number in this rarefied group, had attended a women's college and attributed some advantage to that experience. Reviewing and updating her study in 1999 with three other researchers, Tidball called the advantage "the wholeness of the environment."

What's important, she determined, is the whole package: the mission statement, the role models (a critical mass of women throughout the institution), and the community where women feel they make a difference in what happens. Over time, Tidball researched connections between various measures of success and coed or women's college experience, consistently finding more merit in the single sex institutions.

Tidball has been criticized, supported, and validated. Her original work is now some thirty years old, yet there is merit to it still. Her point is that there is an integrity to a learning experience which values both who and what is taught. The concept of wholeness is psychologically and intellectually valid—and a common-sense reason to explain the academic success of girls' schools.

Girls' schools are in the business of educating girls, nothing less, nothing else. They create a world in which practices and policies devolve from that main purpose. The administrators, teachers, mentors, coaches, and counselors are typically female, thus role models. There is unity of purpose: girls and women are valued, their experiences validated, their values promoted.

Since Tidball's thesis—that in single sex schools, it is the wholeness of the culture, the sense of ownership, and the community that make it effective for girls—other researchers have added nuance: In girls' schools there is "validation for female norms and their consequences," concluded Rachel Belash in 1992. Girls display a "willingness to show affection, even passion, and exhibit a playfulness that encourages intellectual experimentation" in schools without boys, according to Carole Shmurak in a 1998 study.

Sociologist Cornelius Riordan at Providence College found high self-esteem, self-control, and marital happiness among graduates of women's colleges as opposed to coed college alumnae (1990). In a related study, he analyzed the long-term effects of single versus mixed sex Catholic secondary schooling, finding academic advantage to girls' schools. Riordan would argue in 2002 that single sex schools provide an academic culture that "cannot be produced in one or two classrooms within an otherwise coeducational school."

Wholeness begins, Tidball determined, with the mission statement. Ours is fancied up a little, but essentially the same: "Founded on the compelling research about how they learn, the Archer School educates girls—all kinds of girls—to become courageous, committed and capable young women of character to meet the challenges of the twenty-first century."

It is obvious, but nonetheless important, that all the efforts, all the attention of all involved, all the resources of the academic culture of our school will center on the girls who go there. Having such a consistent message integrated throughout all channels of the school increases its effectiveness. It's nice to have a classroom dedicated to girls' learning, but it's better to have a whole school for the purpose. Even if the school is a mismatched collection of rooms and a patio.

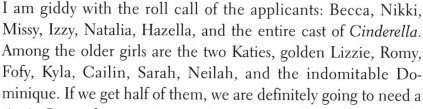

I am giddy with the roll call of the applicants: Becca, Nikki, Missy, Izzy, Natalia, Hazella, and the entire cast of *Cinderella*. Among the older girls are the two Katies, golden Lizzie, Romy, Fofy, Kyla, Cailin, Sarah, Neilah, and the indomitable Dominique. If we get half of them, we are definitely going to need a site in September.

Scott takes Vicky and me on a tour of the facilities at the Methodist Church. He shows us the Methodist gym, a low-ceilinged room with a little stage at one end and wire mesh over the windows and lights. Hmm. Maybe.

Upstairs facing the front are four rooms which smell of paper, erasers, moldy bread, corn chips, and a faint trace of rubber bands. One room used by the Methodist youth has a whiteboard with enigmatic messages: "Zug!" "No trips without slips." "God loves you. Zachariah doesn't."

The Methodists also have a lawyer, Everett Maguire, who assumes poses like a Victorian weight lifter; there is no grunting or sweating, and there is no movement.

Gabrielson Hall, by which imposing name the Methodists call their little gym, cannot be made available to us, according to Everett Maguire. The reverend, who is always very helpful, indicates he is quite willing to move his office downstairs so we can use that room and the youth group rooms for classroom space. Everett says that would be "difficult."

We ask for five parking places in the parking lot. Everett says no, as in none. We ask if we can use the front lounge, next to Gabrielson Hall, as a place for morning meetings for the girls. Everett reports the congregation uses it "heavily," and it would be "improper" to have us in there.

As with Vilma and Rocky Wayne, the rent for the Methodist facility fluctuates. Their team wants to figure a square footage estimate to compare with the fair market price we are offering. This may take awhile. "I think," says Vicky, "what they all really could use is a proper dose of salts."

Lucy is the first candidate to seriously consider the job of becoming head of the Archer School. Not that we aren't doing all the things we can think of to find candidates: Vicky is talking to headhunters, I am reviewing my rolodex of professional contacts who might be weary of university politics, Jim is considering potential candidates from among his cohorts.

"I wish we could get Arlene Hogan," Vicky says wistfully.

Arlene Hogan, revered as one of the 1991 founders of the National Coalition of Girls' Schools, is a sort of mythical being who runs a K-8 school in San Francisco. Vicky and I have seen her at a conference workshop up north, and she is magnificent—the kind of woman other women immediately like, who is obviously a good speaker, a writer, a leader, but who lets you know right away she is not a good cook or a serious housekeeper. We'd love to have her, but Arlene Hogan isn't available.

Nor are there many in the candidate pool. We get some figures from the California Association of Independent Schools (CAIS). There are 148 heads of secondary schools in our state, of whom 58 are female, of whom 15 are experienced (4 years or more), of whom 4 are heads of nonparochial schools. We know all four: they are helpful, thoughtful, supportive, and unavailable.

Lucy is more or less available. Jim says her board of trustees in Anaheim has not yet offered her a contract for renewal, that Catholic schools are sometimes slow with these things, and that she is technically free to accept another job. With a nervous laugh I haven't heard myself use since early dating, I ask if she'd be a good match for us.

"Oh, you'll have to meet," Jim equivocates, "to determine that."

We meet on a windy day in Pasadena at a restaurant of Lucy's choosing with tassels on the menus, cocktails, and custom-aged steaks, whatever they may be. Vicky and I are the vanguard of this venture—everyone else is working but waiting to hear our assessment of the candidate.

Vicky has a preview in the ladies room, a short, chubby blonde in heels and an acetate dress done with large bands of white and black across the middle. "I hope that wasn't our candidate," Vicky says when she slides back into the booth.

"Why? What's wrong with her?"

"Something's a little bit off."

We've been talking about a head of school for months now, and we may have hardened these images into some heroic figure part Mary Poppins, part Dwight Eisenhower: *Wanted, head of new school. Bonded. Experienced. Good refs. Versatility. Sense of humor. Upper body strength.*

Anyway, the person in the bathroom probably isn't even Lucy.

But, of course, she is. She has a soft voice and a sweet smile, and she brings us a sample of her writing. It is an address she gave a few years ago about the kind of girl her son liked to date (the kind who has a voice of her own) and what it is that develops such a girl. The piece has poetry and metaphor, and it is very good. For Vicky and for me, she's produced the perfect document.

We choose something from the tasseled menu. We laugh, tell a few stories. Lucy laughs with us.

When our younger daughter was a baby, she liked to be pushed in the stroller at a fast pace. Sometimes in the park my husband and I would even run with her as we sped on the pathways and she waved her arms gleefully. This is what it feels like we are doing with Lucy.

It is dangerous fun.

I sit at the desk with a pile of application forms, the dogs at my feet, Dreamer curled on the rug, Chelsea laid out on the vent in the floor. The school forms are pages of questions and answers: parents' names *Walter* and *Montana*. There are a few old hippies and ex-hippies in the present mix, so we have a few names like *Tofu* and *Gemini* and last names like *Starbird*. The forms ask about the students' health record, interests, talents, even fears.

Faced with a big pile of official papers, it's almost a guarantee that my mind wanders. After all, what *interests* does a ten-year-old have? Etymology? Indo-European origins? Japanese cuisine? Most of them like Harry Potter and Color Me Mine.

I think about these applicants, *children*, I correct myself. They're trusting us to find the means to educate them. And the people to lead the effort.

I confess to myself I'm a little concerned about Lucy. There is some relationship between leadership and good schools, the exact nature of which is unclear to me. But is Lucy a leader?

"I hope so." I've actually said this aloud, and Dreamer lifts his head from the floor, checks to see I'm OK, and puts his head down.

Although he is only a dog, Dreamer is curious, kind, observant, a self-starter, and always in a good mood — exactly what we want in an Archer student.

The Admissions Committee (which consists of Ruth and Vicky and me and sometimes Megan or Jim or Lucy) meets over several days to review the applications. We have seventy-three applicants, of whom we accept approximately two-thirds, of whom approximately two-thirds will accept us. We mail the acceptances on green-bordered certificates that Ruth makes on the computer. Ruth says there may be thirty-three students for our opening classes.

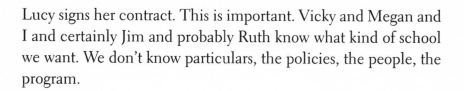

Lucy signs her contract. This is important. Vicky and Megan and I and certainly Jim and probably Ruth know what kind of school we want. We don't know particulars, the policies, the people, the program.

Lucy will attend to the particulars. Or so we believe. She'll hire teachers, staff (we picture one efficient secretary-receptionist-registrar). She'll order desks and books.

For what location? It is March 18, and Vilma is still vacillating, the Methodists are methodically dickering. David is aggravated. Scott, Vicky reports, is writing Everett the Esquire, "parrying a bit."

Finally, when spring has officially arrived and Southern California has gotten out its flip-flops and ultraviolet ray protection, we get a deal. Vilma's space will be classrooms, the Methodists' gym will be P.E., and there will be liberal use of the public library, the park, and, at least for the adults, founders, parents, and teachers, the Starbucks one block away.

I think we have a school.

9

Elite and Connected

Over the summer, we had some changes. We lost a candidate whose family moved to New York, but in a curious balancing of the universe, we gained another student, Ivy, whose family had just moved *from* New York. Ivy is, like our own children, half-Irish, half-Jewish, with a freckled nose, dark, soulful eyes, and a dazzling smile that competes with an idiosyncratic wardrobe; she owns rainbow leggings, heart sunglasses, and a genuine feather boa.

By contrast, Katie, our daughter's friend, has the look of a Nebraska farm girl in the 1950s — denim overalls, apple cheeks, blue eyes with a wry, knowing look around them. It is she, not her parents particularly, who wants Archer.

"The First Class," she says meditatively, "creating the standards."

She likes to lead. "It's new. I'm the oldest, and this feels like family. Like I'm a founder's daughter."

Katie is ready for an all girls school. "Boys — I totally feel that I won't miss males. I think that you can't function without guys — but they don't have to be in the classroom."

Later, this girl who will edit the newspaper and read beyond her years will reminisce about the early years, "Archer gave me the time to figure things out—the Virginia Woolf 'moment-of-being' idea. Not everything was great, but some things were great. Our class was a family."

The polite, sweet-faced girl of the *Will we have cubbies?* comment, small and gentle as a faun, Dominique is one of the seventh graders. She remembers her family was so anxious to attend Open House, they showed up a week early. Dominique was nervous, wanted us to want her, but worried that "I'd get in just because of being Mexican."

Both Dom's maternal grandparents are of Mexican origin. (Later, when she applies to colleges, her grandfather keeps asking, "Do they know about your Mexican background?")

Her mother's first language was Spanish, but Marguerite was not a traditional Chicana. The tiny town of Martinez, California, where all Marguerite's family lives, was too confining, so she left for Paris with $100 in her pocket. She studied, worked, and came home to marry a Jewish hippie from New York, Dominique's dad.

Dominique says after the library meeting, Archer was familiar, friendly, homey. It came to a choice between Archer and Brentwood Schools. "They had too many stairs," she says impishly.

She's ready to be in a pioneer class. Like her mother's experiences in Paris, it's a new adventure.

We want the faces of Archer to reflect the diversity of our town, not the Palisades neighborhood, which seems to be 99 percent white, but the racially, culturally, economically diverse town which surrounds it. We want to be elite but not exclusive.

In print publications like the local newspaper, when the name of a private school appears, it is generally preceded by the adjectives *elite* or *exclusive*. In the world of schools, however, there's an important distinction between being elite and being exclusive, although both involve admitting and omitting certain students.

Exclusivity (limiting the student families to certain social groups) is a means of discriminating on the basis of race, creed, and social and economic class. Until about forty years ago (1963 was a watershed year) private schools typically excluded Jews, blacks, Irish Americans, Italian Americans, and virtually everybody else who wasn't upper-class WASP. This policy has been discontinued in most schools today.

Elitism (limiting the student population to those with academic merit and ambition) is a means of discriminating on the basis of intellectual talent. Policies of elite institutions pursue qualified people versus what once was called "quality people." I've heard admissions directors explain to applicants' parents—sometimes wealthy parents—that it would not do a student any good to be accepted here if she cannot be successful here.

Both policies seek some individuals and exclude others from being part of the school, but one avoids non-WASPS and poor people, and the other tries to omit the frivolous, the fraudulent and the mentally feeble. In Arthur Powell's *Lessons from Privilege*, he describes social exclusivity, which most Americans find "very easy to dislike," versus cultural elitism, which is ignored or overlooked.

Cultural elitism rejects mediocrity in favor of a race-neutral meritocracy underscored by common values and characteristics, the most notable being commitment to academic pursuit. We are expecting students, their families, and the faculty to agree—formally in the Student Handbook or informally by unstated norms—to maintain high standards of scholarship and ethical behavior. Furthermore, we are expecting that cultural elitism and the bond of single sex schooling to unite girls from every culture and background into a community.

Maybe it's a reaction to our own lives: Vicky struggled to go to Wellesley; Megan got financial aid at Vassar and then Yale; I went to state schools first (attending what Pulitzer Prize writer Ron Suskind termed "the unremarkable Fresno State," where former Treasury Secretary Paul O'Neill also attended), but I couldn't have gone to graduate school at the University of Southern California, or anywhere else, without grants and fellowships and the $300 a month I earned as a graduate assistant. We lived on that.

Now we live on more, most especially the rewards of Gary's work in television and film, but we still remember when $300 a month and food stamps were the ticket to ride. And we know others who remember "unremarkable" beginnings—friends, neighbors, family, professional acquaintances, politicians, women, men—whom I ask to donate financial aid monies for poor and middle-class students.

To create an inclusive culture of students and teachers from diverse backgrounds seems ideologically egalitarian and consistent with our inchoate concept that a school can make the world a better place. We agree with another founder, the renowned Deborah Meier of New York's Central Park East Schools: "Good schools, like good societies and good families, celebrate and cherish diversity." With this conviction and by the generosity of virtually everyone I ask, we have a tableau of figures that looks a little like Disneyland's *It's a Small World*, minus the veils and wooden shoes.

It's a Small World has its own song, and by August, so do we. Accomplished, award-winning songwriters Alan and Marilyn Bergman wrote "Within the Walls of Archer," based on our mission statement and photos of our future students painting benches on Vilma's patio. The song is lyrical and emotional, and in the tradition of anthems everywhere it has a note only trained sopranos can reach.

The premier performance of our song is to be Opening Day. We know we need ritual to celebrate our first steps up a Mountain That Hasn't Been Climbed Before and to bind us together as a climbing team. Opening Day is it.

Before the ceremonies on the first day, I prep the new Archer students in the Common Room. The Common Room has green painted shelves for the books we hope will be donated, an old library table and chairs, and a ten-foot couch which had been custom-made for some Hollywood mogul's screening room, but when he divorced either his wife or his decorator, we got it.

In this room there are thirty-three students and a heady mix of smells: scents of ironed cotton, new shoes, hair products, and vanilla and fruit toiletries of the kind that come in pink heart-shaped bottles or in glass containers with little plastic peaches and strawberries on the lid.

The girls enter the Common Room in bunches, bumping each other, hurrying to flop on the floor or the couch, adjusting their socks, shirts, smoothing their hair, eyebrows. They make quick, excited noises to each other as they jostle for position like a chorus line before a big performance.

They are in their uniforms.

The uniforms look like bland golf wear or Weekend at the Gap, consisting of white polo shirts with the school name over the left breast, khaki skirt or pants, white socks, and closed-toe shoes. Once when a couple of seventh graders see an adult walking down a Palisades street in virtually the same outfit, one of them says, "Oooh, someone voluntarily wearing the uniform."

Today the uniforms are as clean and fresh as they will ever be. The whites are white and the colors bright just like a detergent commercial. The girls have hair to match, curls, cornrows, straight parts, a few ribbons. Mothers have taken time this morning in what an anthropologist told me is a ritual practiced all over the world—doing their children's hair in first-day fancy.

My own daughter sits on the floor among the others. She has a new, short haircut, some sticky substance on her lips that looks like pink honey, and a flush to her cheeks that I believe is natural. At home she drolly refers to Archer as the Mommy School, mocking it and, perversely, owning it. But today she is unable to summon such coolness; the patio below us is filling with teachers, parents, and friends, her own father and grandparents among them. Someone down there is testing a microphone, someone else tuning a piano.

I introduce myself to the girls and announce the schedule for Opening Day ceremonies. The girls draw lots to see who will read the relevant pieces: *What Our Name Means, Why We Wear Uniforms, Our Colors, Our First Tradition.* Each girl takes the index card with its brief speech typed on it as solemnly as if this, too, were ritual. One girl, Sarah, says, "I'm going to memorize it, OK?"

When the students appear downstairs on the patio and file into their seats, there is a murmured "ohhh" from the crowd. I glance at Vicky and Megan, who are in the row of seats behind the students. Vicky is in *mufti*, so she calls it, a dark-colored cardigan and skirt and gauzy yellow stockings. Additionally she is holding a white handkerchief. Megan is wearing a light-colored suit and a smile of tears.

The ceremonies begin with a welcome by a parent, a smart-looking executive whose daughter was the sassy Cinderella at open house. Then the four girls variously read or say their pieces before the audience. Sarah's memorization is flawless.

When I was a child, I used to memorize poetry to recite at the table after dinner. It was a throwback to the old country, where my mother said everyone had a party piece—a poem, a song, or a story—to be performed on demand. Though no one asks me for "Oh Captain, My Captain" anymore, I think it did give me confidence in my own ability. This confidence extended to areas my parents never intended, like punching Mary Carol in fourth grade and knocking out one of her baby teeth for saying I wasn't dainty.

Wearing an all-white suit and sunglasses, Lucy steps up on the little platform, and the girls present their classes. One by one they stand before her to have a sash of green and purple ribbon placed over their shoulders; then they file back to their seats. We haven't actually practiced this part, but most of these girls are able to call upon years of rehearsal as princesses, fairies, and brides, so they conduct themselves with regal nonchalance.

Then Lucy begins her address to the school. She keeps her eyes on the legal-sized papers she's brought up with her, and at first it seems that the microphone must be down. Her words slide together without pause, and her soft voice seems unable to enunciate one word from another.

I look at Vicky to see if I am imagining it. Vicky's dark eyebrows are wavy lines sliding toward each other on a furrowed brow. Her face is tilted and quizzical like a student trying to translate an alien tongue without success.

Mercifully, Lucy's speech is short. Most people in the audience still wear the benevolent, indulgent expressions with which they'd arrived. A few, including my father, stand in the aisles smiling and snapping pictures.

If no one seems to have heard Lucy's speech, everyone hears the close of ceremonies. While one of the teachers plays piano, his wife sings the school song. She clasps the mike in a prayerlike fold of her hands and sings like an angel, hitting the high note with sweet clarity. Katie's father, standing near me dressed in shorts and a Hawaiian shirt, brushes a tear from his eye. Megan and Vicky and most of their row weep openly.

I survey the scene and think, OK, we did this school thing. It's not rocket science, just hard work and coffee.

Actually, one of my brothers does rocket science. It doesn't seem *that* hard. He has this lab, and they wear sandals and sneakers and listen to rock music all day while they fool with dials and stuff—exactly as he did in high school.

This is not the other brother, the one who used to dive off the roof into the swimming pool, the one who blew up the bathroom with his chemistry set. Both of them were interesting to live with, especially in adolescence. The memory tells me this will be another experience altogether, this Girl-land.

Classes begin in tentative rigor. Our language teachers are stuck in transit from Europe awaiting visas, so we begin Latin lessons with Admissions Director Ruth Jenson, who studied it in high school, French with the cute boy just graduated from college who is Lucy's son, and Spanish with an administrator who looks vaguely Hispanic.

Some of the other teachers are shockingly inexperienced. Abe Feldman is a kindly, bespectacled engineer who didn't enjoy retirement as much as he thought he would, so he came to teach math. Tanya Reineman, the PE teacher, is understanding, compassionate, and not a bad coach, but her training is in therapy. Ms. Brooks, the English teacher, has never taught before now; she is, by looks anyway, twelve years old.

The diary entry for this phase would be *What They Didn't Know*, if it weren't for the one who fixes her pageboy hair in the morning and then allows it to find its own style the rest of the day, the one with charcoal smudges on her arms and splotches of color on her painting smock. Patti Meyers. Art teacher.

If she resembles Cinderella cleaning the ashes, she is actually one of Archer's godmothers, imaginative, unwavering in her support. "Thank you for this opportunity," she tells me often.

She is a talented painter with a talented painter daughter, and she "got" the research immediately. As she works with students, she is a hummingbird, hovering over each, studying the piece, listening, observing aloud, and then moving quickly to the next. Her class is nonjudgmental, a learning atmosphere sometimes called "connected knowing"; it involves cooperation, collaboration, empathy.

What Patti Meyers does in her classes exemplifies the theory and practices laid out in *Women's Ways of Knowing*, the important milestone in Women's Studies that illuminated the "collaborative, egalitarian" spirit that often animates women's work (including the book itself by four female social scientists). Exploring the parameters of understanding, the authors concluded there is a characteristic orientation, or *mode of knowing*, that is effective for female learners.

It starts from a premise of connection, an attempt to "get" another point of view, to empathically enter another's world. The other world may be that of teacher, classmate, long-dead artist the student is studying, or even an idea or complex of ideas that is a worldview. The mode of knowing exemplified in this work is personal, nonauthoritarian, in which the teacher doesn't dominate but guide.

In her art classes, the environment is one in which everyone shares the experience, everyone understands the process in similar ways, everyone critiques another from the perspective of a fellow artist. Each may be responsible for her own work, but she is also responsible to the group.

Patti describes the comradeship of even individual activity: "They're careful of each other's feelings. They protect each other. If I'm looking at a portrait and I say, 'What is happening here with this connection to the neck?', another student says, 'I like it that way.' The first student says, 'No, you're right. I was trying to do something different, something like. . . . I'm gonna try the shoulder differently.'"

Connected learning is intended to eliminate the negative atmosphere that classroom competition creates for many students, especially in coed groups where research shows boys dominate, interrupt, and tend to ignore girls, especially in middle school.

Few coed classrooms of this period foster connected learning or cooperative interaction among students and teacher, but rather typically consist of teachers conveying information, reinforcing a view of knowledge as objective, impersonal truth. This approach really doesn't work with some students, many of whom happen to be female.

One of Patti Meyers's early successes occurred in the first troubleshooting session with other teachers about at-risk students.

"I'm worried about Ellie," says Abe, the math teacher, speaking of a young African-American girl I recruited from a charter school. "She's in danger of failing."

"She's doing poorly in English," says another.

"In Latin she's struggling."

Then Patti Meyers speaks. "I don't know the student you describe. She's someone else to me—one of the most intelligent artists I've taught in twenty years." She turns to the math teacher:

"Abe, you have to reach her visually, concretely. That's how her brain functions best. We can work on this together."

Other teachers murmur their own contributions: integrating the subjects, approaching the material through physical activity, peer tutoring. It is the research about girls' learning come to life:

respect the student's experiences and perspective and ways of solving problems.

Months later this same student will come running when she sees me in the courtyard. "Guess what, Dr. Meehan?! I got a 'B' in Math and a 'B+' in English," she beams. "Course I got an 'A' in art!"

After her initial difficulties, this girl will become a scholar, a computer whiz, an accomplished artist in several media. When she graduates from Archer, she will go to Stanford on a full scholarship. She will major in history. Four years later, her mother will send me a photo of her at Stanford's graduation: Ellie's in an academic gown, standing beside a renowned history professor, both grinning.

Bless you, Patti Meyers.

10

Bump, Set, Spike

Vicky, Megan, and I have no official job description for our role at school, other than founder, which is sort of vague. It's like being a dog off leash on city streets: there are many interesting things to investigate, there's a world to observe, there are activities that need doing, but we'll get yelled at if we go into anybody else's territory. So we try to stay out of people's way.

We send each other notes by fax with a central theme—the school will succeed.

But we don't expect to succeed in competitive sports—not with thirty-three girls total, some of whom are wispy, sensitive children with dreamy expressions on their faces. So we are pleased to have hired a therapist/coach to prepare the girls for the probable outcome when they play other (larger) schools. By the luck of the draw, our first game is to be played against the behemoth—Harvard-Westlake.

This is a natural rivalry, for Harvard-Westlake as the union of two single-sex institutions, one of which was Westlake, is, in a certain sense, our raison d'être. Harvard-Westlake teams are smart, tough, and as one of our students complains, "full of themselves."

However, it cannot be a fair fight. H-W has 1,539 students versus our thirty-three. They have a practiced team of players, all seventh grade; we have to play sixth graders (at this age much smaller) with our seventh graders to fill the court. Their coach is a seasoned veteran of years of city pennants; our coach is a psychologist in real life.

We have no equipment. We've ordered it, but it hasn't arrived. The manager of the Palisades sport shop lets us use one of their nets and a volleyball for practice. We can only use the Methodist gym on Tuesday or Thursday afternoons, so we draw lines on the asphalt and practice in the parking lot.

League regulations require that the girls know the rules (which they do, more or less) and that they have shirts with numbers on their backs (which they do not; we keep thinking the shirts will come in time, but they don't). The day before the game Betters and I drive around town, going to summer close-out sales at the various Gap stores in our town to collect enough shirts for the team. We stay up until midnight making numbers from black fabric tape and ironing them on the backs of the shirts.

As a team we may look a little ragged, but at least technically, we can compete.

In both the animal world and the human world, females compete. In physical matches, such as dominance competitions of some species, males are direct and aggressive; females are indirect, engaging in what award-winning science writer Dianne Hales described as "subtle jockeying for position."

Among humans in early adolescence, it's not so different. Girls negotiate: "I'll play this position for ten minutes, then you can, and we'll trade off through the rest of the time." Boys regard this behavior as "stupid" because it clearly is not the best way to win.

Competition creates ambivalence in most girls. They like to avoid conflict, to achieve consensus, to get along. They like to win when everybody, that is everybody in their group, everybody they care about in the world, wins. As a rule they don't want to win by dominating or by destroying another. Affiliation is too important to them.

Gilligan's book *In a Different Voice* presents a psychological dichotomy, connection versus separation. Because girls feel connected to others, they care about relationships and about how their actions affect other people's feelings. Males, according to Gilligan's theory, can separate themselves from consideration of others and view their own actions by an objective standard of established rules or laws.

Thus, in a sporting encounter, males compete within the framework of the rules of the game and the strategy of the coach; they don't worry about people's feelings. Girls, however, compete with one eye on the emotional reactions of others, caring about feelings as much as winning. For dads, brothers, and male coaches, girls' different ordering of priorities can be, at the very least, confusing.

One of Gary's oldest friends, Freddie, a successful basketball coach for Jericho High School's Boys' Varsity, describes an eighth-grade girls' game where he served as timekeeper. It was fourth quarter, two minutes to go. The score was 20–19, Jericho girls leading, when one of them committed a foul. Since it was her fifth foul, a disqualifying final one, Freddie blew the horn to alert the referee, but as the ref came to tell her, the girl began to cry and ran from the gym.

The other four Jericho girls on the court ran right after her and as the last girl passed the Jericho bench, the girls on the bench jumped up and followed their teammates out the gym door, leaving the gym floor empty of Jericho players.

"Where are they going?" the referee inquired, looking after them.

"I think they're upset," Freddie noted.

"Do you think they're coming back?"

Freddie made a noncommittal response.

"What should I do?" asked their coach, coming to the table.

"You better get them," Fred advised. "I don't think they're coming back on their own."

Some ten minutes later the Jericho girls' coach returned with his team, many of whom, still crying, huddled on the bench, hugging the girl who had fouled out. The coach, a nine-year veteran, tried for several minutes to get players off the bench and back on the court to finish the game. For their part, the girls were fighting to stay, to comfort their teammate. Finally the coach convinced five girls to take the court, and they played the last few minutes of the game.

When it was over, both teams met on the court to slap palms, and then the Jericho team seemed to form a ball of girls and, arms around each other, tightly entwined, they walked out the door.

"By the way," Freddie tells me, "Jericho won the game 25–23."

We expect to lose today. We just don't want to be taking our lambs to slaughter, so Ruth and Vicky and I call every parent who is a therapist (quite a few of the mothers and one of the fathers) to take a couple of hours off work if they can, to help us console the girls after their defeat.

We arrive at Harvard-Westlake with twelve seventh graders and seven sixth graders. One of the girls, Shannon, has played volleyball as a club sport; Beth and Romy have played in grade school. Our average height is 5'2".

Our coach has not appeared yet, so the referee tells the girls to do stretches. Beth shakes out her hands, Fofy does neck rolls, and Kyla does some dancer's exercises. Many just mill around, with the grim smiles and wide eyes of preschoolers before a birthday party at a strange house.

A visitor asks how they feel. "Nervous." "Very nervous." "They're very good." Shannon, who has a green "A" painted on her cheek, says nothing.

Girls clasp their hands together and crouch across from each other in the dig position, hitting volleyballs marked "H-W" back and forth, except it is mostly forth and rarely back, as they miss with regularity.

Tanya, our coach, arrives and introduces herself to the referee. "We're a brand-new school," she tells him.

"OK, girls," the ref addresses them. "We'll be using the yellow line as a service line. Now do you all know bump, set, spike?"

A few nods.

"Are you allowed to hit it," someone asks earnestly, "if it just comes to you?"

Harvard-Westlake enters the court then. They look tall, powerful, mature. They are wearing black shorts and black shirts with "Wolverines" stitched in blood red across the front. Their coach in solid red shorts and clipped gray hair nods briskly at Tanya and the ref.

There is a gasp from one of our parents, Beth's mother. "I remember her." She glances at the woman in clipped gray hair and shakes her head in wonder. "She was *my* coach in high school."

"Go, Archer," someone yells from the sidelines, and the game begins.

Romy has the first serve. Romy I've known since she was a toddler learning to swim. At three she was fearless, jumping into the deep end of the pool and thrashing about until she got to the other side where she'd reach up, grasping the tile overhang, grinning.

Now she stands behind the yellow line, the ball in her left hand. She moistens her lips. The ref's whistle blows and she serves. A quick volley, and it is Archer's point. High-fives spontaneously erupt on the court and all along the bench.

Romy's second serve is good, but Harvard-Westlake hits it back fast and hard down the sideline, and Archer misses it. This calls forth encouraging hugs from everyone on the Archer court, somewhat confusing the team in black, who has actually won the exchange.

Harvard-Westlake loses their serve in the net.

Shannon's serve is a fluid one, like a stream of water from some rowdy kid's mouth in sixth grade. Her long, strong form stretches and sends the ball into distant pockets of the other court. Point. Point. Her third serve becomes a bump, set, spike exercise for H-W, and we lose the serve.

The sleeping giant seems to wake at this point. Harvard-Westlake's server sends three cannonballs over the net. Shannon stands at the front, arms up, palms taut to spike the ball, but no one on Archer's side can set her.

Tanya calls "substitution," and Shannon and two others come out. Three sixth graders enter the court; one of them, a 4'11" freckle-faced pixie in braids, goes to the service line. She pumps her right arm in a couple of practice swings and hits the ball, which bounces four feet in front of her.

Harvard-Westlake's server gives a lesson. She stiff-arms the ball before her and smacks it over the net. Beth yells "I go," and makes a valiant attempt to set up the front-row players, who are too short to be set up. After several points another sixth grader, Izzy, manages to win one volley to delirious approval.

The score at this point is Wolverines 10, Visitor 7. Shannon and Romy return to the game. Beth serves. Ace. Ace. Loss. On the table behind the mid-court pole, the numbers read 10–9.

Harvard-Westlake serves, and Beth, who slid into position, returns the ball with a mid-court spike that wins the service.

An Archer girl gets two more points, but the warmest demonstrations of affection come on her third serve, which goes into the net. It is 10–11.

Harvard-Westlake's serve takes the front row by surprise. "That's OK," teammates yell at the girls who missed. Another slam, and the score is 12–11.

Then it is Romy's serve again. Point. Point. "What does *side out* mean?" asks Dominique, as the other team rallies. Tanya answers her, as Romy's serve scores another point.

It is game point. On the sidelines Archer parents and teachers hold our breaths, afraid to exhale, to break the stillness. Thirteen-year-old Romy is the only one breathing.

Coolly Romy sends the ball over the net, there is a volley, bump-set-spike on each side, and it is finished. "Oh-my-god," someone whispers, and then the court explodes into cheers, hugs, high-fives, and joyful mania.

The final score is Harvard-Westlake 12, Archer 15.

It is true we lose the next two games and many after with Harvard-Westlake, for years to come, but that doesn't really matter.

It is the upset, the astounding, heart-stopping, amazing, thrilling upheaval of an upset that we'll remember.

By the time girls are past early adolescence, they usually can compete with less emotional baggage than they bring to the event as middle schoolers. In the meantime, we can use their natural inclinations, such as their affinity for relationships, their regard for relevance, and their highly touted communication skills, to reach them. This, of course, applies to academic activities as well as athletic ones.

Girls view their all-female classrooms and their all-female sports teams in much the same way, as networks of relationships. Accordingly, they compete very well academically in teams or small groups where they can negotiate roles, seek and provide each other validation, and come to agreement on how to achieve the goal. We can see this in our middle school.

One of the parents, a father with expertise in computer science, tries to instigate an academic competition by bringing to school two disassembled but functional computers and challenging the sixth graders to see who can make one of them work. Although no one is actually doodling on the table or dressing a classmate's hair, the girls show by their nonverbal communication that they attend to these remarks with politely disguised disdain and disinterest. Then a savvy teacher ups the ante: the class will be divided into two groups, one for each computer, and whoever gets their machine up and running first can choose one of two rewards for the whole school—cupcakes or a free-dress day.

Over the next four days, the two groups of girls work on their assigned computers, and seek and give each other emotional support, just as we saw them do in the volleyball game, until ultimately one group wins the contest, booting up the computer and seeing it work. The girls of the winning team squeal and hug, and then they huddle together to decide on the prize.

Natalia, from the other team, gravely comes over to offer her congratulations. They pull her in to the confab, then grab another of her teammates to help make their decision. In the end, after agonizing for several minutes, the winning group, with Natalia and another girl as additions, announce their choice (and display their age): they choose cupcakes.

It isn't the promise of sugar that motivates them, that brings them in from lunch to work on the computer, but the chance to work together on a goal that may be rewarding for the group. Not the goodies, but the common good. Middle school girls can be quite passionate about their goals in certain settings. I saw that at Julia Morgan.

In 1999, Julia Morgan School opened in Oakland by the efforts of Ilana DeBare and ten other people with the same idea: a school "where girls come first" (which is the title of DeBare's book). Head of School Ann Clarke's motivation was "to save some girls in Oakland; it's a disastrous school system." Originally, the mission was to inspire young women to be passionate, life-long learners while preparing them to be confident, capable, and creative women of tomorrow.

The school is designed, as Clarke says, "for the needs of middle school girls specifically." The *language* of the curriculum is pro-girls: math competitions called "Counting on Girls"; learning projects titled "Early Humans"; and a program addressing problems like homelessness, AIDS, and foster care in the community outside the school walls, labeled "Go Girls" (Go Outside, Get-in-Real-Life-Situations).

The last program inspired students to come running into the Head's office, breathlessly declaring, "We have to change the mission!"

Clarke describes it to me: "I was impressed by their passion. Still, the board writes the mission. We'd gone to press with *confident, capable, creative.*"

"We have to add another *c*," the students told Ann. "We need *compassion*, that's what Go Girls is about.

"I mean how can we deal with the homeless or AIDS without that?!"

"When the girls are aware of choices," Ann says, "they choose their best selves. Incidentally, the board changed it, changed the mission statement."

11

One Star, Two Heads

Lucy has a troop of people who came with her to run the school.

There are two softly upholstered receptionists who sit at the two front desks in the hall, greet visitors, and monitor nail polish violations. For some reason, perhaps pure perversity, the school does not allow girls to wear nail polish, so on Monday mornings after a weekend of Urban Decay in twenty-seven colors, they line up for a tissue and a splash of polish remover from the industrial-size bottle kept on one of the desks. This prevents uniform violations and perhaps something else, I don't know.

There is Lucy's major domo, who decorated her office in white woods and pastels and teaches singing to the sixth graders. He arranges for microphones and potted plants when we have a ceremony of some sort.

There is the Middle School Director. She looks like a grown-up cherub with rosy cheeks and big, round eyes, and she couldn't have been nicer when she introduced herself to Vicky and me a couple of months before school began. We are surprised to learn we need a Middle School Director what with only thirty-three students. At that time we didn't realize that Lucy would be leaving early many afternoons to get to her boat.

Lucy is economical about the effort she expends at work. Many days she arrives after nine in the morning and leaves by three or four, something we do not immediately realize, as we are at our own workplaces. It doesn't seem possible to do this job (planning the curriculum, setting policy, mentoring teachers, etc.) on a part-time basis, but Lucy gives it a sincere try.

And she recycles. For our first Back-to-School Night, she gives a powerful presentation—actually it is the same address she showed me and Vicky in the restaurant some months before—one she'd used at her old school, but she's added the words "Archer" in nine places to make it current.

Lucy has already gone home the day we hear about our bid for the purchase of Eastern Star Home.

I use the term *purchase* to mean *promise to try to get the money*, which is different from its regular usage. This reminds me of a friend from our hippie days who said the bank was mad at him for "inefficient funds"; it conjures a picture of his money lying around waiting for the *cabana* boy to bring Marlboros and a mai tai instead of working for him.

The Eastern Star bid starts with David in a very bad mood. This is because he believes (1) we are on a fool's mission; (2) we have no money and no assets, so we need a long escrow while we try to get some; (3) we want Eastern Star badly. He is correct about 2 and 3.

Eastern Star Home is almost too good to be true. Just west of Barrington on Sunset Boulevard, it is a Spanish Revival building spread across a green knoll, a grand old lady lifting her petticoats to sit on the grass. It is ninety thousand square feet inside, decorated during the Depression by artisans and craftsmen, and six and a half acres outside, most of which are open fields in the back.

Scott and Vicky and Charles and Megan and I dream about this place. I think a couple of us woke with drool on our chins. It is absurdly suitable for us.

And there is nothing else. Brentwood, Santa Monica, the Palisades are full up. They are three Westside communities chock-a-block with upscale apartment homes, bakeries, boutiques, bungalows, condos, and castles. It's all pretty much *better luck next time* if you're trying to find a place for 450 students. Except for Eastern Star.

The Eastern Star board is going to hear purchase offers at nine, ten, and eleven on a morning in December. This contributes to David's bad mood. The other bidders are developers with deep pockets, and we are financially challenged.

"When you talk about our finances," David says, giving me a stern look, "don't go into big, long explanations. Keep it brief and upbeat."

People in L.A. invest their dreams, their history, in real estate. Perhaps because there is no myth of place, *Crossing the Delaware*, say, or *The Battle of Gettysburg*, there are mini-myths of Westside real estate, usually involving movie people.

Jack Warner's daughter lived there. Shirley Temple's dollhouse sits on the lawn. Jane Fonda owned this ficus tree.

This site, the Eastern Star Home, stately and self-contained, is more invested with these myths than most.

"I once ran away from home," says my friend Stacey. "I was about ten. And that's where I went. The Eastern Star."

A couple with a big female Pyrenees on a leash stops me outside Starbucks.

"They used that Eastern Star in *Casablanca*."

"*Chinatown*, Edward, not *Casablanca*." The Pyrenees doesn't look at them, but sits majestically. "It *is* historic."

"Pancho Villa slept there," Edward says, deadpan.

At nine-fifty a.m. we climb the cement steps as a big man, fifty years or so, opens the heavy front doors, eyes squinting in the sunlight. He is paunchy with brown pants and loose limbs and the agreeable amiability TV researchers call rural appeal. He gives me a courtly nod that is almost a bow and peers at David.

"Good. Good. You're here," he says, shaking David's hand. He reaches for my hand with his two large ones, and I realize then who he is: Earl Eckhart. David and Vicky have been talking with him for months. An Eastern Star trustee with some real estate background, Earl regularly communicates with David about the home and its possible future.

"Give us a few minutes." He offers another smile as he turns to go back inside, and in his easygoing, laconic warmth I recognize an ally.

David takes Earl aside to tell him something about the unsavory behavior of one of the developers who will pitch that morning. David does his homework. I take a long yoga breath, mentally preparing for what comes next.

We meet Eastern Star's board members—I don't know how many exactly; I don't know how they're chosen; I don't know much about the Masons, only enough to get through this meeting. I have an impression of a large family forced by the uncle's will to dine together. Perhaps it is the room—wood-paneled with a large cement fireplace, sconces, and chandeliers with the brilliance of a candle in the wee hours of winter. The board members look at us with interest.

I am wearing a vintage skirted suit, chosen because it is inoffensive, navy (a color that denotes credibility), and from the 1940s when Americans were naïve, innocent, and sincere. Vicky wears her lucky yellow gauze stockings with a skirt and sweater; Megan and David wear business suits.

Here in their uniforms, vulnerable, winsome, are two Archer students, Fofy and Natalia, ready with a brief statement. We present them with unstated pride, evidence of accomplishment, as much a compact with the future as the photos grandparents carry of ruffle-haired urchins in bathing suits and cloth caps.

Vicky, David, and I speak our practiced pieces. Scott is there with some drawings meant to show that we won't change much (except maybe the lighting in this room) if the Eastern Star board agrees to our purchase.

Then I stand. "You may be wondering if we have the ability to finance this purchase," I say with what I know is understated calm. "We have the money." I am finished and sitting so quickly, David is startled. He asks for questions from the Eastern Star family. Amazingly, they have none.

We shake hands with everyone. The one I think of as the Matriarch-Queen (she sits with elegant demeanor in the high-backed chair at the head of the table) asks if I live in Brentwood. I nod.

"I was raised here," she says. "It's changed, I think."

"There are a lot of young families, school-age children."

She raises one eyebrow. "So it would seem."

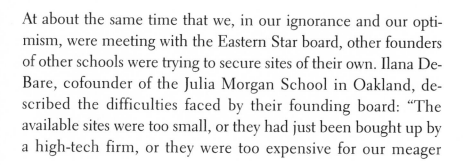

At about the same time that we, in our ignorance and our optimism, were meeting with the Eastern Star board, other founders of other schools were trying to secure sites of their own. Ilana De-Bare, cofounder of the Julia Morgan School in Oakland, described the difficulties faced by their founding board: "The available sites were too small, or they had just been bought up by a high-tech firm, or they were too expensive for our meager budget. If we looked in residential areas, we risked neighbors who would fight the noise and traffic of a school. If we looked in industrial areas, we risked ending up on a pile of toxic waste."

Eventually, after calling every church in central Oakland and Berkeley, after calling local colleges and city councilmen, Julia Morgan's founders got what DeBare called a lucky break: an empty, unused dormitory at Holy Names College, available to rent: "we had, at least temporarily, a home." They opened their middle school for girls, a year after we opened.

Another middle school up north has a site on a lot that until recently was blackberry brambles and brush, on the corner of Jackson and Martin Luther King in central Seattle. The temporary campus of Seattle Girls' School is literal: two portable structures with modular rooms and movable walls. The two rectangular boxes, along with a chicken-coop yard and the use of a nearby park, comprise the physical plant.

The Seattle founders' first task was to convince parents to mentally overcome the reality of the weedy, empty lot in a polyglot, multicultural neighborhood of immigrants (Ethiopian, Singhalese, Vietnamese, Russian, Finnish, and Chinese), plus local street people, and imagine a middle school for girls there. According to one observer, parents were a little dazed at the first Open Houses, as Head Marja Brandon and founders tried to convince them that there would be a wonderful school incorporating the Research in the curriculum for the "future women leaders of the world."

Across the country is Atlanta Girls' School (AGS), founded, like Archer, by three women: fundraiser Candace Springer, Emily Ellison, a former journalist with the Atlanta *Journal/Constitution*, and Brooke Weinmann, onetime IBM executive, now a full-time volunteer. The three had a whole lot of meetings and raised awareness and money (using the Women's Foundation as their bank) from about 1,000 different people, many of whom gave gifts of $1,000 or less.

Gaining a site proved to be more difficult than raising funds however, and, like Archer, AGS lived in rented space in a church for three years. But not before the search for the right site led them to view unsuitable options: a funeral home, a mansion, a recording studio, and — truly — a former gay strip club.

"It went well, I think," Vicky says in the parking lot. She is being WASP-hearty, like those Christmas letters that read "Trey and I are currently living on an ice flow in the Yukon with Berty, Elliot, and Vanessa and our two yellow Labradors, Caleb and Heming-way, while Trey does some fascinating work for the Arctic Cartog-raphers Society."

Inevitably, we know how remote the possibility is that we would ever inhabit the Eastern Star building. In spite of our con-viction that we'd performed not too badly at the board meeting, we are aware that our bid had less merit than those of the devel-opers. Friends, husbands, and David told us as much.

We'd argued that we had many of the attributes of the Eastern Star organization (tolerance, charity, goodwill), that we'd pre-serve their presence in the community, and that we, too, were dedicated to the well-being of women.

This is business, said the scoffers. *Nobody cares about your ideals.*

Alas, we failed to adapt to reality. Because we sorely wanted it, we imagined no alternate scenarios, no future without this build-ing. Perhaps it was superstition.

A dream project, like a young family's bid on the hoped-for house, elicits fear and faith in equal measure. Until, and if, the faith is crushed in the wreckage of loss, fear is not acknowledged. So it is with us.

David, Scott, and Megan go to offices. Vicky and I, unable to assume our places at our writing desks, take ourselves off to Patti Meyers's seventh-grade art class. We are fooling around making Christmas decorations with the students when David calls.

"We, uh, well, we got it." He's actually chuckling. He keeps repeating, "We got it. They accepted our bid. We got it. Eastern Star."

We are not grownup and measured in our response. Vicky and Patti and I are jumping up and down, laughing and screaming. The girls are amused. Ruth comes down the hall to take pictures.

Minutes after David's call, a potential donor calls the school. We've been coaxing and courting this donor for months, and flushed with the aura of victory, I decide to make the ask right then.

"We need you to do two and a half million."

There is a pause.

"We'll do one and a half," the donor says. *Wow.*

So this is life in America's Dream Capital. A good day by anyone's measure. I am thinking, *Eastern Star*!!! Inside my head are think balloons that are comic book exclamations: *Kazam! Pow! Amazing!*

Lucy is not there that afternoon.

Is it illness or carelessness or sloth—or some other frailty, cluelessness perhaps—which create the sense that Lucy is not available to the here and now? Whatever the cause, her absent presence can be ignored no longer.

A week after the Eastern Star bid, we give Lucy a leave of absence. In spite of all that might have been and who Lucy should have been, we like her. When we tell her, she cries. Vicky cries. I cry.

Over the winter holidays we call the one who was runner-up in the head sweepstakes. He has the bona fides to do the job—prep school, Princeton (I believe his uncle was Admissions Director), experience at a number of admittedly distant boarding schools.

The thing is, the guy looks right—tall, maybe 6'9" counting the cowlick, a squint that implies there is deep thought occurring, a dark suit that has been cleaned possibly in the washing machine but not ironed in recent years, loafers, and wool socks that have to be held up by garters. What he looks right for is to be the head-master for Olde East Preparatory or West Upoversome.

He sometimes sits at his desk with excellent posture and an air of waiting. He will take dry cleaning slips from his pocket and stare at them for meaning, like a general reading communiqués from the field. Every day he walks in Palisades Village wearing a slight smile below a worried brow or sits erect in a plastic chair at Panda Café crumbling a poppy seed muffin into his wonton soup.

I must admit, he does give us insight into the American colonists' relationship with George III. On the one hand, he likes being in charge; on the other, he seems to have only a passing interest in our affairs. He speaks often about bringing someone in to run the school, as if that isn't really his job. By May we determine, like the colonists, that we are better off without him.

The Middle School Director, Joanne Schuber, seems to be steadfast, resolute. She wears her dark hair in soft, velvety swathes around her face and mulberry lipstick, shiny and fragrant, as she stands in the hall in front of the mahogany clock, greeting the girls. We discover, however, that she is leaving at the end of the term. George III has made it so unpleasant for her these last few months that she is going back to her old school. We cannot dissuade her; she has already signed a contract.

Although we do ask Ruth Jenson, Admissions Director, to run things for a while as Acting Head, it is surely a violation of the How-to-Start-a-School guide to do it without a principal or head of school. Nor are we recommending it. It's unnerving.

Meanwhile, the students are collecting their favorite sayings, lyrics, and poems for their yearbook pages. Two of them, Rebecca and Lizzie, choose these lines attributed to Katherine Hepburn: "If you obey all the rules, you miss all the fun." Too true.

PART TWO

12

Slings and Arrows

I don't know exactly how many people live in the near vicinity of our new site. There are apartment buildings on either side and across the street from the grand old home on Sunset we still call Eastern Star. In houses north and south of the site and on the adjoining streets are the Neighbors.

They live in meretricious mansionettes—faux chateaux of five bedrooms, four baths, three stiff ficus or pencil-thin palm trees, some stone lions or cement ducks, gates and intercoms and flood security lights that come on when a cat sneezes—on plots of ground the size of Federal Express envelopes. They have little signs in front of the gates that read "Armed Response" and that describe their behavior; they have an irrational fear that our girls' school will undermine their property values.

They also have quite a bit of disposable income. They might have chosen to dispose of it in other ways, but they have a political program that they implement instead. It begins with pink fliers which say, *No to Traffic, No to Archer School*; they hand these flyers to drivers slowing down at the intersection of Sunset and Barrington. Their campaign progresses to large *No!* banners hung from bushes and porches, and ends, as many issues do in our country, in court.

(One of our newly hired teachers arrives at the airport to begin her career in America. Her friend opens the door to her car saying, "Isn't your school Archer? In Brentwood? There are banners against it everywhere.")

For solace and for some understanding, I visit two other newly founded single sex schools which also face opposition, The Young Women's Leadership School (TYWLS) in East Harlem and the Julia Morgan School in Oakland. Leadership, literally the name of the first school, begins with journalist-philanthropist Ann Rubenstein Tisch, who had the idea of a public, single sex school for impoverished girls and shepherded it through two city administrations, two sequential school boards, each of whom had to be courted, and past threatening moves by New York City chapters of NOW and the ACLU to prematurely end this experiment.

These organizations viewed girls' schools, at least public ones, as discrimination against boys. Their complaint, filed in federal court weeks before the school was to open, charged the New York City school district with violating Title IX: if found to be the case, it can mean the loss of millions of federal dollars to the district. The U.S. Supreme Court had only recently ruled that the Virginia Military Institute's refusal to admit women was unconstitutional; it was a discouraging climate for Tisch's school, due to open with fifty-six enrolled students, all girls.

Nevertheless, Ann Tisch, bolstered by allies and lawyers, the latter paid from her own money, opened the doors of TYWLS in 1996. The civil case filed against the school would be returned to the U.S. Department of Justice, and there it would quietly expire. TYWLS will not only survive, it will thrive, winning scores of accolades over the next ten years and inspiring scores of other public single sex schools.

Up in Oakland is another girls' school trying to survive. Julia Morgan is an independent middle school, not sure if it wants to also be a high school, and its small size (less than 150 girls) means money is always an issue. Originally Ann Clarke was merely a consultant, but when the board asked her to be Head of School, she agreed but said she was immediately "terrified" that she wouldn't be able to find donors or, once finding them, convince them to support a girls' school.

The first potential donor with a small foundation, after reviewing the request, said to Clarke, "Frankly, we can't see why we should give you any money." Clarke got feisty, put pictures of the girls in front of him, and told their stories. Before she walked out of his office, she said, "This will be a great school, and you'll long regret that you didn't do anything to help it." Two weeks later, word came from the foundation—*We decided to fund you.*

Buoyed by this success, Clarke went to another potential donor, who said, as frankly as the previous one, "First of all, I don't believe in girls' schools." Clarke got him to agree that he did believe in girls, and from there it was a short discussion to funding scholarships for a couple of those girls. Clarke's ten years as an educator in Quaker schools helped in managing the stress; Quakers, she said, try to find something of God in each person. She'd found it was a good technique for dealing with the children. Also for dealing with the donors.

We will encounter people who oppose us for political reasons, like the antifeminist building manager in Pacific Palisades or some Brentwood School parents who perversely oppose an increase in the number of private schools. We will have critics who argue that boys need our attention, that boys are more in need of good schooling than girls. (We will consider ways to address the education of boys, but at this juncture we are absorbed in the subject of the education of girls.)

There will be those who oppose us on economic grounds (neighborhood house values will inexplicably lower) or environmental grounds (traffic will increase). The intensity and endurance of their complaint, however, argues that the objection is more personal, more emotional: they don't like children or they don't like girl children or children of color or they don't like girl children of color in their neighborhoods in the building known as Eastern Star.

Luckily we've added board members, so we can spread the angst around. At a baby shower for my friend Leslie, I talk with a political consultant named Ann, pregnant with her first child. When she says she might volunteer to help us, I point to her belly and ask what she is having; she ducks her head and chuckles softly, "We don't know. We decided not to ask."

"If it's a girl," I tell her as we're leaving, "you have to give us two years."

After her daughter Lizzie is born, she calls me. "What are you, a witch?" she laughs. Ann will join the board, and when we finally release her from service, Lizzie will be in seventh grade.

We invite to the board Dr. Jeff, a beloved local pediatrician whose daughter is starting sixth grade, and Kathy K., a successful producer whose daughters are yet to be born. These board members and those before and after them serve an idea, an educational philosophy, a feminist ideal. However, their endurance and passion, much like that of those who oppose us, suggest that the motivation is personal as well as political.

There are two homeowners associations, Brentwood Homeowners and Concerned Brentwood Homeowners, who oppose, with various degrees of animosity, us occupying Eastern Star. Joel Garreau, the author of *Nine Nations of North America*, refers to these kinds of neighborhood organizations as "shadow governments" who try to "rigidly control" their residential areas.

What makes these outfits like governments, scholars say, is the extent to which they have the following three attributes:

1. They can assess mandatory fees to support themselves—the power to tax.
2. They can create rules and regulations—the power to legislate.
3. They have the power to coerce, to force people to change their behavior—the police power.

All governments have these powers.

What's unfair, even tyrannical, about these organizations is their undemocratic lack of accountability to the community: their membership is private, and their rules can be arbitrary and their positions based on "one dollar, one vote." Nor are they subject to U.S. constitutional constraints imposed on our representative governments, like city councils.

Unfortunately, this is a time when Not in My Backyard (NIMBY) is a political force across the country, and hostility toward children's activities, sports, and schools springs up in suburbs and cities from New York to Long Beach. Oddly, in our youth-obsessed society, there's a bias against children, as in kids-who-aren't-my-own.

Around the corner from our house is a public elementary school which wants to turn a portion of the schoolyard into a soccer field. *No way*, say the neighbors, objecting to the intrusion into the community of small soccer players and their moms. One man actually argues it will attract child molesters.

Another case in point: an independent, nonsectarian institution, Turning Point School, has bought a church building in nearby Beverly Hills in which to relocate its three hundred or so young students. Turning Point has a roller coaster ride in its attempt to transform an old church into a new school. There are hearings; petitions; testimony by celebrities including Priscilla Presley, who is a Turning Point parent, and Max Factor III, the school's attorney (I'm not making these names up); and public controversy described in the local press as "vehement opposition" by neighbors.

Neighbors object on the basis of noise, traffic, air pollution, and safety. The Beverly Hills school board president feels it is a safety issue. He believes having a new school so close to an existing one (the public school a block away) is "scary."

What exactly is the danger here? Interscholastic rivalries? Teacher scarcity? Double the number of child molesters?

We're talking about minors. In Beverly Hills. Are they going to overload the cell phone circuits in the area? Drive up the price of cashmere? What scary things can they do being near another, existing school?

I argue the case in my mental voice, but it gives me no understanding. People say outrageous things about this small elementary school moving into their neighborhood. They say them again and again at meeting after meeting over seventeen months. Turning Point School counters with proposals and plans and promises. It loses in City Council, 4–1.

As attorney Mark Warda notes in his book, *Neighbor vs. Neighbor:* "Yes, some people do consider children to be a nuisance."

Our first encounter with our own neighbors is a meeting at the community center at the Catholic Church six months after we enter escrow on the Eastern Star property. Scott and some other Archer supporters who live nearby plan to attend. There are issues raised by the group called Concerned Brentwood Homeowners that might be addressed in a frank, face-to-face exchange.

It is not to be. Scott and those who arrive with him are expelled from the meeting as soon as they arrive. After their departure, a guard is placed at the door of the community center.

Then on October 29, an open forum on neighborhood issues is held at the synagogue across the street from our much-desired site. Both the rabbi and one of the organizers invite us to come. It is going to be well-attended, dense actually, with cars overflowing the expansive parking lot and onto the residential streets.

Brentwood's concerned citizens are here, a goodly portion of whom are white-haired or bald or white-haired *and* bald. Or they're the two men entering ahead of me who are wearing standard agent clothes: Armani suits in shades of gray—charcoal (one) or steel (the other), cashmere sweaters, burnt orange or slate blue, no visible shirts, loafers, Rolex watches, haircut from a Beverly Hills salon, not a barber. You'd swear they'd had their hairs cut and faces slapped with scented lotion as they left their cars two minutes ago—and maybe they did.

Our side is easily identified—we wear forest green metal buttons with a white A+ on them. Archer also provides the only non-whites in the audience and the only children. There are students here from the history class.

One of the girls reacts to the audience. "They look at us like we're toxic waste." She scrunches down in her seat.

Ms. Bennett, the history teacher, tries to comfort them. "It isn't personal, it isn't about you."

I'm in a seat on the aisle next to a woman wearing a flowered dress and crocheted vest, smelling of eucalyptus room deodorizer. I recognize the smell, for I use that brand at home.

"I'm here because I'm against the college," she says with a benevolent look over her bifocals, like a grannie editorializing as she reads a bedtime story.

"The college?"

"They're abusive," she says by way of explanation. "They have a See Oh Pee." (She pronounces each letter with a pause in between. It takes me a moment to realize she is not obliquely referring to the police but to a conditional use permit [CUP]. Apparently Mt. St. Mary's College has one, too.)

"They're way over it—hundreds of students," she says, "that they're not s'posed to have."

"Oh. How do you know this?"

"That's what I heard."

I try to look sympathetic, but then a series of white-haired men are addressing the audience. When the college up the hill is mentioned, the grannie next to me goes "Tch, tch," shakes her head, and smiles at me.

Then they get to Archer. The microphone is held by a short, balding man with a monk's fringe of white hair and white skin that blotches red with rancor. Bitterly, he describes us as "another school that wants to locate in our neighborhood." (I know of two other schools within blocks of our site, the tiny St. Martin of Tours and Brentwood School, which has two campuses on eleven acres.)

He enumerates the issues of contention: congestion on Sunset Boulevard, traffic on residential streets that will be so obstructed that emergency vehicles will be unable to get through to save someone's life or someone's house from burning to the ground, cigarette stubs (which may very well cause the fire which burns down the house) left burning on the ground by the boyfriends as they wait for the girls from the Archer School to get dismissed (this is good news to the Archer students in the audience, who exchange looks over these proposed boyfriends).

The speaker is Jon Byk, and he will be the King of Clubs in this deck of cards. He writes a column for the *Brentwood News* entitled "My Turn," in which he defends his position as arbiter of the neighborhood. He has organized the "concerned" group to oppose us, to keep Chaparral—the street on which he lives— "pastoral" (it has no sidewalks) and the mansionettes safe from traffic and the aforementioned boyfriends.

Another picks up the boyfriend theme, telling the assembled that the boyfriends will drive SUVs which their parents provide and these new drivers won't be able to handle the traffic on Sunset and there will be fatal crashes. (This is a version of the child molester argument, casting the objector in the role of protector of children.)

As the last speaker finishes, my elderly neighbor turns to me. "People don't dress anymore even for public events. Men used to wear ties, hats. Ladies, a nice dress, some gloves."

I nod, and she indicates two of our students in uniform seated three rows away. "The twins look nice, though."

One of them is black, one Latina, so I'm confused by her observation. I tell her those are Archer girls.

"Ohh," she says knowingly. "Then they'd better be careful."

I look at her twinkling blue eyes and pudgy, rouged cheeks. "We don't want them here," she explains, smiling.

The people who do not want us here portray us as *outsiders* (code for racially mixed), although many of us, Scott's and Ann's and Megan's and my families, are Brentwood residents. Referring to us as *elite* every other sentence or sometimes *exclusive* or *private* to exclude us from their we-ness, they work tirelessly to keep us from getting approval from City Council.

We work just as hard to be accepted. I drive downtown with three Archer girls to meet with council members who represent districts where these students live. In the car the girls read biographies of the council members.

"Hey, she's African American," one says, surprised, "just like me."

From the backseat her friend expels a sound between a snort and a laugh. "Duh! So why do you think you're here, Lame Brain?"

The Archer students are learning rhetoric, philosophy, and political reality. Some land use law, as well.

We send Scott like a ministering cleric to the homes of various neighbors to drink coffee and show the drawings of Eastern Star and how we'd preserve it. Some are angry agnostics who refuse to meet.

Our girls canvass the neighborhood and talk to people outside Starbucks. Ann, the board member who has been a political consultant, gives them advice, her own girl, baby Lizzie, on her hip:

"Always be polite. Ask them if they have any questions about Archer. Ask them if they'll sign a petition supporting us."

It is Saturday, and these girls have volunteered for this. Three of them confer with Ann, their heads cocked, nodding their understanding, pulling the paper petitions from her hands. They fly off with chirps of excitement, like birds gathering material for the nest.

Shannon is irrepressible. "Excuse me, sir," she urges one old man who has turned away in disgust when he sees the Archer name. "Is it traffic that worries you? Can I talk to you about that?"

I see them walk a little way down the street, and she bends her head toward him, talking and gesturing. Dominique runs over for another petition, and Shannon returns exuberant. "He signed," she says proudly.

In the one-on-one there are sweet harmonies, moments of accord. But I worry that the future is dark with ill will, enmity, and argument and the sides are wildly uneven: privileged against poor, senior against youth, snarly strong against meek and weak. I worry we will lose.

13

Into the Breach

At UCLA I look at a special computer program that color-codes electromagnetic activity in brains, showing two brains, one male, one female, as each solves a math problem. They get the correct answer in pretty much the same amount of time, but in completely different ways, activating different sections of the brain. According to what I see, an idea enters a male brain and stays in one section, maybe bouncing against a wall as in a handball game. In a female brain it's more like cross-training, bouncing up and down and over, crossing boundaries, moving from one section to another.

Rachel Gur, a University of Pennsylvania neuro-psychiatrist, with her husband, Ruben Gur, a neuro-psychologist (that's so many years of advanced degrees between them, my brain cannot compute it), having conducted some of these imaging studies, concludes, "male and female brains do the same things but they do them differently."

When a woman uses her brain, the blood flow from one hemisphere to another is nearly 20 percent higher than when a man uses his. She activates more neurons and tends to be less compartmentalized than he is. That may account for the ability of the so-called male brain to focus intently like a labrador watching a frisbee in hand, whereas the female brain is busy connecting left and right hemispheres, introducing objects, ideas, emotions.

There must be ways to respond to new research and the implications it surely has for learning. Subjects in the cross-training brain meet other subjects, relationships matter, but how are those things accomplished in the classroom? We don't know, and making it happen is not really the founders' job anyway. It's the job of the School Head.

The School Head is the one who hires the faculty who design the curriculum which incorporates the studies that suggest how girls typically learn. The School Head could read the research and figure out what relevance those brain studies have. We need a School Head's help.

The particular help we need is Arlene Hogan. A former president of the California Association of Independent Schools, she is a leader. A founder of the National Coalition of Girls' Schools, she is a feminist visionary. She has a sense of humor and a great laugh. Simply put, she is exactly right.

How on earth can we get her? Maybe we can make what we are look like what she needs. It is a formidable challenge.

Arlene Hogan is the Head, has been the Head for thirteen years, of a proper girls' school in the Pacific Heights section of San Francisco, a city known for its fog, its museums, its Golden Gate Bridge.

We, on the other hand, are Los Angeles.

Specifically, L.A.'s Westside. Although our school is for children from South Central to the San Fernando Valley, we are located on the Westside. Our neighborhoods—Brentwood,

Malibu, Pacific Palisades, Santa Monica—are the kind of places television uses for nighttime soaps.

There's a kind of nighttime soap feeling to the community, too. Plenty of dreams, plenty of drama, plenty of everything.

The Westside is burdened with useless abundance. It is absurdly full of things you don't actually need. Like palm trees. I mean, what do palm trees *do*?

The other thing we have a lot of is intellectual properties. I'm talking about the stuff that comes out of somebody's head. Songs. Books. Screenplays. Writing screenplays is a principal industry on our side of town.

People here do stuff that is essentially inventive. They work for a living, sometimes really long hours, mind you, in their *imaginations*. Every day they go to the factory in their minds, punch in their pretend time cards, and talk to their imaginary friends. You can see them at Jamba Juice or Coffee Bean, in their cars at Sunset and Barrington, moving their arms like they're conducting music—and they may be, they may be.

The woman who heads Disney Imagineers lives here (there's a job description). The woman who created Barbie, the one who created the Franklin Mint, both live here. (Maybe they're all using cross-training brains.)

I don't know why exactly, but women in this town do everything from medicine to mortgage investments; they run studios, networks, synagogues, and a certain amount of city government. This is a great place for working women.

Good place for weather, too. It's mythic, mostly sunshine and sparkling surf, and years go by without a need for socks. Then there'll be one of those seasons out of the Old Testament: mudslides in Malibu, fires in the canyons, quakes and tremblers in the land of soy milk and honey.

I suppose the weather contributes to the feeling of imminent possibility. And the inventiveness of the work creates a sort of any-one-can-play mentality. There are no prerequisites, no pedigrees, no credentials required to do most of the stuff that people do around here. Anything seems possible.

Arlene Hogan as Head of our school seems possible. In the winter of our second year, when Ruth Jenson has been Acting Head for five months, we invite Arlene to come see what we are doing and she comes. Just curious, she says. She has twenty-something years' experience in girls' schools and no intention of running ours.

We take her to dinner at Michael's in Santa Monica: Megan, David, Vicky, and I, our husbands. Michael himself visits our table, charming us with tales of his ten-year-old daughter.

We make the pitch to Arlene that Archer would be a plum assignment. We talk about the community of women leaders and the culture of generosity in a place where people's dreams come true. We talk about Eastern Star. We mention the weather.

We say, this is a lush, creative, productive place. A hard-working visionary like yourself can be big here. (Arlene is about ninety-four pounds, so being big might appeal.)

We say, we really need you. (Arlene has a measure of Irish-Catholic guilt, so we try to appeal to that.)

Nobody discusses the Neighbors, the lawyers, the debt. Regarding the latter, it's normal to have a mortgage, OK, maybe not fifteen million dollars' worth, but still normal. It's normal to run out of money to pay rent and salaries in early October. That's what a line of credit is for, I'm told. When tuition advance money comes in for next year, that money pays rent and salaries—that's normal, too.

As normal as all of this is, we don't tell Arlene Hogan.

In the film version, Arlene takes the Ann Sheridan-Katharine Hepburn role—freckled nose, smashing tennis serve, big brain, but looks like she'd blow over in a crosswind.

Vicky, Megan, and I take the other roles. Three muses. Three stooges. Three characters in search of an author.

Nevertheless, despite our bumbling around, despite the pundits' predictions, despite the reasonable expectations of anyone who knows anything about such things, Arlene Hogan agrees to be Head of the Archer School.

I don't know, nor ever expect to know, why she accepts this position. I only know the school is possible because she does.

Our year in escrow—what once seemed a soft cushion of time in which to leisurely raise funds, apply for and receive permits, remodel, and make a farewell ceremony for the remaining twenty-seven Eastern Star residents—is ending too soon. We've been raising money, but we've been using it to fund our battle against our future Neighbors.

The battle has been fierce, expensive, and even by their accounts, exhausting. They've spent several hundred thousand dollars, I estimate. For lawyers, consultants, lobbyists. For us it's been worse, many times worse: all the professionals in these last three years who've analyzed traffic, egress, ingress, transit and transportation, who've managed the messages, who've represented us in court—the cost of which buys no book or blackboard, no microscope, no computer. Just conflict.

Our opponents have become muscled in the mechanics and theater of conflict, like battle-hardened soldiers who grimly carry out the tasks of war. In the beginning their side made chatty reminiscences of what the neighborhood had been thirty years ago when a house was bought and promises were made, candid confessions of not really liking to have *Others* come into Brentwood. But these personal propaganda were stilled, and now everyone mouths the same speech: We're not against the Archer School, just against having it in our "pastoral" neighborhood.

We have a conference call at Christmastime that involves all board members on two continents, including the two new ones, Dr. Jeff (who is currently in Costa Rica) and Kathy K. (currently in Wyoming).

"Our contract is up," I tell them, when everyone is on the line. "We either extend escrow and pay the penalty for it, or we close. In which case, we the trustees are responsible for the $15 million."

"We're negotiating a mortgage," adds David.

"But," says Scott, "we're buying the walls, windows, and wheelchair ramps, and we still have to convert them into a school."

"Yeah," says Debi, "it's an old-age home. Let's be serious, it has a lifetime supply of bedpans."

"It'll be a hundred thousand dollars," Scott continues, "just to turn those weeds in the back into playing fields. Get rid of the gophers."

The gophers have made the fields their neighborhood by their teeth and the sweat of their brows. They have their customs and courtships and crossroads dances under the clay soil and tufts of grass, the choice Brentwood real estate known as the fields of Eastern Star. They live there, but they are not embraced by the other residents, any more than we are.

Everyone asks where the Eastern Star inhabitants are going (Yorba Linda, I think), but no one asks where the gophers are going. Plus, unlike the ladies of Eastern Star, they won't be leaving by bus.

"Now is when we honor our convictions and carry on — no matter what. Or not," I finish lamely. As one of those inspiring speeches coaches make at halftime, it isn't quite there. But the board is.

"I move we close escrow."

"Second."

Roll call. It is unanimous. We are either prescient or prodigious fools. Time will reveal.

Time reveals something about money, and it's not good.

The big donor who only months before promised us one and a half million dollars rescinded his pledge. Sadly, disappointed, he told us as if he might share some lesson with us. Some understanding of the cruelty of nature perhaps. He had changed his mind.

This is a shock. This Very Rich Person (we heard eight hundred million) with brown eyes and cashmere jackets and tasseled loafers that glide when he walks, this formerly nice man has changed his mind.

What does this say about human endeavor? And commitment so shallow it doesn't last a season? What does this say about us and our unanimous vote to close escrow on a fifteen-million-dollar property?

I drive home on Sunset facing east, in fading light, leaving the school. At the first bend I glance in the rearview mirror, leaving behind the Palisades, nihilistic news, the collapse of our hopes. Ahead I see a blond dog leaning out of a car, a yellow lab, ears flopping, nose to the breeze, and as I pass, a long, dark smile on his face.

That wolfish enjoyment shoots right to my heart. Thus gladdened, I employ an ancient Anglo-Saxon incantation against fickle allies, faithless donors: *Fuck 'em.*

Arlene Hogan arrives in the spring for a visit.

The first day she joins the eighth-grade girls gathered in a circle on the courtyard. Shannon leans her arms over long legs, and Cailin blithely twists her neck and torso in a move Gumby can't copy. The rest sit on their haunches like an African tribe.

Although she is in her mid-forties, Arlene Hogan is a tennis player, a marathon runner, as nimble as they are, smaller than many of them. She sits listening to them discuss the lunch offered from a food service called Beth's Kitchen.

After several minutes Dominique whispers to her, "Who are you?"

On sabbatical from her San Francisco school and before she officially assumes her post, Arlene comes down frequently to perform a series of impossible tasks. When we originally sought a head of school, we knew it was a big job.

The head leads a family, a kind of government, a small business. Family members (that is, students and faculty) must, on occasion, be counseled through depression, anxiety, drug dependence, and emotional distress. At one time or another, they can be expected to offend each other and/or the surrounding community, including nearby residents, parents, and the possible donors of the gymnasium. In addition, just like biological offspring, they will expect to be subsidized in their use of computers, cell phones, coffee, pastry, Kleenex, Band-Aids, and chocolate.

We know, because Jim McManus, our wise and savvy consultant, has told us that the head provides vision and oversees the day-to-day operations (the governing function). The Head also operates like the owner-officer of a small business, raising money, managing the budget, selling the school to prospective parents, providing a public face for it, and answering the phone calls from angry parents or angry teachers or angry neighbors who, in one case, objected to the color we painted the handicapped parking spot.

The Head of a brand-new school has all the above duties plus the additional chores of implementing the Founders' good ideas on educational philosophy, except when they aren't such good ideas and she must politely note that. She must use her professional connections and personal friendships to give the school instant credibility among all. She must determine how to shape the curriculum to address this mission, which has not been done before because this school hasn't been done before.

And she has to hire, inspire, evaluate, and sometimes fire the faculty.

We haven't attracted the most competent of teachers. If Lucy had been producing a situation comedy, her choices would have had a sort of internal logic: Ms. Brooks and Ms. Valladares are brand-new and in their early twenties; they know the characters on *Dawson's Creek*. The rest of the comedy cast are the wacky, amusing sidekicks.

The science teacher, Mr. B, is a young man from Europe, Serbia, I believe, who is focused on endeavors other than teaching. He runs a business, motivational speaking, by cell phone while conducting class.

He once returned a science test with an "A" on the outside page, but the student had not written anything on the inside pages. Deliberately. He is so wrong as a teacher, he is a unifying force in the class.

"Mr. B was really bad," Shireen remembers. "You know, Katie and Fofy and I carpooled, and we *never* talked, then we started talking about Mr. B, he united us, we even went for coffee one time."

Liz grins when she says, "He was awful. But he liked me."

Old World teachers are out of their depth with American students, who encourage each other to be vocal, to initiate and, by their own accounts, "to trick the teachers" when possible.

Sometimes tricking the teacher is just too easy. One day there are seven or eight students sitting on the floor, chatting outside the language class. Another teacher discovers them.

"Why are there students outside your classroom?" she asks the sweet-faced language teacher from Slovenia.

"Oh, they have contagious headaches," the language teacher explains with a sympathetic frown.

"What!!? What do you mean?"

"One got a headache, and the others caught it."

"I'm sorry to tell you this," the American teacher replied, "but there's no such thing."

Two of the language teachers, a married couple from Europe, spend most of their time working on getting their green cards. Teaching seems to be as peripheral to their lives as the occupations of the TV fathers of the 1950s; it is not an identity so much as a backstory, a definition easily discarded in the day-to-day events of the neighborhood.

The Spanish teacher believes she has too many students (twelve), so she dismisses half on Tuesdays and half on Wednesdays. Where they go is up to them. They're expected to work on unspecified "projects." The good conduct kids go to Patti's art class to work on their marionettes; the rebels go to the bathroom to see if toilet paper rolls will burn.

However, the original lot provide a cultural diversity with its own quirks. One teacher writes "Retard" on the tops of homework that is late, but it is months before the girls figure out that is not a personal assessment of their mental facility.

Eventually Arlene will hire capable professionals whose primary interest is teaching (one language teacher, a little slip of a thing, runs off with a Frenchman she'd met in the summer, but there is also Ms. Crawford, who takes her Spanish class to work in an orphanage in Mexico, and Dr. Brown, whose advanced students write a humorous address for graduation entirely in Latin).

However, even among the teachers Arlene hires, there are misfits for us. I suppose you don't have to be an academic seer to recognize that a brand-new school with no campus will attract as teachers the troubled, the untried, and the brilliantly brave. We have more than our share of teachers who are all wrong or caught at the wrong time of their lives or are wrong-headed about girls. We have some teachers who are preoccupied with their private lives or emotionally fragile or suddenly explosive and furious.

Mr. W was a charming, charismatic lecturer who liked to talk about movies and let his history pupils out early; he had ardent fans among the students. Unfortunately, he had a fierce, violent temper revealed in glimpses when he was frustrated. On the school trip an administrator had to accompany the student group he was supervising to ensure there'd be no incidents.

Miss Brooks, much beloved, "like a big sister" according to Dominique, left her job abruptly, moving to San Diego two weeks before school began. Her husband had asked for a divorce, and she felt she had to get away.

Sometimes the lesson was the teacher. Katie says, "I had a lot of trouble with Mr. V [a European teacher too authoritarian for the free spirits of the Palisades]. After awhile I discovered you could start off hating someone and then see them as a human being."

"The relationship between teacher and students," Katie concludes, "was intense."

Some of the other school relationships are intense, even angry: a former employee, who made complicated a simple job, is suing us for dismissing her, alleging racial discrimination; another, who makes her complicated job simple by failing to perform much of it, sues Archer (and Arlene and me, personally) for terminating her contract. Neither suit will be successful. Amid hours of depositions, Arlene and I meet in the hall and share a bottled water. We wonder why this force field seems to attract incompetents and loonies.

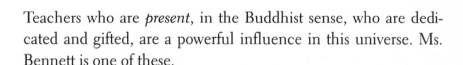

Teachers who are *present*, in the Buddhist sense, who are dedicated and gifted, are a powerful influence in this universe. Ms. Bennett is one of these.

She came from Crossroads School, where she was revered by students and appreciated by all but the one administrator to whom she reported. He was young, new, determined to make his mark; she was seasoned, serious about her work, determined to have autonomy in the classroom. They clashed again and again.

"You have to come to Archer," Patti Meyers told her. "Just see it. You won't believe it, unless you see it."

When Jean Bennett decided to leave Crossroads, she interviewed for Archer at the Methodist Church. She responded strongly to the mission and found Deirdre "visionary" and Arlene Hogan "refreshing," even though she said something startling:

"Don't come here if you're bitter," Arlene told her.

The tight corps of teachers sharing a small space and an integrated curriculum could not absorb acrimony or cynicism. Nor do the students deserve it.

Jean Bennett considered the question. "I'm not bitter about teaching," she said.

It is after school on a Thursday afternoon, and one of the ninth graders arrives to work on her writing. Although she teaches history, not English, Ms. Bennett tackles whatever difficulties students have. This student has been coming two days a week for awhile; she cannot seem to write a coherent paper.

Ms. Bennett reviews the student's latest effort, and suddenly she says, "That's a perfect paragraph! Perfect." She looks at the girl. "OK. Now try for another one."

Later she says, "I had a student who got a 'D,' next report it was an 'A.' I have so many who come in. Girls know that the resource is the teachers."

Ms. Bennett reminds me of my brother's teacher long ago, the one who helped him after school, too. Who took him from a "D" to an "A." Who guided him through some of the pitfalls of adolescence. Who made a difference.

Archer is not the only school with good teachers who are available to their students. I know there are local heroes in other schools and in other towns, but where there are several in the same community, it is a blessing for all. I can't imagine anyone objecting to a school composed of teachers like Jean Bennett and students like ours. Yet, somehow, they will.

14

This Shining Adventure

"When I saw the Methodist Church 'campus,'" Sophie says, "I knew I'd have something concrete to complain about to my parents."

The three upstairs classrooms, the teacher's room, the closet over the sanctuary (which we aren't actually renting), and the gymnasium with intermittent hours do not much resemble a high school campus, but that's what we need it to be, as our first class enters ninth grade. That its primary purpose is to be a facility of a Christian church is not lost on some of the families who visit.

Shireen's uncle is an Orthodox rabbi, so her mother decides not to tell him that Shireen's new high school takes place in a Methodist Church. The mother of another Jewish student physically recoiled from the cross on the wall above the hallway. For some families the Christian symbols are not the challenge; the crowded conditions are.

Students' backpacks line the staircase going down to the dance studio where Shirley MacLaine learned to dance; it's hard not to trip over them. At Vilma's the bathroom for faculty (male and female), staff, and students is also used for photography and art projects; smudges of paint and charcoal appear on the walls, and paper debris overwhelms the gray metal trash can.

The mother of one student is reminded of her experience in a huge, multiethnic, multilanguage New York school, which was "a zoo," so this is not so bad.

"It has a kind of random chaos," another parent says, "which we hope is a sign of creativity."

Random chaos is not the effect we are trying to convey. A new school must necessarily be creative—that's the whole point—but it doesn't do to underscore the instability of the place. Moreover, this is earthquake country.

A year before we opened, a relatively modest earthquake was felt very near here. Fireplaces crumbled, buildings collapsed, patios and walls and sidewalks cracked. This is a place where disorder and disarray can mean danger, where overturned tables in the courtyard and rubble in the alley can signify instability, risk, peril.

Students start their day in the locker room (formerly a supply room in Vilma's old office), which Katie points out is "filled with food and junk." On designated days they have assembly in the former dance studio, sitting cross-legged on the floor, some with their arms around each other, passing Fritos and bottled water between them.

Academic classes are held at the church. Art and science lab are conducted back at Vilma's. Sometimes students conclude it is just too tiring to go back and forth.

A young mother at the Village School is quoted in the *Palisades Post* as approving of "a uniformly polite group of girls, studying together in front of the Methodist Church, walking arm-in-arm throughout the village."

Arm-in-arm, yes. But in the five minutes between classes, the girls are not walking. They run from Vilma's space to the park to the Methodist church. They carry their possessions in fifty-pound backpacks or little baggage carts like homesteaders racing for forty acres of Western land.

The girls who have been here for two years already accept the circumscribed conditions in which they find themselves. Like the teachers, they adapt. However, one or two of the new admittees are not so sure about this.

"When new people come, they are freaking out. Other people were used to space," Katie says. *This isn't high school!*

In spite of the fact that this is not at all what we promised her when she signed on, Arlene Hogan takes it in stride. When she arrives early for a school musical production, she discovers the maintenance crew failed to appear and there are papers, plastic bottles, and smelly garbage littering the brick courtyard where guests are to congregate. Arlene and Ms. Willerson's fiancé clean quickly, gathering clutter without complaint, dragging the garbage bins around back.

Amy Willerson improvises. Slim, dark-haired, dark-eyed with a pale, heart-shaped face, this teacher looks barely older than the girls who crowd around her holding notebooks and book bags, chattering, laughing, gesturing as they move through the hall and down the stairs to the Methodist Church gym, where play practice can occur at certain circumscribed periods of time.

It is not a traditional setting in which Ms. Willerson teaches theater. There are no sets, sound equipment, lights, costumes; no stage. However, her field is creative arts, and the challenges are incorporated into the lesson plans.

"There's so much energy," she says. "When we perform, the cast has to do everything—build the sets, choreograph, clean up.

It's not about glitz, that's for sure." She pauses, amused. "They love power tools."

Moreover, the necessity to own the process, to create what Ms. Willerson calls "an environment where flexible people and a sense of humor can flourish" is its own reward.

The student production showcased two weeks before Willerson's wedding. She was somewhat distracted by impending nuptials; the girls wrote, directed, acted the show, and designed and assembled the sets and costumes.

"When the scenery fell over, the students improvised, blaming it on Clara," Willerson remembers.

Clara?

The main character.

"Everybody wants the toys," she says of other schools, which have stages, auditoriums, departments, "but this is really hands-on." She gets a crooked smile on her face. "For me it's really, *How can I resist this shining adventure?*"

Evidently the Methodist Church itself is not totally comfortable with a high school on the premises. Although the custodian and office people who work there are generally tolerant and good-natured, the church objects strongly when students hang *The Archer School for Girls* sign in the upstairs hallway.

The church is even more upset, we are told, that some of the girls threw bits of ripped notepaper from the classroom window of the second floor. I think it's a pretty minor act of teenage rebellion, but I guess I can see why the church doesn't want it. I don't know if they're aware of what's occurring in the bridal room.

The small, windowless chamber where brides can dress for their weddings is irresistible to some Archer girls. It is the site of life decisions, alliances, pronouncements, friendships: *What exactly is 'unprotected sex'? What can I do about my parents? Why do we have to tuck our shirts in?*

When the high school is granted a day for off-campus lunch, some go to Gelson's Market for salads and bring them back to the tiny, airless room to eat them. Students describe it as "a haven." "A refuge." "Our own world."

"A couple of times I smuggled in Sam, my boyfriend," Cailin reports. "We could hide him in there."

For his part, Sam, the smuggled one, was impressed with the girls, if not the space. "The girls at Archer have always seemed wonderfully close. . . [At] Harvard-Westlake there was closeness, there were deep connections but, on the whole, it was not as cozy. Archer is cozy—that is rare."

It was cozy in the bridal room. It was cozy in theater class and photography. Sometimes it was even cozy in PE.

There is the same scarcity of resources in sports. "When I got here," Raissa Adolphe says, "there were no courts, fields, gymnasium." For emphasis, she adds, "No equipment. No facilities."

Miss A, as students call her, is blonde and wiry, a dynamo who embodies kinetic energy. At Archer she describes teaching dance exercise, which had to be on the grass. *Nobody teaches this way,* she thinks. "Next thing is, the church says, 'we're seeding the lawn, you can't use the grass.' So we go to the sidewalk."

I see the sidewalk dancing when Dreamer and I walk down Via de la Paz from my office. The girls take both parts, some leading, some following. "OK, switch!" Miss A yells. Fire trucks go by and honk. Some girls wave.

Most athletic activities occur outdoors. "The curriculum works," Miss A states, "but we are constantly adapting."

Regarding the Methodist Church gymnasium, which we are leasing particularly for sports and drama, Miss A has learned, "you can *be* there but you can't *do* anything there."

There can be balls in the gym but they can't bounce too hard or hit the walls. The ceiling is too low for volleyball. There can be music, even movement, but Quiet, Quiet. Sometimes preschoolers walk through the gym on their way to recess. Our girls are not allowed to talk to them.

Miss A likes Advisory Time because it's only six students and her: "We have frank discussions about parents, behavior. . . . they are opinionated." Sometimes they give her advice. *Miss A, you really shouldn't say too much. . .* "They're giving me rules!" *This is how it is here.*

Miss A, a Canadian, was unfamiliar with any of the local schools. She didn't know which schools had good teams or, like Marymount, were Westside volleyball champions. When Archer plays Marymount, the first two games are 15–0, 15–0; Archer is trounced.

Miss A goes to the Marymount coach and requests that the third game might be what L.A. calls a friendship game. "Can you play your bench?" she asks Marymount's coach.

"I have been," comes the reply.

Finally, long after the initial game with Harvard-Westlake, there is another win. Our team competes against one from Viewpoint, a sizable school (more than five hundred students) but not monstrously big. When Archer takes the match, there is unabashed jubilation until Miss A cautions her team, "Pretend you always win. Be gracious."

We need Eastern Star. It is obvious to everyone that we cannot continue to have a school in the park, the library, Vilma's space, and a few rooms at the Methodist Church.

Our competition is getting more of everything. Crossroads School has two or three gyms now; we have zip. Brentwood School got maybe one hundred more acres; we have zip. Harvard-

Westlake has a country—the edifice and palace grounds in Bel Air and what looks like a CIA complex in the valley. We, again, have zip.

Well, that's not true.

What we have is purpose. We know that most teenage girls neglect intellectual pursuits, hide their achievements and goals, suffer low self-esteem. It doesn't seem to be happening here. It may even be that privation contributes to the girls' sense of accomplishment.

Shireen wryly observes, "There were no chairs the first week of high school. That was a growing experience." She gives a Mona Lisa smile, "For photography, we had to go to the bathroom for water. Starting everything made us strong."

The oldest of three girls, Shireen is first-generation American. Her family is Persian Jewish. Lili, Shireen's mother, says, "We always lived a life a little outside."

Living "a little outside" the human pageantry of shared food, shared space, and shared leadership of the ninth-grade class is probably neither possible nor desirable. Shireen participates in all the privation and privilege of being the class that is the first.

One of the teachers describes the difficulties for these classmates: "No role models. The biggest challenge for the ninth graders [is] being the pioneers. . . inventing high school from the bottom up."

Girls need role models. Real, actual women and adolescent girls who enact successful roles as athletes, scholars, scientists, and leaders in many endeavors provide the paths for those who follow. It is especially important for girls to have women as role models and for girls of color to see women of color playing nontraditional roles.

Sociologist Janet Chafetz described it simply: women in nontraditional roles can exert "a formidable influence" simply by being in the presence of the young. Girls need to see powerful women doing important work in order to know they can achieve their own potential. By the same token, Chafetz argues, the absence of women role models "implies the opposite."

TEXAS ROLE MODELS

On a January day in Dallas when the grass, the brick, and the limestone walls around the 100-acre campus are all the same dried-prairie color, I visit the Hockaday School for Girls. It's quite a campus, more than 340,000 square feet of rooms to clean every night (as one woman in the lobby phrased it) for more than 1,000 Hockaday students. There are lots of tall windows, some super-sized ones in the mouth-gaping dance studio and in the front lobby, where there's a couch with a live calico cat to keep visitors occupied.

There's a four-thousand-square-foot fitness center, three full-sized basketball courts, two racket ball courts, an all-weather track, three playing fields, an indoor swimming pool, the dance studio, a complete ceramics studio, two libraries, labs, and other studios and theaters. I believe I'm suffering from Edifice Envy.

But I'm also suffering from Role Model Greed. At older girls' schools like Hockaday, there are built-in role models, beginning with the historic founder, Ela Hockaday, who started the school in 1913 to prepare girls of "strong potential" to assume positions of responsibility, based on four cornerstones with a Texas drawl: *character, courtesy, scholarship, and athletics.*

More recent Hockaday role models are teachers (68 percent with advanced degrees), trustees (55 percent female), alumnae who are pleased to give their school the biggest endowment in the history of girls' schools (seventy-five million dollars in 2002), and the girls themselves, one of whom nonchalantly told me, "Girls here do everything." Pressed a little, her companion detailed *everything:* "class work, clubs, council. . . sports, of course (she was in an athletic uniform), and, uh, community service."

Our role models come from the Big Sisters Program we imple-ment, assigning each girl a mentor, a woman prominent in busi-ness, the professions, or the arts. We have illustrious visitors, too, like political path breakers Ann Richards, Carol Moseley Braun, and Pat Schroeder; like local leaders Leticia Quesada and ABC chief Jamie Tarses; like artists Judy Chicago and USC's Ruth Weisberg.

We have teacher role models like Miss A and Ms. Willerson. "More than at any other school," Miss Adolphe says, "you have an impact."

Ms. Willerson felt it as "a powerful connection" with the girls. "They feel ownership," she said. "They think around the prob-lems. They mentor each other."

She influences them, and they impress her. "If one is sick, they stand around her, they get her work, they cover for her in class," she smiles sweetly, "even if they aren't on speaking terms."

They can be big sisters to each other and to the younger girls. And some girls are not only path breakers at school but pioneers in their homes, too.

There is Lauren, as willowy and fresh as a young plant, evi-dence of the optimism of new life even in the concrete-and-asphalt world of Compton, a city of storefront churches and stucco-faced bungalows with front yards of clay soil and orna-mental cement borders and backyards bound by chain-link fences. She is the only recruit from Compton, so we send a taxi for her every day because it is cheaper than hiring a bus.

Entering Archer had been Lauren's last resort. After extensive gang warfare in her public school, she'd applied to a program which placed minority kids (in L.A. that would be *majority* kids) in private schools. She wanted to play basketball. She visited what she wryly referred to as Archer's "campus," looked at the poor, sorry gym, and revised her plans—she would go to Archer to learn computers (of which we have at least five).

Lauren works hard at Archer with very little support from her family. Her father is absent, and her mother is emotionally unstable. When her mother evicts her in a fit of pique, Lauren will move in with Ms. Bennett, her history teacher, and live with her until college.

There are recruits from South Central L.A., four Latinas, Susan and Esmerelda in ninth grade and Maria and Perla in seventh. When we accepted them and gave them full scholarships, their guidance counselor called, his voice choking with emotion. "This validates my whole life," he told us. "For twenty years I've told kids, stay off drugs, stay away from gangs, do your homework, and your life will get better. You made it true."

The better life in America begins at five-thirty in the morning, when they rise to meet the neon-green station wagon that serves as our bus. When they leave for Archer, their families are vulnerable, for the girls are the ambassadors, interpreting the culture, reading official documents, making appointments at the doctor. Sometimes they also shop and clean and babysit when they return home.

Susan and Esmerelda are currently learning salsa dancing in front of the Methodist Church. I'm sure they are wondering why they've left South Central to come to Pacific Palisades and do Latin dancing on the sidewalk. Without boys.

Then there is Liz, smart and funny with a rebellious irreverence that is undermined by her fresh-faced looks. She wants to be *noir*. When she met Dominique, after ten minutes of Dom's ebullience she said to no one in particular, "This girl should have pompoms permanently attached to her wrists."

At the all-school picnic at Leo Carillo Park, the ninth grade, at Liz's urging, is making Mexican food. "It's easy," she insists to the doubters. "You buy tortillas, open a can of refried beans, grate some cheese."

Susan and Esmerelda go into the park bathroom to wash with soap and water and then prepare guacamole, peeling the avocados and mashing them back at the picnic table with their bare hands. Other students exchange looks, appalled. Ms. Bennett considers how to intervene to get any of them to try the guacamole.

No need. Liz has observed the covert glances. "You know," she says to her classmates, "we're lucky we get guacamole made in the traditional way—wash your hands with soap and water, mash it, add the special spices. It's *authentic* guacamole."

Everyone tries it.

Liz is surprised to find herself in what she calls "an intellectual, philosophical, emotional community. . . . I've never been friends with girls before, only guys."

She is amused at the contrast between the context and the content of her new school: "We're on the orange couches in the lounge, arguing the relative merits of Athens versus Sparta—I mean, we don't have *desks*. We're . . . arguing about people from two thousand years ago and I'm really into it. It's like that damn quote: *How can I resist this shining adventure?*

"The campus," Liz says with a sardonic smile. "Pretend school—four rooms at the church."

Not for much longer. Not if we get the money. If we get the permit. If we get the building.

15

Nefarious Activities

All new schools face obstacles of some sort: financial insecurity, political opposition, powerful dissent. We happen to have all three.

The letter that most troubles me is from someone named Freda Hermann, who writes to city officials, ordering them to "Stop the Archer School." The letter is reproduced in our initial Environmental Impact Report (EIR), a 798-page document which, we hope, portrays us as a nice, quiet school with very little traffic and no satanic rituals.

Tell that to F. Hermann. She argues that the students of *Brentwood* School go to Chaparal Street to "park cars, cavort, and engage in nefarious activities." She suspects there will be more of this sort of thing with Archer, given "the increase of teenage girls and their attendant activities."

Attendant activities that are *nefarious*, as in *wicked, vicious?*

I'd say she's kidding, but the tone of her message belies it. Elsewhere she refers to "reckless teenagers" and their inevitable "litter, smoking, etc."

This is not an isolated complaint, but one of seventy-six I can peruse in my copy of the preliminary EIR. Most, like Freda Hermann's, are intended to prevent the Archer School from moving to Brentwood. This one particularly troubles me because it represents a world view that is antichildren, antischools, anticommunity. I suspect that most of the "Anti" letters have these biases, but this is probably the most blatant.

There are no young scholars or promising athletes in Ms. Hermann's world, only "reckless teenagers." Schools don't educate tomorrow's leaders; they create "accidents, traffic jams and driving delays." This world is a perilous place.

Although the letter writer refers to her neighborhood as "a residential community," that doesn't imply, as we thought, an environment of homeowners, apartment dwellers, shopkeepers, and temple- and churchgoers who would welcome a girls' school in their midst. No, allowing a school in "this hazardous location" would be tantamount to "signing the death warrant of pedestrians as well as drivers."

Unfortunately, Ms. Hermann is not alone. Other than one letter, which begins, "I am very excited about the prospect," and another which states "We need the school" and explains why, most of the rest of the testimony is decidedly anti. Some, like Ms. Hermann, are against the other schools (Brentwood, Mount St. Mary's, Sunshine Pre-School) and by extension, ours.

"The level of driving exhibited by parents dropping off or picking up children [at these schools is] abominable," declares one. There is more specific description of this abominable behavior and then the conclusion — "No, a new school is intolerable."

Most of these people view the prospect of the Archer School in the neighborhood as "a dangerous situation" due to an increase in traffic. "Are you suggesting moving Los Angeles proper to Brentwood?" asks one.

Others see graver dangers lurking, such as "increased vandalism and other types of low-grade crime, which is a particularly acute problem in all-girls schools." What?!?

We meet with our lawyers, consultants, and traffic experts and discuss how we can counter this message. We want the neighbors to know we will bus most of our students; a few will carpool or walk to school. Nefarious activities will not be allowed.

Our architect, Scott, calls Hugh Snow, president of the Brentwood Homeowners Association, but the BHA won't discuss the EIR (too lengthy to review in time for the hearing). Instead, its board votes to oppose the school. Scott argues for negotiation, at least on the points of concern not addressed by the EIR.

"Why spend the time on other points," asks BHA's president, "if the school will not exist at the site?"

"I don't think," Scott tells us, "he considers the possibility that Archer could succeed without BHA's endorsement."

My husband and I take two of our opponents to dinner at Divino's, a restaurant near Eastern Star that has good food and a good proprietor, that is, one who supports our school. Chris and Jennifer Lewis, who are reportedly investing a fortune in the campaign against us, are colleagues of friends of ours. They live in the neighborhood on a drive of private estates above Chaparal Street. Although they are good eaters and pleasant company, they seem to be unmoved by our protestations that we will neither devalue their property nor create more traffic on Sunset.

Arlene and I attend a neighborhood gathering on Saltair Street, where other opponents live. The red-haired crone who owns Sunshine Pre-School on Sunset rushes in, takes a drink from our hostess, and informs us that she once applied to increase enrollment at Sunshine. She didn't get the permit, she tells us meaningfully.

This woman will prove to be an unrelenting adversary, an outspoken opponent who drapes a *No to Archer* banner across Sunshine's entry and who lambastes our efforts to join the neighborhood in her opening speech to new preschool parents. The preschool with its perky name so at odds with its personality reminds us of the L.A. dump where garbage is tested for radioactive waste; its name is Sunshine Canyon Landfill.

If the other guests at the Saltair house are not open to persuasion, nor are they as openly hostile as Miss Sunshine. *Miss Sunshine* is the students' name for her, demonstrating in the musical they will write an ironic understanding of the character. A senior citizen given to leather pants or tennis outfits, she figures large in the girls' experience, not only because her public presentations are vitriolic but because in one instance she will actually step on Dominique (who is sitting on the floor in front) as she goes to take the microphone.

After the injurious engagement on Saltair, Arlene continues to attend gatherings at whatever homes will have her, but I do not go with her. I find it debilitating and depressing. No matter what we do, they rail against us.

One event, the July 9 hearing before the Zoning Administration, particularly attracts the anti-Archer militants who rail against us. It is held in the Grand Ballroom of the Olympic Collection, which is as unsuitable as it sounds, a vast, sterile space with folded metal chairs set up in rows. The only music in the Grand

Ballroom is the robotic pip from cell phones, which interferes with the public address system.

Here Dan Green, the Zoning Administrator (ZA), presides at a table with stacks of paper and a bound copy of the Environmental Impact Report for what will be eight hours of testimony, much of it intemperate, angry, and aggrieved, punctuated by hisses, catcalls, and clapping. It is not yet 10 a.m., and Dan Green is already looking harassed.

In the Anti contingent are Jon Byk, Chris and Jennifer Lewis, Miss Sunshine, and a few of the privileged Brentwood residents with personal training programs and Altoids in their sweat suit pockets; their protests (usually about traffic) are polished and particularly damning because they are probably parents of school-age children (in another private school).

For the most part, however, the nay-saying neighbors are white-haired and white collar—I recognize two real estate developers, several talent agents, and, sadly, a colleague from UCLA. I assume they're worried about congestion on Sunset: "It would be madness," one of them will say, "to let Archer School add hundreds of bodies to further clog the boulevard."

Sounds like we're creating a human barrier in the middle of the street, a line of female scholars, donnish robes dragging on the ground, as they stand and recite—in Latin—formulas and parodies and stanzas of prison rap: *Gallia in partes tres. Amo, amas, amat.*

On our side of the battlements are twelve students, two teachers, five professionals (attorneys and environmental and transportation experts), a handful of hardy neighbors, and parents. The parents, working-class women and men who've taken the day without pay, are going to sit in these metal chairs for eight hours, except for the one moment they stand in answer to the ZA's question, "Who is here in support of the school?"

There are no celebrities, no rock stars, no movie producers. We hear an enduring complaint that our side is endorsed by movie producers who, "with an infinite amount of funds can buy or play with zoning," even promise jobs to heads of homeowner associations. It is completely false, but we can do little to stop it, and it is a rumor that persists for years.

Arlene and I are wearing tailored suits, the students are in uniform, the professionals in business attire. No one is chic or cool. (Well, except for Lisa, our primary attorney, who is both chic and cool: size six Italian suit with curves, sexy high heels, and those rimless colored glasses that perch on the end of an aesthetically perfect nose; she's in uniform, too, what she wears walking the halls of that large-but-understated cement edifice on the Westside where her law firm exists.

Lisa sits by Arlene and me in the front row. On the other end of our row are Scott, who is here to talk the architecture of historic preservation, and Sam Ross, a balding, genial man who is our expert on traffic. Sam is newly married, and through all proceedings, however rancorous, he maintains the quiet cheerfulness of one who is well loved.

Behind us are eight hundred people, some who are here on our behalf, some who scowl or turn away.

One who scowls, but without menace, is Fred Gaines, our opponents' attorney. Fred is intense, acerbic, given to sarcasm, even in public. He will say, "The EIR overlooks *tiny little things* like the opening of the Getty."

(At a later meeting in the august setting of City Council, Fred Gaines will actually say, "Every party needs a pooper, and today it's me.")

Joking remarks are alien to us here. We have promulgated and placated and acquiesced to get this far. We're serious.

I'm to talk about this: *Why a school? Why girls? Why here?* It's a simple speech, two and a half minutes, prepared with the team at Lisa's law office.

I say my name and begin: *If we start backward by looking at our best citizens, the peacemakers, the path breakers, the innovators — at the core is education; each had a —*

Dan Green interrupts me. "We don't want to hear this. This is not germane to this hearing." He looks sternly at me from his table in the front of the room, and I pause and look away like a dog who has pissed on the floor. There is stifled applause from the Neighbors, a stunned silence from our side.

I go ahead to the part about Eastern Star and the Brentwood community but again Dan Green interrupts. Lisa steps up to confer with her client, advising me to step away from the mike and let Arlene do her part. I am finished for the day.

What does it mean that I'm prevented from speaking? I believe it's important, relevant to this process, that we are a school, not a crematorium, not a porn club. A school. In a neighborhood of shops and houses and places of worship.

But I may be wrong. Naïve. Maybe the whole thing is about cars on Sunset. Maybe Sam Ross, our traffic consultant, is the only one here who can help us.

The next eight hours are jammed with remarks both germane and inane; some of the testimony is from pros and some from amateurs, like the woman who presents a drawing she's done of our site with a huge gymnasium which will block the light in three municipal districts.

"Is this to scale?" asks the ZA.

"I'm not an artist," she says dismissively.

On chairs in different rows, initially unknown to each other, are two pro-Archer neighbors with nothing to gain by being here but the sweet sense of acting honorably. Morris Rosenfeld, a retired economics professor, lives across the street from Eastern Star; he is passionate when he speaks of good schools and neighborhood value, when he states that Archer will be "an asset to the area."

Randy Sherman, the head of a citizens' environmental group, touts another asset Archer will provide—an example of environmentally friendly leadership. Because of our commitment to busing nearly all our students, because we de-emphasize L.A.'s car culture by restricting student drivers to car pools which will park off campus, and because we agree to fund some street improvements at five intersections on Sunset Boulevard, Sherman is visibly angry with the Anti campaigners, who are trying to ruin "the best solution for Brentwood and for the traffic on Sunset."

There is another, Mary Ann Sickle, a retired school librarian, who says that good schools make good communities. These three say their pieces determinedly at meeting after meeting.

To you three an Irish blessing:

> *Health and long life to you,*
> *The love of your heart to you,*
> *A child at the hearth for you,*
> *Land without rent to you,*
> *And may you die in Ireland.*

Into the room comes Cindy Miscikowski, the City Council member representing Brentwood. She is blonde, round-cheeked, smiling with wide mouth, seemingly energized by being among her constituents. (She had been Councilman Braude's assistant and reportedly wanted this job for many years.)

There is hushed quiet as Miscikowski asks permission to speak. The ZA nods, and Councilwoman Miscikowski says these words: "Both sides have requested my support. I recognize the legitimacy of both. I decided to support Archer School because it is appropriate for the Eastern Star site." There are hisses and grumbles and catcalls as she continues to speak. Something about negotiations, more meetings (Arlene involuntarily recoils), and holding open the record until July 31. I don't hear the rest, only these words.

I support Archer School.

Health and long life to you, too, Ms. Miscikowski.

How did we survive this period?

Our own friends and families were an unfailing, if sometimes offbeat source of support in our founding endeavor. Vicky's husband John wrote letters to editors and attended an untold number of rallies, receptions, assemblies, and wine servings; at one he said, smiling, "This could work." Megan's husband David did child care and occasionally dinner, as well as the requisite number of meetings. Even their two daughters, aged four and six, excused their mommy's late evenings if the reason was school, one of them saying, "Just this once. . ." as Megan went off to the hundred-and-forty-seventh encounter with the Neighbors.

We were fortunate too, that nature provided us a comic vision, one of the requirements, according to Jill Ker Conway, former president of Smith College, for running an academic institution. "Faculty meetings," she said of her own school, "always provided plenty of material."

Neighborhood meetings did the same for us. And shared depositions, deficits, defamations. We needed irony and distance to survive; with comic vision, we could embrace the dark as well as the light.

One time during budget difficulties, a day of angry phone calls from parents about the buses, and news of a fresh skirmish in the civic struggles, Megan put her hand on Arlene's shoulder and asked, "Can't you sometimes resist *this shining adventure?*"

Vicky was habitually wry and darkly humorous in her view of our attempts to negotiate and renegotiate space for the school: "Every time David turns over a rock, there's a lizard underneath. So I say, quit turning over rocks. He, being trained otherwise, continues to turn."

My contribution was dogs, the steadfast Dreamer and two Newfoundlands, delightful, drooling, bumbling giants: Teddy, furry-friendly and one hundred and sixty pounds; and Corduroy, the new puppy, a baby bear invited to the picnic, unruly and irresistible even as he's overturning tables of potato salad. It's hard to have righteous indignation around clumsy characters like these.

Plus I live in the midst of comedy writers. Both our daughters make droll observations at various times, mostly about my compulsive tenacity and the obsessive pinheadedness of our opponents. Gary, at a neighborhood conclave which droned into exasperating tedium, observed to the room, "If I weren't in show business, this would be the stupidest meeting I've ever attended."

16

Comedy Saves

August is oppressive, with empty skies and long, hot days of unrelenting glare. On the Thursday that the *Brentwood News* hits the asphalt driveways of our neighborhood, we retrieve it with a sense of dread. It seems to contain only rejection and recrimination toward us and, now, toward Councilwoman Cindy Miscikowski, as well.

One couple writes that Miscikowski is willing "to sacrifice the needs of an entire community for her own political ambitions." Another charges her with (unspecified) personal gain.

We are accused of trying to "invade" Brentwood. (We live here. And so does Cindy Miscikowski.)

At the July 9 public hearing, Dan Green, aware that he was sitting on a wasp's nest, closed with the comment, "I'm glad I don't live in Brentwood." People laughed; I didn't find it completely funny.

The good news comes August 22. The Los Angeles Office of Zoning Administration, in the person of Dan Green, approves our conditional use permit. Unfortunately, there are fifty-one conditions. The product of negotiations, the conditions restrict

Archer's size, cars, hours of operation, even landscaping. Who knew the people with stone lions and cement chickens in their yards even cared about such things?

To date, Arlene has endured more than twenty hours of tea and crackers with the neighbors and, since July 9, another twenty hours with representatives of the city and neighborhood associations. In an interview in *Brentwood News*, Arlene sounds like a weary Caesar: "We were called to the table, we went, and we gave."

Concessions are costly. We give land in front of the building for a left turn lane onto the property, and we agree to make street improvements on Sunset Boulevard at five intersections (which will cost almost one and a half million dollars). The landscape buffer—mature plants, and parking for the Neighbors on Chaparal—are other expenses.

Still the neighbors are not pleased. Brentwood Homeowners Association wants us to construct homes on our playing field "to act as a buffer for the existing neighborhood" (and give them more members?). Concerned Brentwood Homeowners want us to locate at another site. The two neighborhood groups appeal Dan Green's decision. In the fall we won't be moving into Eastern Star. We'll be defending ourselves before the Board of Zoning Appeals.

The neighborhood, says Jon Byk, has been "raped," a rather insensitive metaphor, I think: "Imagine how emotionally stultifying [it is] to be confronted with the invasion of your neighborhood by a school that you don't want."

Byk is a marketing and advertising writer who for two years has conducted a public relations campaign against the school. Now he complains that neighbors have been "unable to overcome oft-repeated clever PR spin" because it converted some to our side. (It will be revealed that Byk and company are trying to buy Eastern Star and develop it.)

We have one friend on Chaparal (the "Street from Hell," one of Archer's young staff members calls it). His name is Steve Wyler, and somehow he is able to buck his neighbors and applaud us for working "so determinedly" with the surrounding community. Steve Wyler is the one sane voice in the posse which plans to string up all the strangers in town.

There are times I picture that posse, the angry townspeople opposing us, and I fantasize about the gunslinger we'd get who'd make *them* get out of town by sundown. I'm pretty sure there are some Brooklyn cronies of my husband who could do the job. Some dead sushi in the mailbox, perhaps.

We are not doing this gracefully. This opposition stuff. There are people who like adversity, people who *thrive* in adversity (lawyers, arms dealers, agents); there are people who become more spiritual in adversity (St. Augustine, Mother Teresa, Joey Tribbiani on *Friends*), but not us. We're fadin'.

We find ourselves spontaneously weeping at McDonald's commercials and waking up in the night to mewing, whimpering sounds, which I find is me. In her house it's Arlene.

Luckily Arlene is who she is: the oldest, the example for the younger sisters; the first in her family to take the long subway ride to St. Brendan's Girls' School because her working-class Irish family believed in sacrificing for education. And she's from Brooklyn—she doesn't like to lose.

The price is extreme stress.

Megan and Vicky are doing better than we are because they can use drugs. Megan uses the drug of work (or Hollywood's version of it, which is meetings, phone calls about meetings, and lunch meetings). Vicky uses coffee—café espresso, which is a dense, dark, foreign-looking drink served in a little cup, which resembles one from a doll's tea set.

Arlene's response to insult and injury is to surround herself with canines. When she arrived here from San Francisco, she had two old, quiet cocker spaniels as befit the predictable life she had in the north. Then our daughter talked her into getting Grace, a Newfoundland puppy, soon-to-be a drooling, licking, bounding, 135-pound bear-like creature. When things get really rough, Arlene and I take Teddy, my Newfoundland, and hers to the green fields of a dog park near Eastern Star, where other dog owners offer counsel, sympathy, and help in wrestling our dogs back into the car.

When we aren't petting, feeding, or restraining a large dog, we go for the chocolate. At Archer there are Musketeer bars, Hershey's kisses, schoolboy cookies, brownies, chocolate of every kind and quality. When things get really grim, even the men eat it. I watch, fascinated, as John, an investment analyst, and Robert, a real estate mogul, eat chocolate *tofu drops* as we discuss neighbor relations and interest loans.

Because we are conducting a campaign as well as classes, because we must hire experts as well as teachers, because we are fighting for the school's very life, we are helplessly—almost hopelessly—in debt.

In panic and near hysteria, I confide my fears to Gary. I'm visiting him in New York where he's doing a show called *Spin City*. The school needs a loan to cover our costs, I tell him, but the bank won't do it without some outside collateral. I suppose the bank questions that we'll ever get the permit.

"We can do it," he says quietly. "We'll mortgage the house."

I'm silent. Tears flow unchecked down my cheeks. I see his face, so dear to me, the expression, serious, grave.

"We can't let them win," he adds. "This school will change the lives of thousands of girls." Then he sees my face and his mouth softens, he crinkles the laugh lines around his eyes. "We can always go back to living in a tent. Like in the sixties. That wasn't so bad."

There are no other options that I can see. We have a modest-sized student body of diverse economic capabilities. We have a small staff of teachers, administrators, volunteer-parents. The development director, hired from a tiny school back East, pursues computer games, long conversations on the phone with his mother, cocktails promptly at five, but no donors. In May he quits altogether.

Our board members, perhaps regretting earlier enthusiasm, are subdued.

I chair the board, a full-time job, as it happens. Full-time, unpaid. Megan has another of these unpaid positions, chairing Annual Giving with Dr. Jeff. One night I see her as we are both leaving the parking lot at twilight.

"How'd we do on the Giving Campaign?"

"Nearly one hundred thousand dollars from the parents. Not much help toward the debt, but 100 percent participation. 100 percent of the staff and faculty, too." She gives me a mischievous look and adds, "Even the development director."

Rob Everett, a highly sought, Harvard-educated, prospective teacher, interviewed at the jury-rigged, jigsaw campus in Pacific Palisades. He described what happened next:

Deirdre Gainor suggested that I go take a look at the new campus—noting that it was finally being adapted to school use after a protracted legal battle—to persuade me to be part of a new adventure. When I drove up Sunset that afternoon and saw the Eastern Star building, I . . . nearly wrecked. That building?! I didn't believe I had the address right. I strolled, awestruck, through the building along with a young student applicant and her mother. The little girl whispered to me, "I hope I get in." I replied, "I hope I do, too."

Debi, a lawyer specializing in financial matters, puts her practice on hiatus for six months to supervise the adaptation of Eastern Star from a home for old ladies to what we hope will be a school for young leaders. She comes every day to scrape walls for painting, check the gas heaters, the plumbing, and the work the backhoe is doing on the athletic fields.

On Saturdays and Sundays in jeans and green t-shirts which say *Archer* on the front, she works, and her teenage daughter provides child labor. This commitment cannot be good for Debi's legal practice or her daughter's life as a teenager, but neither Arlene nor I say anything. We need them too badly.

I've become sick.

When Gary and I were hippies we spent day and night together, talking ideas, waiting tables for capital, reading Kurt Vonnegut and books on Oppenheimer, Einstein, and Lenin, listening to music. Doing nothing much but be in each other's company.

Then I went to graduate school. I took to it, won awards for research, but I got mired in the political morass of it and, crying on the bed one day, decided I wouldn't finish. "You can't *quit*," Gary insisted. "You can't."

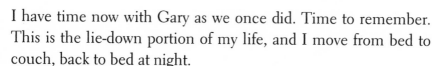

I have time now with Gary as we once did. Time to remember. This is the lie-down portion of my life, and I move from bed to couch, back to bed at night.

I've always had the vigorous energy of a three-year-old. I've clog-danced off beat and slightly off center every St. Patrick's Day. Now I feel the vitality draining out of me from a mysterious disease that feels like it's replacing my blood with a slow, dense substance that drags my limbs down.

No one seems to know what I have, but it is making me insubstantial, a shirt drying on a clothesline in the wind. My body is ash and bone, no weight. After I wash my face, I look into a hand-held mirror and see only eyes and lashes, like a Keene painting. Sometimes I can't hold the mirror. Dancing is definitely out.

Gary drives me to clinics, centers, hospitals, only for us to find that the medical world is baffled. At UCLA for one test, it's eight o'clock at night, no one but the medical technician is there with us, and I can't get my arms over my head for the body scan; Gary has to don the lead apron and force my arms through the x-ray machine. The tests are inconclusive.

Finally two physicians diagnose it, a rare autoimmune disease and a related condition that inflames the muscles of my body. It is fatal about 40 percent of the time, usually in the first few months. Although we are past that critical time, I still seem to be fading.

Gary cooks, cleans, and carries, ferrying me to chemotherapy once a month and keeping me company for the six or eight hours that the magic poison drips into my arm. In between sessions at

Cedars Sinai, he offers jazz, reminiscences, and amusing observations about the world, like a personal *Tonight Show* for an audience of one.

The two physicians we see (kind men—one of them calls every other day) seem to like Gary more than anyone else in their day. He asks after their children, grandchildren; he has tales to tell them.

For us Gary holds the fears and harbors the hopes and tries to transform all this into comedy. He has a hundred stories for me, but I see underneath and they are based on one message: *You can't quit.*

I am a stone statue, unable to sit, eat, talk much, or read. I occupy a silent netherworld, mostly awake, dreamy. I have time for meditation.

What I don't have is anything like normal time with our teenage daughter. She invests in substitute mothers—a manicurist from Russia who only has sons, a yoga instructor, her Latin teacher—women who are available and able. When she passes our room on her way downstairs early every morning, I wave. "Elvis has left the building," I murmur to my husband, who sleeps beside me.

Our older daughter has become a comedy writer like her father. She leaves her television show in the midst of production to spend a week sitting with me, reading me magazine articles about sofa styles and lip gloss, gossiping about politicians she knew in Washington, D.C., when she was a Congressional Page. She is afraid—I see glimpses of it in her dark eyes—but she is trying to be intrepid like the main character of *Brave Irene*, which we'd read together when she was a child.

Friends call, write cards; Dr. Jeff makes casseroles; Megan brings her crème brûlée; Dreamer keeps a constant watch by my side with such wary concern, we begin to refer to him as *the Doc-*

tor. Sixth graders from Archer visit, each coached with a brief story to tell, a happy incident to report. Arlene comes almost every day.

The Archer School for Girls is real. Some teach, some pay tuition and worry about attention deficit disorder (ADD) and teenagers with cars; others are the recipients of the worry, the lesson plans. They chew gum and smoke filtered cigarettes, blowing the smoke down the toilets in the bathroom; they design rockets and test them in the canyon behind the church.

I have long had a dream that they will design rockets. It is symbolic, it seems to me, of reaching for the stars. It is mathematics, physics, aerodynamics—stuff girls aren't supposed to be good at doing.

They do have their own girlie spin on it. The rockets are elaborately decorated. Inside the noses, which will be ejected in flight, young engineers write the words for things they reject: some write *War, Racism, Poverty.* One writes *Big Thighs* (I predict she will be the comedy writer).

Through the battles and the challenges on campus and off, these girls, their teachers and administrators, and their parents have become a community. Most of us can recognize a community when we're in one: it has shared values and goals, a sense of belonging among members, sometimes rituals (for us, those would be Fall Outing, Founders' Day, Arrow Week, the school song sung off-key at assembly, the Maypole Celebration, and anything with sugar).

At Archer, students adopt honesty, respect, and responsibility as official shared values, and they talk about applying those values to interactions with teachers and among themselves in the classroom, in peer counseling, on the sports court, on the bus. There are unstated values, too, shared by this communal body, which include a commitment to hard work and high expectations to become what a girl named Sofi identified as "tomorrow's dreamers and tomorrow's leaders."

The other shared value is single sex schooling. The union of all girls creates not only a certain harmony of purpose but a unique society that at times is disparaged by the outside. Where girls wait for our bus on a street in their neighborhood, they are in uniform with our name on their chests. There are times that circumstance gives rise to remarks from other teenagers about their (better-than-everybody-else's) social class, their (worse-than-everybody-else's) physical beauty, or their (different-from-normal) sexual preference. Mostly our girls ignore or laugh it off, but they are aware of being part of an obvious group.

"Yeah, like you're really cool," one eighth grader reported about her bus stop exchange with Brentwood boys, perhaps rewriting her part as she added, "look where you go to school."

If Gilligan first noticed that adolescent girls have an urge to be part of a caring community, that they develop their identities in relationships and in caring for others, other educators provided evidence that such connection affects learning.

Women's Ways of Knowing, which built on feminist theory such as Gilligan's, offered empirical data to support what coauthor Nancy Goldberger identified as the authors' "breakthrough insight: Women don't just learn in classrooms; they learn in relationships, by juggling life demands, by dealing with crises in families and communities."

In a classroom in a school that feels like "a caring community," students want to learn, according to studies conducted by the Developmental Studies Center in Oakland, California. In elementary, middle, and high schools which felt like "supportive, friendly environments" to the students, female and male, children were motivated, achieved higher test scores, and had higher educational aspirations (among other measures) than their counterparts in less friendly institutions.

A caring community is a good place to learn.

My own conclusion: A caring community is also a place to heal.

The treatment is working. The medicine, meditation, imaging, soup, letters, chocolate, prayers and wishes, flowers, phone calls, visits, stories, and living with Gary are making me better.

I expect to be clog-dancing by summer.

17

The Moon in a Silver Bag

These days are over-full of moment and event. We experience them numbly, absorbing them without acknowledging their import or their impact.

I am recovering from the unfathomable autoimmune disease that keeps me on the green couch in the living room, when the report of the Zoning Appeals Board approves Archer as an appropriate use of the Eastern Star site. On December 18 we again assemble all our experts, parents, supporters, some administrators, and students, and we beseech City Council for its blessing.

Amy Willerson, theater teacher, was there. "I was stunned at the venom [of the Neighbors]," she recalls. "It is amazing to me that people could be against a school like this. It was hard not to take personally."

She worried about the students taking it personally, too. So she assigned them the writing and producing of a musical about Miss Sunshine and the Neighbors. "Let them have a cathartic experience," she offered.

Students wrote and performed a satirical, fairy-talesque story of three girls on a quest to find a place for their school. They used popular songs throughout, particularly their own version of an R&B song then in vogue, "Never Gonna Get It." In defiance of the lyric, the three protagonists do get it eventually.

"It was hilarious," one girl told me, when she and four classmates visited shortly after the performance. "I mean, really, it was soooo good."

What was also so good was that City Council approved the Archer School's permanent home on Sunset Boulevard by a vote of 13–0. Unanimous. So, it's finally done.

Except—there always seems to be an *except* to the Neighbor troubles—Concerned Brentwood Homeowners, now calling themselves Concerned Brentwood Residents, sue, seeking an injunction to keep us from occupying Eastern Star in September. Now we appear before Judge Robert O'Brien of the Second District Court of Appeals. Who denies their injunction, affirming our conditional use permit. It is three weeks before school is to open.

One week later, my mother dies on a ship halfway between Ireland, where she was born, and the United States. She and my dad went to breakfast and, walking the decks after, stopped in a little pub for an Irish coffee. Some 1940s music was playing, and she danced with my dad. On the way back to the room, she got chest pains and died.

We have the memorial service with an Irish harpist, the funeral mass, the burial. At my parents' house afterward, we hold a California wake with lots of food, Napa wine, lots of family (a great many people named Kevin), friends, my mom's exercise class, her yoga teacher.

She'd had what our generation would consider a difficult life—the early death of her father, the subsequent poverty which that bequeathed, the discrimination against immigrants she encountered in American schools—yet she seemed to have danced through the years with the "moon in a silver bag," as Yeats described it. And each of her three children thought he or she was her favorite.

My younger brother's case for being the favorite is aided by being named Thomas Kevin, after her brother; my middle sibling's case is enhanced by his McGourty features, after her father; mine is abetted by Archer, for our mother, a devout Catholic, also worshipped education, especially for girls, especially those who might be impoverished and/or immigrants, especially those who might themselves have the moon in a silver bag.

I wish she'd lived to see Archer grow up.

The first day of school at the new campus is the day after we return from the funeral. The construction crew is driving away as the teachers arrive; the crew has worked through the night. There is no toilet paper in the bathrooms, so Anne, Arlene's young assistant, runs to the market to buy some.

"Who would think of toilet paper for the first day of school?" asks Amy Willerson. "But of course you do need it."

Arlene has already addressed another need. We are required by the permit to pave the parking lot, but there is a strike in Los Angeles County among asphalt workers. No one in the county will lay asphalt.

Tom Bookman, the construction chief, finds a company outside the county which will come in at dawn on the first day of school. The police will come, he tells Arlene, because it is illegal to do construction that early in the morning. "So when they come, you act indignant and say, 'Tom, you should have told me!' and I'll say, 'Aw shucks, I'm sorry,' and meanwhile we'll get the asphalt laid."

The police come, watch the charade, deliver the rebuke. Smile at Anne. Depart.

After the young teachers have run through the halls (the sixth-grade faculty, with two dogs, a golden retriever and a yellow lab, following), touched the fountain and the courtyard bell like kids in a game of tag, and gloried in the high-ceilinged spaces, the students arrive at the new campus. The buses unload at the front door, girls bound out; some, like a slinky, uncurl down one set of steps and up another, others, like rubber balls, bounce and squeal.

Almost overnight the centerpiece room of the Eastern Star home is transformed from an old-age dining facility, where the highlight was fruit Jell-O for lunch, to the site of Patti Meyers's advanced drawing class, with girls standing at large easels in the brilliant southern light of long windows, classical music accompanying the broad strokes of their brushes, their brows serious as they concentrate on the line and texture of a limb or a strand of hair on the live model posed before the gigantic stone fireplace.

The physical space, which all of its existence has been dedicated to the well-being of women, which gives us not only courtyards and crannies but seven women's bathrooms (and one men's), has integrity. Every space, every hall and wall is dedicated to one purpose, which is the advancement of the young girls within. The entire campus echoes M. Elizabeth Tidball's "wholeness of the environment: the whole package, including the mission, the role models, and the merits of a women's community."

Although girls can make their own space in a garret (or a dance studio, as we have seen), I think the high, painted ceilings, artisan tiles and multiple fireplaces, and all the nooks and corners where they lean together on couches, talking and reading and eating (there is food everywhere at Archer, always), take this girl-nurturing to the ninth power.

A group of girls in the hallway outside the office Arlene has awarded me are loudly proclaiming their favorite places on the Archer campus, which proclamations are nearly poetry when written down: "Everywhere, every corridor you go down. . . the courtyard. . . the fountain. . . Every corner you turn is. . . a place to hang out. . . to talk, to text, to be together."

Some see in the freshly painted rooms and graceful arches a rebuke for previous nonsense and nonchalance. It is time to get serious about school, SAT scores, grades. The rebels especially.

"In the little bridal room [a reference to a hideout in the Methodist Church], I established myself as a rebel—against the authorities, talking back," remembers Sophie. This girl breathes drama and passion into the mundane minutiae of regular attendance and standard handouts and homework. Now, at the new campus, Sophie regrets inventing herself as an acting-out adolescent.

"Academically, I wasn't doing well," she admits to me, recalling missed classes, dress violations, tank tops, flip-flops. She reports that she begins to cry when she thinks about college. "I wanted NYU but I said, 'NYU, ha ha ha,' because I believed I'd never get in. But I said I'm gonna try really, really hard."

Minka is another rebel who converts. Somewhat. Minka is Snow White as a Harley-Davidson biker chick: pale skin, ebony hair, tiny little halter tops tight on the bodice, exposing out-of-uniform tattoos.

Minka has come to Archer as punishment. She'd been at Crossroads celebrating life and Kurt Cobain, but she flunked Latin, so her mother sentenced her to girls' school.

"I'd been wearing uniforms (in grade school), so I said no more uniforms. Didn't want an all-girls' school," Minka reminds me. "Also my mom really wanted me to go to Archer and yeah, right."

She chafed at rules, restrictions about removing nail polish, the requirement for the girls to have "natural" color hair. After spring break in eighth grade, Minka returned with snow-bleached locks, Shannon with dread black, both testing the limits of what nature provides. Ruth Jenson, in the mode of adults who ask silly questions, blasted at them, "Don't you know the meaning of subtle?!"

Well, no. We're teenagers.

For a year Minka stormed the halls, a wrathful waif, dripping scorn and gloom on the Middle School carpet. And then, as if Snow White's time in the coffin was suddenly over, she woke one morning, smiled surrender, and ran for class president.

The transformation came when Minka decided that instead of challenging the rules, she'd try to get them changed. She and Romy, who called themselves "the original Archer bad girls," decided between them, "We're going to make the uniform cute." They redesigned it, made mock-ups, and photographed the new ensemble in a glossy book for the administration. Minka was one of CalArts award-winning high school photographers, and the results were like something *Los Angeles* magazine might do. The uniform got changed.

Like a lapsed Catholic who still genuflects in the aisle of the church, Minka absconds with the key to the school's front door, which she discovers in a desk drawer in her junior year. She isn't sure why she takes it. Maybe a faint declaration about who is who and whose school this is now. "I wanted it for our class," she says a few months later, "but no one even noticed it was gone. Still. . . "

The rocket program evolves into a robotics team. Twelve students in three groups—mechanical engineering, electrical engineering, and animation—work together to design and build a robot from scratch to compete in a national robotics competition. Teachers Jennifer Chalsma, who is an electrical engineer, and mathematician Lisette Valladares, along with a host of volunteer mentors, including my brother Tom, who runs a lab at the Jet Propulsion Laboratory (JPL) in Pasadena, guide the Archer girls as they apply engineering and computer programming to their design.

It is quite a commitment. During the first trimester, while team members are training, studying the competition, and learning key principles of design and construction, they are also designing team uniforms, mentoring middle schoolers in the Lego League, *and* raising funds. Of course, they are expected to stay current with their other subjects.

The first robot, named Hypatia for a fourth-century female mathematician, is entered in a NASA competition against more than three hundred schools. The Archer team discovers in the pre-trials that Hypatia cannot compete as designed. They decide to redesign and retest the robot at Nationals in the seventy-two hours before deadline. Some are scouts and gofers during the intensive redesign; others, including the two teachers and Rebecca, the team captain, do not sleep.

Competitors from other schools are wandering around investigating designs. A crowd gathers at Archer's booth, clearly impressed with the fever of activity, the risk the team is taking, the support the girls give each other. One group solemnly marches over during the second day of competition (Hypatia would place one hundred and forty-fourth eventually) to give Archer a peer award: "Best Use of Plywood."

If it were my award, it would be Best Use of Research. The robotics team exemplifies brain research and social research that describe the ways girls learn, emphasizing the concrete (physical manipulation of robot parts and programs), the complex (many, detailed, sensitive choices and trial and error), and the cooperative (helping each other, mentoring and being mentored, role modeling). It is inductive, which is the kind of reasoning girls favor. It affords them an opportunity to sacrifice, risk, and lead, which they seem to relish.

"We were the only girls' team from the West," Roz, a robotics team junior, informs me. "I think there was a team or two from back East—and we said we can get more; we can mentor other schools. Next year there will be three teams from schools we helped."

"Girls are practical," says Archer's Karen Neitzel, whose Ph.D. research is confirming this observation. "They like problems which are real, like the Oil Spill Project where they learned how to save plants, what life forms need, what chemicals are [produced]. They get very involved. . . . Problem solving like this validates how they see the world."

Karen Neitzel is a young, fair, blue-eyed athlete who is also a computer geek. To allow for a more intensive pursuit of intellectual questions than high school schedules typically allow and, paradoxically, a more relaxed classroom climate, Archer adopts a block schedule—fewer classes of longer periods. Among other tasks, Neitzel administers the scheduling; she describes the schedule of longer periods as opportunities for realistic problem solving: "We do a lot of group work, project-based investigation. In Chemistry girls mixed colors based on elements in the Periodic Table; they compared natural compounds, then used them in Ceramics class. They like discovering how things work."

In tenth-grade English class, students put Dr. Frankenstein on trial. Besides reading Mary Shelley's novel carefully and thoroughly, they interview medical ethicists, scientists, and psychologists; research cloning and the Hippocratic Oath; and learn debate and courtroom procedures. Obviously, this is multidisciplinary.

For that matter, so is the real world. It isn't separated into disciplines. The cook who doesn't do fractions, a little chemistry, and a touch of art isn't very good. The doctor who doesn't consider the whole patient or the lawyer who doesn't try to see all viewpoints aren't doing their jobs.

I suspect disciplines, compartmentalized expertise, were devised for the sake of educational institutions. It's complicated and turf-invasive to organize an integral curriculum, one that satisfies students' natural drive to understand their world and to try to improve upon it. Integrated learning and the intellectual rigor it can foster require the time, from both teachers and students, to pursue an inquiry in depth.

Creating such a curriculum requires some sacrifices on the part of teachers and administrators—who have to coordinate, cooperate, and combine efforts, usually on weekends or in August when others are vacationing. At Chicago's Young Women's Leadership Charter School, for example, faculty spend a full three weeks, compared to three days in other Chicago public schools, in professional development, planning, and collaborating. They meet throughout the school year to talk and to share their own ideas and areas of expertise about real questions in the real world that real students care about.

In the Chicago River Project, YWLCS students apply mathematics as they chart the river's flow, depth, and density; they use science to ask questions about composition, to measure properties and chemicals. "I'm not so ready to drink it," laughs one of the girls.

In math class at YWLCS, the teacher eschews memorization and repetition to build students' multiplication skills. Instead she hands out ceramic tiles, asking students to devise as many ways as they can to create rectangles, thus applying basic mathematics in a concrete way. In other math classes students consider the geometry of a honeycomb, how to maximize profits from a cookie store, how to measure the settlement of peoples in the American West.

An integrated curriculum asks students to be as flexible as teachers, to be active in their own educations, investigating problems they are invested in and taking some responsibility for the culture of the school. After all, the girls themselves must answer, to themselves first and then to others, *Why am I learning this?* In asking and answering that question, they internalize the knowledge if, especially if, the reason for wanting to know arises from their own *need to know*.

At Archer some ninth-grade students started with the question, *What can we do to help tsunami victims?* From there they considered, *What causes tsunamis? How is food distributed in organized societies? How do emergency organizations work?* They covered quite a few disciplines in answering those questions, and at the end of several weeks, when they sent off boxes of clothing and supplies to victims of a recent tsunami, they "owned" the process in which they'd participated, and they owned at least a little of the culture of Archer.

The feeling that they are creating their own school, with what we hope is wise counsel and expert guidance from adults, gives girls responsibility for all aspects of school life, including extracurricular activities. They figure out ways to be inclusive, making contracts with each other to share scarce resources.

Sometimes the scarcity is the students themselves.

Archer is still a small school, just over two hundred girls. Sports teams are not competitive yet. Dominique describes being on the varsity soccer team: "I stand up at all-school meetings, beg and plead kids to come out for the team."

One time there is a varsity game, and the star player, Natalia, gets sick during the day. Our team will have to forfeit if we can't field the minimum number of players. Dominique spies Rebecca shooting baskets.

With the native courtesy of her Mexican forbears competing with her natural exuberance, she catches the basketball, exhorting Rebecca, "You've gotta play." Rebecca is an outstanding basketball player, but she doesn't know soccer at all.

"You can be goalie. It's like guard. You can use your hands."

Dominique and other soccer players rummage through lockers looking for shin guards and cleats. Rebecca is outfitted as goalie, so they can play on their new, grassy playing field. They don't win the game. They don't forfeit either.

18

The Abyss

In the next year, the last year at Archer for the oldest girls, the founding classes become more daring and paradoxically, more bound to each other.

They are paratroopers hurling themselves from planes, holding hands; in their unconventional pursuits their gifts are parachutes: improvisational comedy (Romy, Cailin, Sophie, Liz), documentary film (Lauren H), figure drawing (Neilah, Aly), robotics (Emelda, Susan, Ivania, Lauren L, Rebecca, Hazella).

Even the classics: one playwright in the senior class writes a one-act play about four high school girls; in it, the Greek chorus speaks Latin. The joke is surely lost on the audience (except for those the playwright has specifically told), but it's there for those who look.

The startling difference between these girls and students we know in other schools lies in the risks these girls take. Girls this age are typically cautious, critical of their own abilities and academic performance; these girls are daredevils, intellectually, socially, and emotionally. Their teachers encourage it.

In theater arts, Amy Willerson says sometimes they are "flying by the seat of their pants." Audauniform, the student-named improvisational comedy troupe, offers one opportunity to fly. In improv the comic actor faces the fear of being seen as a fool, relying only on her wit and the other performers to save her. Usually she doesn't need saving.

At a school assembly, Audauniform demonstrates an improvisation called "What's Been Returned?" wherein Romy is a store customer and Cailin the clerk at the returns desk. (Romy does not know what object the audience has chosen but is instructed to act as if she does, entering, "with deliberate choice," pushing a big box or holding a tiny one in her fingers.)

CLERK [knows object]: How can I help you?

Customer struggles under weight of a very heavy, imaginary box. Audience laughs.

CLERK: You returning more than one thing today?

Customer pretends to lift a jewelry box from inside the other box.

CLERK: I don't think it would fit in there. What seems to be the problem?

CUSTOMER: It's too small.

CLERK: Hmm. That seems unlikely. Open wide.

CUSTOMER opens mouth: So maybe it's stuck between my teeth?

CLERK: Well, that would be peculiar. Did you try plugging it in?

CUSTOMER: I hadn't thought of that. Standard batteries?

CLERK: Yep.

CUSTOMER: Can I use it anywhere other than my teeth?

CLERK: Not as far as I'm concerned.

Audience laughs.

CUSTOMER: OK, cool. So. That's why I'm returning this electric toothbrush.

Audauniform uses verbal and nonverbal communication and careful listening to create character and suggest situation. It depends on trust, not only between troupe members but also between players and the audience, who have an implicit contract to support each other while the players risk being fools. Playing the fool, mocking the self may be a good skill for getting through adolescence.

In Jean Bennett's honors seminar on Cleopatra, there are other ways one can play the fool. Using historical method and original documents and artifacts of the legendary queen of Egypt, students try not to be blinded by their own perspectives. Or duped by the objectives of others.

Lauren, who is black, wants to investigate the idea that Cleopatra was, too. Despite the articles saying "Whites have stolen our history" which she finds on the Internet, Lauren concludes there are not enough data, so she writes instead on the underwater excavation of Cleopatra's palace.

Lizzie and Cailin read Roman materials in classical Latin. They, daughters of writers, discover a private truth. The writer, in this case Julius Caesar, has the last word.

The Cleopatra class learns that three world-class museums are featuring the kind of work they're doing: Cleopatra as stateswoman, political theorist, economist, first of the pharaohs to learn the Egyptian language. It would seem to be a validation of their scholarship, but they see it as evidence of their leadership. *We so knew that.*

There is a playfulness and celebration in some of these intellectual adventures. Cailin emails Shelby Brown, Latin teacher:

> Dr. Brown, did you hear about the Roman centurion who went into a bar and ordered a martinum?
> "Don't you mean a martini?" asks the bartender.
> The centurion says, "If I want a double, I'll tell you."

Getting girls to risk requires an emotional climate which is relaxed and forgiving. Then mistakes can occur. Archer teacher Patti Meyers has a mantra, *A Mistake Is an Opportunity*. She teaches art as improvisation, telling students who tell her they made a mistake, "I want to see it because it's the most interesting part of the project. It's information, valuable information."

In this environment there must be acceptance and support for taking a challenge. It can't be *that's not good, you're wrong there, that doesn't look right.* Too much judgment, even if it's not essentially negative, is a forbidding environment for creativity.

In creative groups, such as advertising teams or the writing staffs of comedy shows, members pitch ideas, one after the other. The word "no" is rare, as ideas overlap, building on each other: *How 'bout Bob is a priest? He's a Buddhist. Bob's a vegetarian. Who works in a meatpacking plant. For a butcher. Who's a Buddhist.*

The atmosphere in a classroom where students are challenging themselves, like that in the writing room of the show about

Bob, cannot be critical, for that dampens creative impulse. Only in settings that bolster their confidence can students venture, risk, chance failure.

MISTAKES AND STANDARDS

But how can teachers evaluate if the students aren't critiqued? Patti Meyers uses constructive feedback during the project, and she says, "Context and boundaries are important." By setting clear objectives, studying the work, listening to the artist, and making informal observations, Patti can assess the girl's progress and the understanding she has of what she's doing.

Then there are the portfolios. Students in Patti's classes create portfolios over a period of time, sometimes with the advice of peers. In this way they do what artists have always done, organize and evaluate their own work and set their own goals for future projects which seem warranted by this body of work.

The practical effect of this approach is that the student has a body of work that she and others can assess. A local gallery owner told Patti that "guys kept coming in with portfolios, pushing us to show them." No girls. Patti challenged Archer girls to change that, aware that team competition works with them.

Now they are presenting portfolios to gallery owners and artist representatives. One girl convinced a local store to let her paint a mural for them for a small fee; another, Liza, approached the manager of a coffee shop and got him to agree to exhibit her work.

Across the country is Chicago's Young Women's Leadership Charter School where the director, Margaret Small, treats students as professionals in what she calls "a culture of success." In lieu of grades, girls have categories of mastery: high performance, proficient, not yet proficient. Girls in study sessions say they're working on their *Not Yets*.

Founder Joan Hall, a partner at a prestigious Chicago law firm Jenner and Block, says she and the other founders wanted a school for girls which would emphasize mathematics, science, and technology. She *thought* she wanted to see a school which would promote tough standards, high test scores.

"I've changed my ideas," she now says. "It's not just about test scores. Girls who leave us [YWLCS] have the ability to stand up in a group, to present ideas, to become useful and informed citizens. That's what we're about."

Does it work? Gillian, a fifteen-year-old sophomore at YWLCS, says it does. "The best thing about the school is the grading," she says. (The worst thing is the lunch, but that's another conversation, and anyway, Gillian's mom is an award-winning chef, so maybe her standards are a bit high.)

The grading, the basis of evaluation being strategic objectives in which students may have been rated high performance, proficient, or not yet proficient, has the feel of a process that is ongoing rather than a door that has closed. Teachers actually have Not Yet parties, which are workshops for students who want to improve themselves in some skill or deepen their understanding of some concept or idea.

"No kid is a loser," says Margaret Small. "This isn't a job where they can be fired." As a result, the girls tend to hang in there. The school has an enviable graduation rate of 85 percent, compared to the average Chicago public school's of 50 percent. Forty-one percent of the graduates say they're interested in careers in math and science.

And 100 percent of last year's graduates got into college. One hundred percent. That's a statistic that represents high performance for the school, teachers, founders, and funders. And for Chicago public schoolgirls.

Senior year begins for us with the Senior Ring Ceremony and the senior uniforms designed by Minka and Romy, the SAT classes, the college applications.

For Shireen the anxiety of being accepted by a good college is complicated by her Persian Jewish family, where the "idea of college was not discussed." She murmurs, "Girls from my culture did not go away." But it is too late. Shireen has gone on a college trip with Romy and Rachel. "Rachel's mom said I wouldn't like any of the colleges, so my mom let me go."

When she visited Emerson in Boston, she remembers, "I loved everything about it. But I didn't tell my parents."

Shireen applied early and was accepted by Emerson and Pitzer, one of the Claremont Colleges just outside L.A. She applied nowhere else.

Shireen's mother, Lili, describes her feelings about the dilemma. "She wanted to go away. I wasn't sure it was right for her. There's value in being among family. I was very conflicted."

Three days before the deadline for accepting or rejecting Emerson, Shireen's mom said she'd make the decision for her daughter.

Shireen was very upset. She was so nervous she called Lizzie and Liz and insisted they do something: "My friends know me," she says. "I knew they wanted what was best for me." (As a parent I cringe at this, but what can you do?)

Her classmates are sympathetic but also practical. Lizzie goes online to garner arguments from websites; Liz calls Emerson and Pitzer and gets appointments with each for Shireen and her mom.

Shireen remembers a two-hour meeting with the man who was Emerson's head of admissions in California. Lili thinks it might have been four hours. To every concern, every question, every anxiety (the distance from family, the urban environment, the sophisticated city of Boston so different from Pacific Palisades), he'd listen. He said, "Yes, you're right to worry about that. We worry about it, too."

"He made us feel that Emerson was going to be there for us like family," concludes Shireen.

Ultimately, for Lili, doing the right thing for Shireen also was about family: "My mother-in-law allowed all her five children to go away to study, four to Europe, one to another town in Iran. I thought if she could do it, I could, too."

It is Passover and Lili offers me an array of tiny figs, two kinds of pistachio nuts, apricots she has dried herself, olives, home-made candy. She is beautiful, with lustrous hair, a shiny plum-colored mouth, still young, already missing this firstborn of whom we speak. Lili gives me a wry, knowing look, mother to mother. "No matter what you do, they blame you." Her dark eyes are laughing.

Seniors become emotionally close to each other when they get near graduation. They accept, even celebrate, the idiosyncrasies that once annoyed them. The gregarious cling to their friends as they gather at Starbucks, in the patio, outside the college counselor's office waiting to hear about acceptances, rejections, and scholarships. The loners in a spirit of loyalty seek the sisterhood of others and are embraced by classmates they avoided or who avoided them. It is powerful, profound, and predictable.

There is an intensity here that ratchets seniorocity up a notch.

"These girls are our lives," insists Katie. "Everyone loves each other. Senior year. . . strong emotions. . . because these are the most important relationships."

"Being seniors, everything clicks," Dominique explains. "We appreciate each other, know we won't always be together, got over issues, stuff that separated us." In characteristic exuberance she adds about her friends from Archer, "They will be the brides-maids at my wedding."

Sophie sees it as embracing what she scorned. "By twelfth grade there is no rush from walking around in flip-flops. The uni-form. . . I don't want to take it off."

Minka has a date to the prom, a tall Huck Finn type she met at CalArts Summer School. "But," she insists, "all that matters is the dress." She smiles wickedly. "You have to have the dress."

Two of the girls make their dresses. From shower curtains and masking tape. Rebecca sends up the dress mania of the seniors (she is a junior) by wearing a tutu over her uniform to all-school assembly. And she dances, somewhat like an ostrich leaping pot-holes. Girls are spouting with laughter. The juniors, who are pretty tired of the seniors by now, are laughing the hardest.

It comes suddenly. June seems to be immediately after September this year. June is the month my mother was born, and I think of her, wishing she could be here to see these twenty-eight seniors, costumed in calf-length white dresses with impossibly wobbly shoes. ("Too virginal," complains one.)

Vicky and I provide white-food lunch (lest anyone spill on her-self), so it's chicken salad, tuna salad, hummus, and jicama—it almost looks like food from the 1950s, except there are no saltines or white gravy noodles or potato chip casseroles.

Immediately after, the girls fix garlands of flowers in each other's hair and paint their eyes, some with subtle competence, some with the skill and enthusiasm of preschoolers finger-paint-ing. Some are adventurers even in this, their daredevil heels, in-discreet décolletage, and ornamental eyelids decorated like Disney deer or vampire ladies, bespeaking the exit from the house before their mothers were awake.

The day has been overcast, typical of June, but the sun comes out in time for the senior picture, so they are squinting as they look toward the future.

The ceremony occurs at two.

I'm not ready for this. Nor is Arlene. We're anxious and excited when we meet in the hall, like co-conspirators before a big heist. She reminds me that I sent her a poem when we were trying to get her to come here.

"You pretended it was special for me, but I think you used it before."

I shrug, caught. It is an edited, slightly altered quote from French philosopher La Rochefoucauld:

> They stood at the abyss.
> Jump, she said.
> We can't. We're afraid.
> Jump, she said.
> We can't. We're afraid.
> So she pushed them
> And they flew.

These baby birds are about to fly. Off to college by September. Their record of college acceptance is extraordinary: Kyla realizes her lifelong dream to go to Spelman, Emelda gets a scholarship to Stanford, Lauren to Princeton; Romy, the comic whose college essays are excellent, even if her grades are erratic, chooses Antioch; Minka is going to Bard, where most of the students are also iconoclast artists; Sophie, the actress who vowed to "try really, really hard" and who had a "brilliant" audition, is admitted to New York University's coveted Tisch School.

Vicky's daughter is going to Brown, ours to Harvard; Katie and Liz are off to Vassar, Dominique to Boston College, Shireen, of course, to Emerson.

I stand at the podium in an academic gown speaking each girl's name into the microphone as she comes to take her diploma. Some hug me, some hold their hands out solemnly for the leather case, some weep. I can't look at Arlene at the other end of the stage, or I will weep also.

When it's over, I put my arm, still draped in black gown, over Arlene's slight shoulder. I say quietly, "What an adventure."

She shakes her head, smiling. "It's not over, Kemo Sabe. The abyss? Still there."

"You know," I tell her, "that guy who penned the abyss poem also wrote, 'Who lives without folly is not so wise as he thinks.'"

She is reaching for a brownie when she answers. "We are *very* wise."

Arlene goes off to greet some beaming man and his beaming mother, wife, and Archer daughter. A group of girls, emerging seniors who will be graduating next year, come over to me. They look like trouble, mischief written in quirky grins and innocent-seeming smiles.

"Hi, Dr. Meehan," says one. "We were wondering—"

"We wanted to ask you," says another, her eyebrows arching inquiringly. The three of them look at each other for confirmation or courage, swift exchange of eye contact, slight shrug of shoulders, leaning toward me just a little.

"We love Archer," adds the third quickly. The other two nod vigorously.

The first begins again, "I have a brother, Andrew."

"I have two brothers."

"I have a bunch of cousins—Jason. Jackson. Jimson." She's smiling to show she's winging it with the names, but we can all see where this is going.

"What about the boys, Dr. Meehan? What about doing an Archer School for them?"

I would tell them I'll get right on that, but I try to avoid sarcasm with kids; it's disrespectful. So I just smile and say what adults have always said when they mean, *I'm tired. Don't bother me. No.*

"I'll think about it."

When we truly finish here, I truly will.

19

To Seek My Fortune

On a bright, gently warm day ten months later in March, when the sounds of cars and SUVs on Sunset are muted by the garden of delphiniums and the iron fence and young orange trees just planted at the front of the school, a group of seven or eight girls gathers on the veranda to say good bye to their robot. I'm the only adult there just now: their mentors are at work at JPL and UCLA, and their teachers are momentarily back in the classroom. The girls want to show me the robot before the FedEx truck arrives to take it to the competition.

Gently two girls roll it out of the crate, and two others open and hold the heavy front door as the eighty-eight-pound robot named Calliope is carried to the entry, where it is lowered onto the floor. It's a raw-looking thing, a painted box the size of carry-on luggage on wheels, with an arm on one side and a red popsicle light on top. It doesn't look as polished as R2-D2, but I can tell by the grins and glad eyes that the team is extraordinarily proud of it.

Rebecca takes a small box a little bigger than a cell phone, moves a lever on it, and lo and behold, the robot moves, scuttling down the corridor. Sparks flicking in its wake. *Uh oh, sparks are not right.* I'm the daughter of an electrical engineer, and I know electric fire is supposed to be confined inside protective casing, not shooting out onto the floor.

I turn to the nearest child, the happy face of Maria, one of the team engineers, and say with dismay in my voice, "You better go get a teacher." But Maria's smile only widens as she walks toward the robot. I wait, as do her teammates and history teacher Rob Everett, who has joined us, coming to see what the group is doing gathered in the front hall.

Maria reaches into her back pocket and casually retrieves a small gray screwdriver, bends to the robot to reattach something, a strap maybe, and, beaming, nods at Rebecca. Silently Rebecca manipulates the driving mechanism, and the robot travels down the hall, minus the sparks, merrily unaware—I assume a robot is unaware—of the human drama that its imminent destruction would have caused.

I stand there, shaking my head slightly, wordless.

"It's exciting and sad," one of the girls will say later, "to put the robot that you've spent six weeks of your life creating into a crate." For me watching, it's only exciting. Maria aiming her brilliant smile at us and reaching into the back pocket of her uniform pants and pulling out that screwdriver is just a complete thrill.

My father attended one of the robotics competitions, driving over the mountain pass to San Jose. The college arena reverberated with the sounds of thousands of people, hundreds of robots, and a booming public address system that was loudly calling play-by-play, interspersed with beat-strong music meant to keep competitors keyed up. The Archer girls were gathered in the prep area, the air around them tight with nervous energy, silently altering something on the robot minutes before a match—there is always some last-moment adjustment—and I looked over their heads and saw him there.

Although he was in his eighties, nearly bald, with little tufts of gray in his ears and crinkly lines around his eyes, and the industrious girls, by contrast, were younger than most of his grandchildren, as he stood there watching, captured by wonder, completely absorbed in the process of someone trying to make something work, he seemed a boy.

He'd always loved figuring out things like how radio waves transmit (he was eleven), how cars run (he was twelve when he fixed some man's engine with a coin and a wad of gum), and then, like the Archer girls, how rockets conquer gravity (he was a space guy at twenty-nine).

He got annoyed with people (me) who couldn't use things properly or who moved things like screws and springs lying on the floor of the living room next to the broken bike (mine), which would be fixed, maybe not in my lifetime.

On an October afternoon, three years after the San Jose competition, my father died. It was not sudden. He'd had heart problems all his life, but his absence seems temporary, as if he'd only left the room to get a pair of pliers.

He was not finished. Around the house, always, were projects pending: electric engines; electrodynamic devices for mail, music, photography; sport cars; computers in semipermanent processes of improvement.

His education, too, was ongoing, although his formal schooling ended with high school and a few courses in physics from Brooklyn College. He was an orphan, and like my mother, he had to go to work instead of college, so he studied at the kitchen table. In his seventies he studied French at night and taught weather for the Coast Guard.

Continuing education, what we sometimes call *lifelong learning*, a dynamic process of trying to figure things out, was central to him and what he was seeing as he watched the young engineers, scientists, artists in that arena. It was fun to see.

I am continuing with my own education, teaching a section of something named Life Skills at Archer. The topic is "Images in American Media," and tenth-grade girls are discussing Barbie as iconic symbol. Natasha, with a nostalgic half-smile, recalls a period in her life that was dedicated to make-believe and fantasy occupations: "I mean Barbie could be *anything*—doctor, astronaut, fashion model," she chuckles. "I mean as long as there was an outfit for it."

Jamilla, an African-American girl with ample proportions, argues mildly that Barbie is "pseudo" with her large breasts, minimal rib cage, tiny, tiny feet. *And* long blonde hair. "I guess she looks like Paris Hilton," she adds dryly.

If Barbie were a live person, she'd be, um, nine feet tall, a girl says.

I had a black Barbie, says another.

Jamilla grins. "Did she have nappy hair?"

Barbie seems to be a pertinent topic for this class on media literacy. The girls clearly know her. Some couldn't give the first names of our two U.S. Senators (Barbara and Dianne) or Secretary of State (Condoleezza or "Condi," as she'd be in the toy world), but they know who this doll is.

Since being advertised on *The Mickey Mouse Club*, an after-school program on ABC fifty years ago, the figure has gone from toy to media personality to marketing phenomenon. I tell these students that at one time in the early twenty-first century world-wide, *two* Barbies were sold every second of the day, and they nod knowingly.

"I had like fourteen of 'em," Jessica states. "Only one shoe, though. One teenie shoe. It was like Cinderella."

I don't actually expect these tenth-grade girls to know as much about Barbara Boxer, U.S. senator, as they do about the pubescent Barbie, with her ermine capes and ocelot bikinis. I recognize the appeal of pretty, of apparel that is fuzzy, slinky, sparkly, or pink, of princess stature (Barbie has good posture, I give her that).

I'm a child of the 1960s, a mother of girls, but I do live in the Real World.

What I mind—what worries me, as a mother, as an educator, as a citizen of the Real World, is what we're saying to our young with these toys, these images.

It's not that Barbie aims for success; it's that success is measured in cars and clothes, an ideal that's unattainable, unfulfilling, and expensive. It's not that she is an unrealistic representation of a human female; it's that she manifests the epitome of the psychological disorder which results in a young female who starves herself, surgically balloons her breasts, removes several ribs, and shrinks her feet by what method I don't know.

And, Barbie, at least for this generation, has been everywhere, marketed to, purchased for, played by two-year-olds, four-year-olds, and virtually every eight-year-old girl in America.

"The sheer extent of children's immersion in consumer culture today is unprecedented," sociologist Juliet Schor tells us in *Born to Buy*. Where previous generations had toys and teddy bears and comic books, they also had activities such as chores, church, clubs, sports, and books which occupied their time. Now, Schor reports, "most of what kids do revolves around commodities."

Barbie, Material Girl, champions commodities. She has airplanes and cell phones, sports cars and computers, wardrobes of skirts and shirts, shoes, boots and baubles, bridal dresses, lab coats, and stethoscopes. In short, Barbie has every*thing*.

Barbie's land is a culture of things (and the things aren't books). The focus is on get, not think. It is nonacademic, and as more than one educator has observed, consumerism is a culture inimical to learning.

We in the learning business, especially the single sex learning business, are fighting back. Among other things, we are offering courses in media literacy as part of a curriculum that is relevant to the age and the gender, for adolescence is the age of defining the self as separate and unique, and girls are the object of many of the mediated messages (and all of the ones featuring pink.)

Students who are sophisticated, marketplace savvy, and aware of the massive number of messages directed at them can be inoculated against some of the appeal, like those students in this class who are ironic about the iconic Barbie. They know, even if unconsciously, that if their brains are full of ad slogans and beauty products, there's no room for geometry.

Tools of analysis provided in the context of classes like the one at Archer, such as the discussions about the values and images portrayed by Barbie or a pop lyric or a TV character, can provide to the girls themselves the means to read cultural content, reveal the deception and hypocrisy hidden in many messages (wherein *girl power* represents shopping choices, for example), and determine what portrayals of female protagonists, if any, fit their emerging selves. It is their own savvy which counters the ardent appeals from advertising and gives girls that mental shrug when discussing their own attraction to it.

Barbie can be anything—as long as there's an outfit for it. . . . Did she have nappy hair? . . . I had, like, fourteen of 'em. Only one shoe though. Like Cinderella.

Besides courses in the Life Skills curriculum, which many coed schools also offer, often in single sex classrooms, girls' schools counter the materialism of marketplace messages in another way: we and all the forward-thinking girls' schools I examined are organized around rigorous courses of academic study which allow less actual time in the marketplace and create a pro-academic climate. Such a climate, educators like Cornelius Riordan and Rosemary Salomone have argued, undermines the anti-intellectualism of a culture of continual consumption and values girls for their inquisitive minds rather than their exquisite makeup.

A father of one of our students described the different daughter he had after she'd left a traditional, upscale coed school for a girls' school:

"Last year she'd get into the car, slam the door, and start complaining: 'Those girls! They think their $400 designer sweaters are so great and anybody'd be a fool not to see it,'" he informs us.

"This year I pick her up, she slams the car door and starts complaining: 'Those girls! They think the Spartans are so great. And not the Athenians?! What is wrong with them!?'" He laughs.

We founded this school because of the research. Naïve, idealistic, inexperienced, Megan, Vicky, and I envisioned girls in an environment in which learning is integrated, as it is in their brains, connected to a caring, just society, as it is in their souls. We thought if the research were addressed in the classroom, the students would thrive, risk, lead.

The opposition almost undid us. For four years we battled for our conditional use permit, we struggled with so-called neighbors, we were sued.

The students attended hearings, circulated petitions, cajoled city council members. They also did their science, their sports, and their homework in history and English, mathematics and art; some of them wrote a musical, mocking the narrow-mindedness of NIMBY, celebrating girls and their education.

Eventually we saw that our purpose was not the research. The research is the transportation system, like the buses that pull up to the front doors. It is a means for minds to be engaged, for girls to confront and shape their world.

The purpose is the girls themselves being the best they can be. Given a chance, they create worlds that are better than our dreams for them: consider the cool confidence with which Maria repaired the robot, as the adults around her, including me, fretted and worried, unbelieving; consider the wisdom and humor the girls bring to a media literacy discussion.

There is a Scottish folk tale in which the young hero of sixteen or so says to her mother, *Bake me a bannock. Roast me a collop. I'm off to Seek My Fortune.* Along the road she meets her sisters who have gone before and they give her food and shelter and secret charms against evil; she rescues her prince; she grows up.

But for the bannock and collop (which I think are bread and bacon), this Scottish girl puts me in mind of the female heroes of Archer, the girls of the founding classes. They are discoverers, designers of their own destinies, and, because of the four-year civic struggles, war buddies. They will go to the mat for their friends.

When Liz's mother dies in their first year of college, she calls two of her Archer friends to tell them. "I know you can't come here. It's three thousand miles away and you have finals next week. But my mom died. I wanted you to know."

Both of them call their parents and ask for frequent flyer miles. They take the red-eye to be with their friend as she chooses music for the service, talks about her mother, cries. On Sunday they fly through the night to be back at school for their finals.

(We would hope they'd support their friends. Any good kids would. They are being responsible students and daughters, as well as friends.)

Although the first classes are gone, having assumed roles of adulthood, the younger girls inherit the legacy like siblings moving into their elder sisters' rooms. They climb mountains. Literally. At Joshua Tree National Park they scale cliffs, acting as lifelines for each other. Two of them play guitar and then go home to incorporate math, music, and the mountain into a song. Another student writes a poem that is published in the literary magazine using geometry terms for states of being.

"They take what they learn," a math teacher says, "and make it their own."

I think about Archer and what it means, and what it doesn't mean: Not just another single sex school but the first to test the research; the leader, mentoring other schools; the biggest risk taker. Not just another private school but a community where almost a third of the students are children of color, almost half are middle-class or poor.

And not just a school that fulfills its mission (although I want that), but a school recognized as outstanding. For those I love who came from Brooklyn (Gary, Arlene, my Dad), I want us to be better than the other schools—especially coed schools. I want Archer to beat those guys.

And, so far, in some things, Archer does beat the coed schools, public and private, small, medium, and large.

In debate the Archer team is nationally qualified in 2002 and league champion in 2003. The following year they are nationally ranked in both speech and debate. One Archer student out of 127,000 test takers receives a perfect score on the National Latin exam; another places sixth in the nation in the National French Contest.

In 2003 our Academic Decathlon team, competing in a series of testing and speaking events, places first in our division. The next year the team travels to Alemany High School elsewhere in the state, where they are told that the organizers of the event have moved them from Division III to Division II, a more competitive group. The girls maintain their composure and get to work, eventually winning more than thirty medals, including six team awards. The following weekend at the awards ceremony, they hear the official declaration: they are now Division II champions.

We have National Merit Scholars, a Coca Cola Scholar (250 finalists out of 250,000), and millions of dollars awarded (about a million every year) in scholarships from colleges and universities, from Barnard to Princeton, Stanford to USC.

Archer's middle school teams are Pacific Basin League finalists in four sports in 2001; Miss A is league coach of the year. We are soccer champions in 2003. In 2004 the junior varsity volleyball team is 10–0 for the season, and the team is Delphic League Champions, a first for any Archer JV team. The girls organize a tennis team with a math teacher as coach in 2004. In 2005 they are first in the league, advancing to the second round of playoffs, another first in Archer's history.

The best thing, according to Coach Adolphe, is that half the school comes out for teams.

In the arts Archer has more students accepted to the competitive CalArts Summer Institute, in 2004 and again in 2006, than *any* other school statewide. Archer's competitive dance team is

California state champion. Even the Student Store wins an award, which results in a $10,000 grant in 2004 from the Women's Foundation of California.

The Student Store is the research redeemed in yet another context, the corporation. Girls in business. Student entrepreneurs write a business plan, keep accounts, research and market merchandise, manage and staff the store, *and* sell shares in their company.

In a manifestation of girls exceeding our expectations for them, the Student Store returns stockholders 15 percent on their investment, and the student board of directors awards $1,000 grants to three graduating seniors and an additional $2,000 to Archer's financial aid endowment. The second year the board increases the financial aid grant to $5,000.

Somewhat bemused, the store's faculty advisor, Steven Denlinger, credits the school for the leadership skills taught by this opportunity: "Archer allows girls to make choices and then allows them to be accountable for their actions."

I am trying to account for my own actions, my own part in this experiment. I'm intrigued by the Student Store and impressed by the dance squad and the tennis program, which have basically created themselves from nothing. I'm taken with the robotics team.

It too has awards and honors: The prestigious Engineering Inspiration Award (2002 Southern California Regional); the NASA/Drydon Award (2004 Edwards Air Force Base). And a long list of media stories—ABC *Evening News with Peter Jennings*, NBC *Today in LA*, Telemundo, CNN, *Los Angeles Times*, and CNN again.

One student complained that at the competition, "I knew that I was in for a challenge, but I was not expecting to have to deal with television producers asking us to 'pretend' that we were doing something." She says later, "Even though I was not expecting these obstacles, I learned to deal with them."

The team also "deals with" the Southern California Regional Robotics Forum, which it founded to find and fund robotics mentors. The team itself mentors three other schools and nine squads of middle school Lego Leagues, the training ground for robotics. Since most of our robotics team members are students of color, they are obvious role models in these schools where minority students are the majority.

A member of Archer's inaugural robotics team, Lauren volunteers as a mentor to high school students during her academic years at Princeton. She concludes, "When I got to Archer and realized that I was in an open and supportive environment, I felt I could let my guard down. . . . I am trying new things all the time, stepping outside my comfort zone, and breaking boundaries."

I want also to be breaking boundaries: I am the daughter of two people who couldn't go to school because they didn't have the means, the mother of two daughters with lovely minds and lofty aspirations, the wife of a man who believes in me.

Every one of them, at one time or another, at some point of this journey, said exactly the same thing: Never give up.

With that mantra I take myself off to see what I can see at other schools in other towns, to meet with other girls, other heads, other founders, for I hear they too have been told to *never give up,* and I want to see what they've created.

20

Signs of the Times

Creating a new school was like going flying with my dad in his
Cessna. He focused intently on what he was doing, reading the
dials in front of him, scanning constantly, glancing around to see
if there were other planes in the area, all the while checking for
storms in front of us. The weather up ahead was the future, but
he was mostly focused on where we were.

As founders, we focused on the task of fulfilling the mission,
barely aware of the storms in the future or what was happening
on the ground. We didn't track the climate in other places, the
politics, power shifts, and potentates of single-sex education. We
were too busy flying.

When we landed on something like solid ground, though, I set
off to explore the worlds beyond, hear the tales of other travelers,
especially those who started schools like ours, in this country, for
a diverse collection of girls, preparing for college, for leadership,
for adulthood.

As an educator, I was curious; as a feminist fan of girls, I was
hopeful; as a mother of daughters, I was anxious to know: Was it

difficult to start a girls' school if the climate was unreceptive or the need unrecognized? What does the new kind of girls' school look like? How is it distinguished from established schools like Spence in New York City or Hockaday in Dallas or Winsor or Westridge or Emma Willard?

Knowing how hard was our own founding, the sheer number of new schools was unexpected: thirty-five and growing. That several conquered the cumbersome and cutthroat conditions required to mount a new single-sex institution within a *public* system was unexpected and oddly moving.

I chose to visit six, public and private, by recommendation, asking friends in the education business; and by design: middle schools and high schools and combinations, with some geographic variety because, to some extent, every school reflects its region and the local history and culture. I traveled to New York, site of the first girls' public school in a hundred years; to Chicago and to Dallas, where two more succeeded in going public, following the New York school's example; to Oakland, an independent middle school on a sylvan college campus; to Seattle, where school-in-a-box almost literally describes the facilities; and to Atlanta, a 6–12 school, tech-smart and Southern.

The schools I saw are as different from each other as east from west, island from plains, rich from poor, yet they have a purpose in common: to educate girls. There is focus and consensus in this simple proscription: primarily, they say, we explore the means to reach and teach girls, females of a certain age and stage of development. The schools may espouse other purposes—to create tolerant individuals or compassionate citizens, for example—but their primary focus, what is valued, is girls.

Furthermore, the schools share a conviction that this learning environment encourages girls to hold high academic standards, to contribute in some way to the community at large, and to become successful women, even leaders, in the competitive, heterogeneous world they enter on graduation.

These societies have other attributes in common, which I take as important to understanding how the path-breaking professionals "turn the system upside-down. . . [and] get girls to study things the culture says they're not interested in," as Chicago's Margaret Small put it. They operate on the belief that the culture denies girls the joys of discovery and mastery of academic, scientific, and intellectual pursuits; they try to address this denial, especially in science, math, and technology, which girls aren't expected to embrace. They follow the research results and implement new approaches, adapting to new understandings of ways girls learn.

Because the resources of these new schools are stretched so thin, they don't typically have much that resembles art or sport in the usual sense. However, they are housed in clean, light-filled, sometimes elegant buildings, and they have the necessary elements, every one of them: computers and books, smart boards and science labs (in high school), and most important, qualified, dedicated teachers.

The schools are small (at four hundred and seventy-five students, Archer is the biggest), they are inclusive of many cultures and races, and they are innovative, exploring and employing educational research especially as it addressed their favorite subject—girls.

My own acronym for what I was seeing was SIGNS: small, inclusive, innovative, girl-nurturing societies. (A counselor at the Atlanta school said they were "girl-nurturing, not girl-smothering.") Our school and virtually every one of these six were started not to enclose girls—wall them off from prevailing winds which were clearly harmful—but to give them wings that they might ride. After a bit I began to look for a glimpse of the wings, and at every one of the seven schools, they were there.

~

There is a self-conscious purposefulness, a *mindfulness*, that characterizes new schools, that animates their choices, from the words that describe their mission to the faculty they hire and the photos they hang on their walls. Old schools, even those in the middle of strategic planning, rely to some extent on their own history or unexamined habits and traditions to create their worlds. New schools must necessarily decide everything from nothing, which decisions and early experiences will define them.

Like an anthropologist studying new societies, I observed, questioned informants, and interviewed chieftains, warriors, and poets, seeking to discover their values and beliefs and to learn about tributes and emblems of their success.

The warrior-chieftains at The Young Women's Leadership School (TYWLS) in East Harlem are Principal Kathleen Ponze, a genial, crinkly-eyed realist who multitasks like it's her birthright, and Chris Farmer, the young, sandy-haired, male, college guidance director. The fact that there is a college advisor is unusual enough for a public school (his salary is funded by private foundation money), but his caseload of fifty or so students, versus four hundred and fifty elsewhere in public education, is a measure of the commitment to what TYWLS calls the "culture of high expectations."

On the walls of hallways are framed photographs of the heroes of this society, the ones for whom the high expectations are held: the students who have themselves elected and been selected to attend the school.

TYWLS is a school of poor kids (85 percent qualify for free lunch), and it works, according to Principal Ponze, because of great teaching, parental support, systemic support (translation: money from outside, as in foundations and rich friends), and college guidance embedded in the program.

She talks about how hard it is for the students, how many obstacles lie in the way of their success: "You can't do it alone. And some problems you can't solve. Even after the (essentially) private education, they still have mountains to climb."

The students require time, attention, a chance to talk about things. ("They love to talk," Ponze says.) They demand a lot of the teachers, and, in turn, the teachers need support, comfort, professional recognition. "If you don't feed the teachers," she laughs, "they'll eat the students."

In the midst of our discussion, a harried drama teacher interrupts Ponze with the crisis of the moment: the janitors won't let the teachers hang the banner announcing the evening's dramatic program. "Don't worry about it," Ponze advises, "Chris and I will hang it later this afternoon."

Whatever impediments the system and the circumstances have imposed, the school has fended off the forces of darkness and achieved enlightenment; their students graduate and get admitted to college—that is, *all* of them. A goodly number get college scholarships as well.

TYWLS attributes its success to its core values, says Ponze, the first of which is single sex education. From that value comes the mission and the female role models who visit, like black astronaut Mae Jamieson; from that comes the culture of high expectations: *You can do this*, they're told. *You can go to college, too.*

Some of those who poo-poo the TYWLS phenomenon argue that it is size, not single sex, that accounts for its results. At TYWLS, its small size *is* impressive: three hundred and fifteen students, about the same as New York's Spence or Palo Alto's Castilleja, for grades seven through twelve. The classrooms are peopled with sixteen to eighteen girls, and advisory groups for addressing personal problems are somewhat smaller.

The small size of the school, classroom populations, and advisory groups is a feature of the design, just as it is in a private school like Spence, a few blocks away. It allows faculty and staff to know "every student in the school personally, intellectually, and emotionally" as TYWLS school materials state. However, size is but one aspect of the whole culture, one ratio in the partnership required for the business of raising expectations and ultimately student performances.

Perhaps the reason the small community is not emulated more in the public sector is that it is expensive. TYWLS and other schools like it are supported by public funds bolstered by big dollops of private funding.

Young Women's Leadership Charter School (YWLCS) on Chicago's South Side is another expensive public school, a burden settled on the 5'5" frame of a fifty-eight-year-old woman with cropped hair, faint lipstick, and powerful energy named Margaret Small. She directs YWLCS with a straightforward mission ("a rigorous college preparatory education focusing on math, science, technology, and the development of leadership skills") for three hundred and forty girls in grades seven through twelve.

Modeled after the school in East Harlem, YWLCS is a charter school, which means the Chicago Public School system gives it $6,000 annually per student and says *good luck*. It costs the school at least $10,000 per student, so YWLCS has to get help from funders, volunteers, and parents to stay open. Nor is the money they raise enough.

"We have to hire baby teachers," Small tells me, "because we can't pay for grownups."

YWLCS designs its own curriculum, determines the length of its school day, hires and fires its own teachers. This autonomy, necessary to such a school, can be problematic for others in the system. Especially teachers.

"A school is only as good as the people who work there," says Small. "They must be well qualified, highly committed, visionary, and they have to care about the kids." She could easily add *be willing to work long hours, collaborate with others, do lots of things not on the job description* (like watch a baby while a girl writes a college essay).

The faculty spend a full three weeks, compared to three days in other Chicago public schools, in professional development, planning, collaborating. One teacher quit, saying, "You expect way too much." Indeed, exhaustion and burnout account for some of the teacher turnover, which can be 20 percent each year.

What's extraordinary, however, is that students stick. "Their lives are really hard," Small says gently. "They have infinite need. Society is collapsing around them. Some of them deal with exploitation, humiliation, brutality; some with homelessness, families who can't afford carfare to get them here."

Although they are in what YWLCS calls "a culture of success" (similar to TYWLS's "culture of high expectations"), these girls have been given few of the elements that lead to success, including the experience of previous success in their families, their neighborhoods, or their earlier schooling.

Students at YWLCS are racially diverse and mostly poor; more than two-thirds live below the poverty level. They've never done science experiments, do not know how to explain an answer in algebra. The teachers, even the math teachers, find themselves teaching reading and writing at some pretty basic levels before they can get to the curriculum.

They get to the advanced work by using girls' natural strength: communication. "Girls are less linear, more emotionally mature, more social than boys," offers Margaret Small. "We use that in math and science, problem-solving in groups."

Internships and external panels, in which they present portfolios of their work to professionals, bridge the worlds of school and work, so YWLCS students can see the value of what they're learning. And one graduating student said, "They don't let you drop out here."

This school works by overcoming the usual disasters of public education—low interest, low attendance, low scores in science and math, a high dropout rate, teacher ennui. It's not hand-picking the best and brightest either, but working with students assigned by lottery. Yet of sixty neighborhood and charter high schools in Chicago Public Schools (CPS), this six-year-old girls' school is number one in percent graduating and number one in college enrollment.

The newest of the schools I saw is Irma Rangel School in Dallas, in an old dark brick building with classical lines and lovely windows and a surround of trees, with a hum of activity that makes it feel like being inside a hive. Irma Rangel only opened in 2004 so there have been, as yet, no records of college enrollments or accolades to cite.

It is a college preparatory (magnet) public school, with a mission to nurture the intellectual curiosity and creativity of young women, especially in the fields of science, math, and technology.

Principal Vivian Taylor Samudio decided the first priority was that girls be taught by positive example. "My first challenge," she declares, echoing Ponze and Small, "was to get teachers who were enthusiastic about girls." Because the school is a science-math-technology magnet, she wanted "to be sure the girls saw women teaching science, math, and technology." Taylor Samudio adds, "Then they could say, 'Hey, she can do it, maybe I can, too.'"

The girls can see a role model in the principal herself. Taylor Samudio, trim in a skirted suit, stylish short hair, perfect makeup, looks like a successful executive at one of the more forward-thinking Dallas businesses. She is the ideal ideal, the perfect role model for the students—a woman of color (African American) who is a professional person in authority, married, and mother of one son, and when she speaks of Irma Rangel girls, she's ebullient.

She knows all (200+) of them. "Sometimes they come into my office and they say, 'You doin' OK? Are you feelin' stressed, Ms. Samudio?' And I think, 'Oh my, they're reading me.'" She adds, "They want to make it OK."

The school itself is more than OK, in part because of considerable funding from a local foundation established by Sally and Lee Posey of Dallas. The foundation provides the means to have smart boards in every classroom and a laptop, which can go home with her, for every girl. There are other key features: the school's overall smallness, small classes (eighteen students or fewer), training for faculty and principals, and a single sex student population.

Again and again, social science researchers like Cornelius Riordan have argued that the most important argument for single sex schooling is that it provides "successful role models of their own sex." It is especially advantageous for girls, Riordan has said, because in a girls' school "all the top students in all subjects will be female. . . [and] the teachers are predominantly women."

Besides the principal and teachers, there are Texas women of accomplishment throughout Irma Rangel School, in the classroom, in the library, in the halls, and on the walls. In the front hall are two posters titled "Women in Science" and a framed picture and paragraph the size of a crib blanket of the legislator for whom the school is named.

Irma Lerma Rangel was the first female Hispanic state legislator elected to office. One of her legacies (she died in 2002) was public support of college education for everyone who graduated in the top 10 percent of the class from a Texas high school. This initiative opened the door for many, many minority students and probably encouraged some to stay in high school.

There are some photos of local paragons and paladins in the library. (Ms. Ruiz, the librarian who can point them out, is probably a pretty good role model herself, as a young, attractive, educated Latina.) On the bulletin board is a newspaper photo of Dallas Mayor Laura Miller with Irma Rangel students; as she shakes hands with one of them, she is urging the girls to "be nice to one another" and focus on their studies so that they might become "successful leaders of Dallas."

On November 24, 2006, the U.S. Department of Education began implementing new rules interpreting Title IX, the landmark civil rights legislation of 1972. These rules will allow—and implicitly encourage—American public schools to be single sex.

This is a good ruling for The Young Women's Leadership School in East Harlem, for Chicago's YWLCS, for Irma Rangel in Dallas, and for all the public girls' schools around the country that have championed single sex schools when the trend was definitely against it. Moreover, it is good for the populations those schools serve, which include a diverse mix of backgrounds and abilities, more diverse than in other (nonpublic) schools.

The early successes of these emerging schools and the evident excellence of their elder sisters like Western Girls' School in Baltimore, one of the oldest, public, single sex schools in the United States, argue that girls, particularly minority girls from lower-income backgrounds, benefit from the academic climate, leadership opportunities, and role models of single sex schools. Indeed, some recent research has shown improvement not only in academic subjects like math but in attendance and behavior as well. Given that poor children of Hispanic and African-American minorities are most at risk and members of two of the fastest-growing populations in this country, that research is a big argument for single sex schools for girls.

How do they achieve their success? In a school like Chicago's YWLCS, which faces so many obstacles, the degree of difficulty is 10. How does this school teach its students, and what can we learn from YWLCS? What is to be learned from the new middle schools in Oakland and Seattle and from the six to twelve independent girls' schools in Atlanta?

W. B. Yeats, at different times, observed the "poor have only dreams" and "education is not the filling of a pail but the lighting of a fire." I, therefore, am seeking dream catchers and fire starters and the material they employ.

21

Science, Math, and Joy

In January 2005 Larry Summers, president of Harvard, spoke at a national conference (NBER) on the topic "Diversifying the Science and Engineering Workforce."

He claimed he intended to be controversial, that he was making "some attempts at provocation" when he made his remarks. After front-page stories in major newspapers, faculty protests at Harvard, repeated apologies from Summers, and the appointment of two faculty committees on the subject of women in science, I'd say he succeeded in being provocative.

Basically Summers suggested scholars pursue certain questions about women in higher education in the fields of science and engineering:

1. Do women really want high-powered commitments?
2. Is there different availability of aptitude at the high end? (Are there just fewer women geniuses in physics, for example?)
3. Are socialization and discrimination keeping women from the prestigious jobs in these fields?

These questions are not idiotic, but they are inane and unscientific. They are *inane* because they provide a stereotypical, inaccurate, and unsympathetic picture of women in science (women don't like it, aren't good at it) at a conference promoting diversity. Summers's "speculation" about the subject was *unscientific* on two counts: (1) the question of innate differences is impossible to determine scientifically since boys and girls grow up in a society that treats them differently; and (2) the statements ignore a body of evidence on the culture of the fields of math and science, the systematic discouragement of women, and the discrimination and prejudice against them from graduate school and beyond, which ignorance violates scientific practice.

Maybe Summers is just obtuse. Harvard, the most renowned university in the country, has a less than stellar (one woman scientist called it "abysmal") record on women in the faculty; they are "underrepresented," and they're not getting tenure, according to the university's own committee reports. These committees, appointed by Larry Summers, made several recommendations Harvard could adopt to remedy the problem.

Summers agreed to implement changes to increase the visibility and influence of women on Harvard's faculty, particularly in science and engineering. He pledged $50 million as "an initial commitment" to that goal. Eventually, faced with negative response from faculty and public, he resigned. After an interim appointment, he was replaced by historian-scholar Drew Gilpin Faust, Harvard's first woman president.

Margaret Small has a bad cough, she should probably be home nursing it, but she's at school, treating her nose with Kleenex, her throat with tea and cough drops as she takes questions from teachers, staff, students, and me. Small has come to this place in her life via roads less traveled by most women: she's been a machinist and a member of a trade union; she's attended schools in Maine, North Carolina, New York; she has a Ph.D. in mathematics. She thinks math and science should not be considered the domain of men.

"Larry Summers had it wrong," Dr. Small argues. "There's nothing wrong with the brains [of women], it's the *culture* of hard science" that we should examine. "The culture is male-controlled, unfulfilling." Small demonstrates her point with evidence: 50 percent of U.S. medical students are female; these women will soon be one-half of all our doctors; that schooling requires expertise in math and science.

There *is* a science/math/technology gender gap in the twenty-first century. It's in school, where girls' interest in science and math, equal to boys in the fourth grade, diminishes every year after. It's in careers, where the highest paying entry-level jobs (computer science and engineering) have the *smallest* numbers of women, less than 20 percent of the workforce. And it's in girls' heads, where they think they aren't good at it and shouldn't like it.

"We fight the perception," Small says ruefully, "that these subjects are too hard, are boring, that math and science are highly privileged intellectual fields, inappropriate for [these] kids." She leaves the room to cough a little, drink some tea, and when she returns, she adds, "In engineering, in physics, in biological sciences, they aren't there but not because they lack the *ability*."

The Chicago school that Margaret Small runs teaches a system called the Interactive Mathematics Program (IMP), which seems ideal for girls. In traditional teaching, Small observes, "the math doesn't seem to mean anything. It's very disconnected. They want it to relate to something, to build connections, which is more in line with the way young women learn."

The IMP curriculum integrates problem solving with traditional math (read, the regular arithmetic, algebra, geometry, trigonometry), and the addition of probability, statistics, graphing, matrix algebra, even perhaps something called combinatorics. The IMP technique involves students in an inquiry of some open-ended problem, such as how to measure shadows or population growth, exploring solutions much as working mathematicians and scientists do. It's collaborative and grounded in communication: girls discuss problems, write clear descriptions and proposals, express mathematic concepts which may be applied, and then present their findings to the rest of the class.

To prove they have the ability, everyone at YWLCS works to show regular girls achieve in subjects they aren't supposed to know or like. In eleventh-grade science class, wearing gloves and aprons and goggles, girls perform autopsies on odd-shaped, gray organs the size of footballs, pig hearts. "This is not nasty," exclaims one eleventh grader. "This is a lifetime opportunity that kids don't get in other schools."

I suspect there are also some "lifetime opportunities" at Atlanta Girls' School (AGS). With its electronic boards and ubiquitous laptops, it's the most technologically sophisticated secondary school I've seen, considerably quieter than the average school, and except for the single sex student body, one of the most diverse independent schools in the country.

Much of the written communication and many of the class exercises use electronic webs, linking subjects, teachers, students, and worlds using computer technology. Students make Power-Point presentations before the class, do research on the web, and email questions to their teachers, up to nine p.m. They email their homework assignments, too.

If YWLCS is making science and math girl-friendly, AGS is doing the same for technology. When I tour classrooms I see connected learning, I see teaching "the way girls learn best" (just as Archer says it does), and I see a commitment to a community that is diverse and respectful of differences. The founders were clear they wanted a girls' school for all Atlantans. Today there are 175 students, 41 percent of them children of color. And at the head of this Southern institution, a smart Yankee.

Sue Thompson, fair, tall, blue-eyed, wears lip balm as her makeup, her strawberry blonde hair short and curly, her ample body in black pants and a wrinkled velvet jacket in a raspberry wine color. She came as the Interim Head to look the school over and was able to remind the interview board that if this was a college-prep school, it should probably say that in the mission statement. The AGS promotional material now states the mission on the first page: the first sentence is "AGS prepares girls for college."

The missions of middle schools are more immediate than college preparation, yet they still educate *the way girls learn best*. The middle school motto of the new generation of girls' schools might be *connect and conquer*. In the research and planning stages of these new schools, founding directors tried to determine what the developmental and educational research showed and to design a culture to fit the needs of girls ages ten to thirteen.

One of the first things they recognized at Julia Morgan School in Oakland, according to Founding Head Ann Clarke, was the importance of interpersonal relationships to these girls and that the school should teach through that: encourage the attachments they form to each other through teams and group work, ties to adult guides (teachers and other role models), connections to the larger world outside.

The second point about the culture Ann makes is that it should be a blend of fun and work—a relaxed atmosphere, a safe place (it's OK to fail), which fosters girls' voices and allows them to sample different versions of themselves, to try to understand, who am I? Who could I be?

Julia Morgan School starts the school year with Family Math Night for new students and their families, and the girls run around getting material for graphs on the new population and meet everybody in the process of getting answers. *How many here like chocolate or vanilla? How many are average height for their generation?* Then they play board games which have math questions, and then, consuming the lesson, they eat something chocolate or vanilla.

In spite of games and silly names (Gaming Girls is a competition to create cyber worlds, for example), in spite of traditions that sound unserious (parading on the Mills College campus at Halloween dressed as goddesses, playing chess as human chess pieces, building tiny architectural models of Buddhist and Shinto temples in the seventh grade), there is rigor to this program. There are standards and measures, some objective ones set by teachers, some set jointly by the individual girl and her advisor with an eye toward what she needs to know.

Rigor in the curriculum, Ann Clarke argues, is pretty important. *"Be anything you want* only works if you have the tools to do it."

Subjects like math and the humanities are integrated into project-based curricula to help students see how questions are related and to provide time to explore problems deeply. The process asks students to be independent, focused learners, responsible for their learning and for evaluating their learning; they run the parent-teacher conferences.

Middle school girls are at a crossroads, where their concepts of themselves are more fragile than in earlier years. They *need* to be in charge to contact that earlier version of themselves as curious, capable people. Middle school, in general, is more informal, more unpredictable, more dynamic than high school years. At these emerging schools, it is energetic and noisy, too.

When I ask Marja Brandon, head of Seattle Girls' School, "what makes a good school," this is her first response: "Joy. The noise of joy." She explains, "It's natural to want to learn. Our brains are wired for it. . . . To create a school that rides the horse in any other direction is absurd."

In this school whose physical presence is little more than two portable structures with modular rooms and movable halls, there is a kind of irreverent, backslapping, noisy joy, not surprising in middle school, not surprising in student-cultured, collaborative learning.

Seattle Girls' School has an integrated curriculum with chickens. The fifth-grade theme is "All Creatures, Great and Small," and includes questions about animal life, habitat, ecology, scientific theory integrated with conceptual Latin, poetry, and literature using live poultry as subject matter.

In the coop in the side yard live four chickens the fifth graders have raised from eggs. Recent actions by one have shown him to be a rooster—a "man chicken" is the term one girl uses, dimpling and smiling slightly as she leans over the coop—not allowed within city limits, so he will have to be traded.

In the sixth grade in late spring are Grand Rounds. In one room girls are reciting original poetry; in two others they show original media presentations on their research into topics like diabetes, infectious disease, and AIDS. In the fourth room students in blue hospital scrubs Stand and Deliver. Each has a specific expertise; each is quizzed by M.D.s, mostly women, wearing white smocks. A physician with a stethoscope around her neck asks the appropriate (sixth-grade) specialist, "How does the ear work?"

The girl takes a breath and answers to the room, which, incidentally is full of guests, parents, reporters.

"Do you accept only extroverts?" some visitor invariably asks.

"No," answers board member Julita Elewald, "but they are confident, aren't they?"

In the seventh grade the organizing principle is "Seattle"—the land, the community, its future. They consider the interrelationship of the business community, environmental activists, children, and families.

The eighth grade takes flight. The topic is the "World and Beyond" and appropriate to Seattle, original home of Boeing and Varrier, it translates as the science, the math, and the literature of Aviation. Every eighth-grade girl goes to flight school; every girl copilots a small, four-seat aircraft; and together they make a plane—they stretch canvas over the wood-fiberglass frame of a fifteen-foot ultralight which they store in their hangar-like classroom.

Archer's middle school resembles those at Seattle Girls' School and Julia Morgan School. One year the sixth-grade curriculum at Archer focuses on world hunger: students create world maps of malnutrition, investigate technologies like water filtration in their science class, write and act out monologues, conduct surveys of famine with charts and graphs, and finish by making ceramic bowls to sell as a money-making project for a local relief agency.

Based on the concept of "active learning," which has students assuming responsibility for their own academic achievements, our parent-teacher conferences, too, are student-led. Parents have an opportunity to meet with their daughter and her Archer teachers and hear the student articulate educational goals and assess progress.

"Girls like to be in charge," Vivian Taylor Samudio says about her middle schoolers. "They are great organizers."

What I like about these emerging girls' schools is that they are avowedly academic but not test mills. Their missions are radical and countercultural. They are promoting new definitions of female adolescents: girls who are geeks (Atlanta, Irma Rangel), girls who like to dissect pig hearts (Chicago) and program robots (Archer), girls who overcome the limitations of being shy or fearful or passive and stand up and fly (New York, Oakland, Seattle).

The old, established schools I visited (Hockaday and Spence and, earlier, Castilleja, Emma Willard, Westridge, and Winsor) are evolving as well. They are evaluating their missions and educating themselves (and sometimes educators) about girls' needs and abilities in this new century. The older schools often have more course offerings, because they have more money, more faculty, more opportunities to cross-reference courses; and they have better facilities. They can host swim meets and educational conferences both.

However, the new schools have a mindfulness that may be absent from the old schools, and the latter are more likely to have some antiquated notions among their traditions and even among their curricular items, a class on "mankind," for example, or an annual fashion show, things the twenty-first-century schools would not offer.

And in the future?

Schools with integrated curricula; with advisory groups addressing such interpersonal issues as sexism, racism, and materialism; with school cultures which value girls and young women as fully actualized beings capable of being courageous, caring leaders—these schools will be relevant long into the future.

Some schools with the above traits will be coeducational. But even if coed schools incorporate the inspiration and motivation of single-sex schools and somehow meld *learning like a girl* with *learning like a boy*, there will still be a need in society for a place that is wholly dedicated to educating, that is, challenging, guiding, nurturing, girls.

That's why Jim McManus' opinion is so heartening: "The schools that survive are those that get into people's hearts. Something about Archer," he says with a smile in his voice, "I'd bet on 100 years."

I'd make that bet on Archer, too. And on Atlanta Girls' School, Julia Morgan, Irma Rangel, Seattle Girls' School, and The Young Women's Leadership School. And Chicago's YWLCS? 200 years. If Margaret Small stays as director.

22

Where the Boys Are

So what about the boys? If the girls are off to Archer or Seattle or Irma Rangel, then what's left for the kids with the Y chromosome? Boys' schools, by default?

Boys' schools have been called the dinosaurs of the American educational world. In public, private, and religious spheres, their numbers have dwindled. Once the mainstay of male education in the United States, the institutions, often with spacious campuses, big endowments, and lovely sports facilities, were pressured by forces legal, ethical, and economic to go coed. Most of them did.

They had been, in some cases, citadels of certitude and privilege, dedicated to producing erudite gentlemen who, it was assumed, would become ruling elite in the likely future. Some, even today, can be justly criticized for perpetuating stereotypical views, for reinforcing exclusionary tendencies among students, even—in the case of some military-type schools—for fostering a culture of violence, cruelty, and degradation.

Most boys' schools that are still around have changed. Just as girls' schools have evolved from creating ladies to creating leaders, boys' schools have eschewed rigid definitions of manliness to embrace sensitivity, tolerance, and respect for women. Many of them have female teachers and administrators, providing positive role models of the other sex.

Still, it is generally assumed that boys do better in coed schools than single sex ones. Boys behave better around girls, it is thought, and without girls in subservient roles as a willing audience for their achievements, boys will degenerate into violent, sexist, irrational beings out of *Lord of the Flies*. This is the Better-Coed-than-Dead argument, I guess.

At the end of the 1990s, however, researchers like Cornelius Riordan began to express doubts about how well boys were doing in coed schools, worrying that boys were having problems with reading, writing, and other academic achievements in what he termed the "silent gender gap." About this time, there was new concern that coed schools, especially the elementary grades, were neglecting boys' needs, were not treating boys fairly. Some educators and parents cautiously suggested that single sex education might make sense for boys.

Boys and girls, they pointed out, are developmentally diverse and quite out of sync with each other. Most boys lag behind most girls developmentally. Although boys perceive spatial relationships vividly and achieve large motor control early, their relationship to the physical world makes them less able to sit quietly, listen closely, and, in general, behave like girls.

For their part, girls typically use language more deftly, understand complex concepts sooner, and manifest small motor control at an earlier stage than boys. During reading circle at the library, girls might be moved to sketch or color; the boys, meanwhile, might be moved to wrestle. In early grades, the school environment is conducive to the orderly, attentive female members of the class, not to the physically active male members.

Boys' schools take into consideration normal male behavior and design the day around them. They can be counter-stereotypical, providing role models of men who mentor, who challenge, who inspire, sometimes by their evident affection for Cicero or the piccolo, for physics or Sandburg or ceramics. Confronted with manly examples of adults who have chosen without reluctance to teach and to pursue a passion that is slightly recompensed but, here at least, socially respected, they learn that within the parameters of the male role, there are many options.

An educator named Diane Hulse, studying middle school boys attending a boys' school or a coed school with similar demographics, came to the conclusion in 1997 that the boys' school boys were "less aggressive and less susceptible" to the peer pressures of teenage culture and more positively engaged in the academic pursuits of their school.

Five years later, after what she termed "an extensive review" of the research literature, Hulse urged parents to look at boys' schools, for in the nurturing kind of boys' schools, she concluded, "many of the problems faced by boys in coeducational schools seems to diminish." A boys' school can be, in the words of another cogent observer, Rosemary Salomone, "a protective space where boys can pursue their own path to self-fulfillment free from the distractions of girls." I took myself off to search for such a place, and I wound up at New York City's Allen-Stevenson School (A-S).

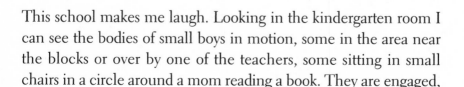

This school makes me laugh. Looking in the kindergarten room I can see the bodies of small boys in motion, some in the area near the blocks or over by one of the teachers, some sitting in small chairs in a circle around a mom reading a book. They are engaged, and they are moving—wiggling, tapping, bobbing, nodding, drumming—even those in chairs. "During the story," my guide explains, "the boys can move around but they aren't supposed to make contact physically." I guess that eliminates pinching and punching, for a moment or two.

It is pretty much the same thing in the third-grade classroom, where boys are doing projects on butterflies which they studied on a trip to the Museum of Natural History, some imitating with their own bodies the movement of these creatures in flight, doing a slow-flapping arm wave like Queen Elizabeth visiting the Australians; other boys intent on details are drawing the distinctive markings in comic book color.

Fifth grade is in the gym, where aerobic exercise is a contest: answer a question put by the PE teacher, something like, "Who knows how many of Mrs. McCauley's sons attended Allen-Stevenson?" My guide, Jean McCauley, is smiling at this. A few hands shoot up. The boy who answers correctly gets to choose the next exercise. I am unsurprised (I have brothers) that he picks something challenging enough to elicit groans from the rest of the class.

I picture the same scene with fifth-grade girls: a girl choosing something easy or something funny, like finger aerobics or rolling necks, shoulders, toes, trying to please her teacher without alienating her classmates. Eleven-year-old boys fear being considered weak; eleven-year-old girls fear being isolated— they're not going for the groans of their friends.

The classrooms of older students at Allen-Stevenson, grades six through eight, are smaller—in some cases eleven or twelve students around a table—and although they are dressed in ties, shirts, and slacks, they are expansive, sprawling, one leaning back in his chair at a dangerous angle, one beating rhythmically on the table with pen as drumstick.

In the hallways of this too-small building (nearly four hundred students in a place designed for two hundred), boys are blurs, a glimpse of music cases, books, and backpacks, traveling hurriedly to orchestra or art or an academic class. At lunchtime the blurs move into hyperspeed—fueled by the kinetic energy and testosterone of boys who bounce, bound, and sally, fling words, things (like crumpled paper, pens, caps) over heads and across lockers, just miss the interception—and achieve stratosphere.

We pass a bulletin board at the Allen-Stevenson School which claims, "There are many ways to be a boy and many ways to be successful." It would seem that all the ways involve moving.

"Their rhythms are honored," says one of the teachers at A-S, stopping to talk. "They have wiggle room." Evidently this is meant literally, as I'd seen in the kindergarten classroom, and philosophically, as in there is more than one definition of appropriate behavior for a young male. The student is not told that an Allen-Stevenson boy does sports or passes silently in the halls, but rather, that there are many options.

Most developmental studies comparing the sexes, ages five to fourteen, show boys having higher energy levels but shorter attention spans than girls. They're more active than girls and their female teachers. ("I'm used to their exuberance," the kindergarten teacher commented.) Where their rhythms are honored, they are not as likely to be what used to be called "behavior problems."

Boys at this age don't hear as well as girls, so when the activity raises the noise level, that only makes it feel more natural. This is, of course, assuming they aren't being rowdy or disturbing out of frustration, aggression, or anger. Their energy and high physicality can be channeled in a single-sex school with nobody having to say "sit still." That alone reduces frustration.

Single sex schools are able to teach boys according to their natural timetables, respecting their rhythms and, it would seem, their hearing. In addition, psychological goals such as impulse control, high self-esteem, and the understanding of nonverbal communication that contributes to "emotional literacy" can more easily be accomplished, some psychologists argue, among all-boy groups led by caring adults.

It is worth noting that caring adults are an important dimension of any successful program with any combination of students. Other considerations are class size, teaching philosophy, mission, curriculum, and emphases on subjects such as science, math, literature, and the arts. In a boys' school like Allen-Stevenson, there is a broad range of academic and curricular options, including those which might be otherwise female-dominated, such as the arts.

Here on the A-S campus are boys in the orchestra (I count seven violinists and two flutists in the ensemble) and boys in chorus (they have an anachronistic attachment to Gilbert and Sullivan) and in one of the art rooms, boys draw, model, paint, mold, and build in a variety of media. A bulletin board in the middle school hallway announces highlights of varsity and junior varsity sports and next to that, the winners of the poetry contest, with one of the winning entries printed alongside. (At another boys' school the Headmaster brags that the winner of the poetry contest that year is the star athlete as well.)

Studies confirm that among comparable students, boys in single sex schools are twice as likely to study art, music, foreign language, and literature as those in coed schools. In the latter, girls dominate activities considered expressive, such as drama, literary magazines, school dances, and community service. What's left for boys in which to excel, what's urged on them by the coed school culture, is athletics and athletics.

In a coed setting, boys' behavior is more rigidly defined; there's more pressure to conform to the stereotypical male role: dominate, influence, bond with males, display no feelings, play ball. In mixed sexed classrooms males have been found to talk a lot, although not *on subject*, and to ignore, discount, tease, or harass females in their midst. A boys' school is something of a recess from these demands, what Salomone calls "protective space."

David Trower, Headmaster at Allen-Stevenson, cites counter-stereotypical behavior at the school: "Boys sew, paint, talk about feelings. Project Charlie is a kind of group therapy." Trower is genial and warm, and with his dimpled face and almost military brush cut, he's a cross between a cherub and a colonel.

The military aspect of Trower's image is misleading, however; though he is the head of an all-male institution, it is too flexible, too comfortable, too nurturing to be martial. It is rather a harbor, a safe haven, for boys where (1) their physicality is challenged rather than contained; (2) instruction embraces action over lecture and reportage; and (3) the meaning of boyness is textured and complex.

"For young boys it is pretty evident they learn differently [from girls]," Trower states. "For high school it is debatable." Since his school only goes to ninth grade, this assertion may be more about politics than educational policy. At any rate, the relevant research offers support for what Trower calls "doing right by boys" by giving them their own school.

Their own school in this case resembles several other old, upscale (elite), prestigious, independent schools in this Upper Eastside Manhattan neighborhood of brick and brownstone buildings on tree-lined streets. Inside, the Headmaster's office is an asylum of wood, windows, books, many decibel levels quieter than outside the door, where there are kids and construction workers using all the gear of both occupations.

Trower, who has been at A-S for more than fifteen years, describes his job: "I put out fires and hold the big picture." Just now, in the midst of what appears to me to be a huge, much-needed remodeling, he adds, "My main job is to get us through construction."

Can they learn how to be boys without girls around? Much of the male role is defined as *not girls*. When they are in preschool, they learn not to play in the doll corner, it's where girls play. In elementary school sports and play, they learn to be tough, to suffer pain without complaint, disappointment without tears, because only girls cry. In academic pursuits they learn it's okay to be mildly able in history, science, and math but not in English and French (which are for girls). All the signposts of masculinity are in opposition to females. What happens in single sex schools?

What happens when girls are removed from the scene is that boys learn a broader definition of masculinity than one based on opposition to females. A single-sex school is not a monastic institution where the other sex is banished from sight. The adults provide opportunities to counter both monastic auras and sexist ideas. Faculty and staff at enlightened schools include both women and men, wherein students see men being nurturing, women making decisions, and both sexes working together as equals for a common goal.

But what about the argument that there are two sexes and they need exposure to each other? They do. They need to know how to treat each other fairly, generously, compassionately, but competing with their own gender for the attentions of the other doesn't ensure anything good.

In secondary school, relations between males and females are complicated by hormones. Adolescence is a famously difficult stage physically, socially, and emotionally; and again, the different rhythms of the two sexes are not harmonious. In their relationship to the other, females seek intimacy, males seek sex. Furthermore, the different agendas in the same room make it hard to pay attention to anything else.

In single sex settings, physical interaction, romance, and sex (the activity, not the variable), which have considerable importance in coed schools, are less central, less polarized as opposites, less salient in defining masculinity or femininity. Students from boys' schools, according to at least one study, actually have more egalitarian attitudes toward females and support concepts like equal opportunity, parity at work, and co-parenting.

Why would they have more egalitarian attitudes? Three factors may account for this finding. The first, according to two different researchers, is *role models*, the presence of successful, nurturing males and strong females in single sex schools in the persons of teachers, coaches, counselors, administrators, and staff.

Second, boys' schools have become more sensitive to changing male and female social roles and more liberal in their views about the "appropriate" spheres for women and men in parenting and the work world. Some, like Allen-Stevenson, try to remove gender bias from the culture of the school.

The third factor? Jean McCauley and I think it's the demise of enforced social dances, those awkward, awful, unsettling encounters which emphasized boy-aggressor, girl-object moments punctuated by boredom and embarrassment. Jean and I share memories of our own and our children's experiences with these mixed sex disasters.

What's happening today in boys' schools is more natural, less forced: girls and boys together after school in drama productions, neighborhood projects, debate or chess club tournaments, community service, or robotics competitions. A boys' school like A-S may have a sister school with which to partner, or students can meet in all-school events.

It would seem, if Allen-Stevenson is a model, that male-female interactions like these can normalize encounters between the sexes, as well as counter the anti-intellectualism typical of the adolescent subculture. It would seem that all boys, all the time with a few women teachers and girl helpmates for variety, some good role models, and a culture of tolerant diversity in definitions of maleness can be a healthy way for a boy to learn who he can be.

Back at Archer a few months later, I witness an Opening Day ceremony. Girls are gathered on the front lawn wearing their uniforms with green t-shirts celebrating "ten years of excellence," as they say on the back. Up the tile steps in the front hall are the new seniors, each with a fistful of green pencils with the celebratory words. They witness the youngest girls raising the flag and the entire school singing the school song, and then they line either side of the entry, and as the girls from the lawn enter the building by class, the seniors hand each girl a pencil as she goes by. The morning ceremony ends in the back by the fountain, where parents and trustees witness the cutting and distribution of a heavily frosted cake which says *Archer School, Ten Years of Excellence.*

I can't believe it's been ten years since we opened.

I can't believe we can truly claim the excellence we are touting, although there's considerable evidence that we can. My new mission is to gather the evidence from the last few years, assess the progress and the regrets, and determine what still needs to be done.

I also can't believe how different this event might have been at a boys' school: the pencils are obvious projectiles and instruments of ear adornment; the march into the back courtyard, an opportunity for scrimmage and other antics; the cake? I can only imagine.

Afterword

A school year ends in graduation. A journey ends in homecoming. There is a rhythm and a circularity to both. There is both sorrow and joy, for they represent the marking of change, and change is always tinged with loss.

The students, who are, after all, at a beginning, a Commencement, are leaving friends and memories. Loaded down with wishes and advice, they are starting over. Sofi, Archer's student speaker at graduation this year, urges her classmates to "seize life's opportunities and act" because when you don't act, you act. "With inaction, you open the door to evil and evil is always more than happy to enter, to put his feet on your coffee table, to copy your homework and to drill for oil in Alaska."

I'm filing this advice with that of other Archer girls, like the Student Store supervisor who told another student, "Do your part. And if someone's absent, do her part also." Or the robotics captain who worked all weekend to get the robot ready for competition who matter-of-factly told another girl, "There are no queen bees here. Only ants."

For me it is the journey's end, home from travels to other schools in other places, home from meeting kindred colleagues, almost as if I'd been to a reunion where I discovered unknown cousins who make their tea in the same kind of pot and share a penchant for Irish blessings and old goddesses. I found fellow travelers and saw sights both wondrous and trite, the latter exemplified by the school maintenance crew who wouldn't lend their ladder to hang the drama teacher's banner for who-knows-what peculiar, bureaucratic reasoning.

The journey I made at the end is a mirror to the one I made at the beginning. Then I was searching for a good school, wondering if it mattered so much if it was single sex. Later, telling the story of Archer, seeing its success, I went in search of sister schools, wondering if they were good and if it mattered so much if they were single sex.

The journey taken over eighteen months in lurches and stops, like a vehicle with standard transmission driven by a twelve-year-old, had moments of madness. In Texas I named the rental car directional guidance *Mr. BusyPants* for its bossy insistence until it made me really lost, late, and cranky. I stopped talking to it and tried to kill it by drowning its voice with Country and shrouding its face with a sweater. I'm not pleased with myself for that.

Too, there were moments of delight: an African-Latina girl at Spence answering my probe about the uniform by telling me, "You can wear colored shoes, colored sweaters. . . colored skin"; the Seattle Girls' School student reporting that one of the hens had developed into a "man-chicken."

There were shared tears at several places, usually over the desperate circumstances of some of the children's lives. Margaret Small recited the painful litany: "exploitation, humiliation, brutality, homelessness, families who can't afford carfare for them to get to school."

Once they get there, school can mitigate, and sometimes over-come, the awfulness of some of these lives, the empty materialism of others. They are in a community that validates the values and ways of behaving that are naturally theirs. They are in a school cul-ture that values girls for what they do rather than what they have.

In a tenth-grade Life Skills class, students comment about solv-ing problems by centering on *think*, not *get*. Harvard professor Eleanor Duckworth, I tell them, describes learning as "the hav-ing of wonderful ideas." "It'd be hard to argue," notes Natalie dryly, "that it would be the having of wonderful strappy heels."

What I found among the girls I encountered at each of these schools is the immeasurable joy of ownership they feel for their schools. What *can* be measured—the accomplishment and atti-tudes and career aspirations, the grades and test scores and gradu-ation rates—argue for the starting of more single sex schools.

What I found is that science, math, and technology can be conquered where the curriculum and method are geared to girls, centered around problems that matter to them. This was true for middle school girls in Seattle and Oakland, for high school girls in Atlanta and Dallas, for public school girls in New York and Chicago. And, of course, for Archer girls in Los Angeles.

What I found is that Archer is not unique. In all the schools I visited I saw inclusive leadership, I saw innovative, constructive learning, I saw role modeling and risk taking. I also saw what other people have noted at girls' schools, other people being the people who are the professional observers who make a little note at the back of their jottings about the bonds of community.

It begins with those who go every day into the classroom, fac-ing adolescent energy, emotionalism, and angst armed only with naked resolve and lesson plans. At every school I visited, faculty endure long work hours, take special training, and toil together on weekends and holidays challenging themselves to bridge disciplines, theory, and relevance, for which efforts they are, by their students if not the outside world, respected, applauded, and sometimes loved.

They, in turn, challenge their students to think, to risk, and to be accountable for their visions of truth. They allow them to have *wonderful ideas*. They take the students into their hearts and, in at least two cases, into their homes.

They pass the hat in faculty meetings for the student of impoverished means who is going to Smith or Barnard for the summer without money for carfare or lip gloss or pajamas; they tell her the school has a small grant budgeted for this.

They grieve at the passing of a girl's parent, always too young, invariably the very one who remembered to ask after one's own well-being at the parent-teacher conference.

They are supported and abetted by remarkable women: Arlene Hogan, her protégé Ann Clarke, Sue Thompson in Atlanta, Seattle's Marja Brandon, Chicago's Margaret Small, East Harlem's Kathleen Ponze, and in Dallas, Vivian Taylor Samudio.

Explaining the determination of Texas women, Ann Richards once said when the men went off on the cattle drive, women were left to hold the ranch and protect the kids with nothing but a dog and a gun.

In Dallas the one holding the ranch is Vivian Taylor Samudio. In Chicago, it's Margaret Small. In Oakland, Ann Clarke. At Archer, it is Arlene Hogan.

Our biggest supporter and the most important figure in this wild adventure has been our head of school. Once we had the able Arlene Hogan (and lost her unable predecessors), we got the school we sought.

So, too, has it been for the other schools, most of whom had some ordinary human in the job until they found the other-worldly Margaret or Kathleen or Sue, who knew how to scale glass mountains and root out ogres under the bridge.

"Most schools fail," Jim McManus told me, long after we'd founded ours. Schools last if they have a clear idea of who they are, if there's a need for who they are, and if there's a bond among the members.

Cornelius Riordan, himself a sociologist, remarked some years ago on a panel about education, "You don't have to be a social scientist to identify the characteristics of a *good* school." On most of our lists, whether we're parents, teachers, students, or the aforementioned social scientists, is the idea of school as community.

We were engaged from the beginning in creating what we off-handedly referred to as a *community of learners*, a place where *the best teachers can do their best teaching*. It's taken several years (at least seven) to attract the best teachers, let alone unite them and those they teach into community. We may be there now.

Teachers I interview refer to Archer as "innovative" and "inventive" and, at the same time, "a supportive environment," "nurturing," "a family atmosphere." This feeling of community, suggests Rob Everett, history teacher, may originate with "a sense of mission, a sense of founding" the school inspires.

Nor is it fancy (desks, windows, facilities) that makes it special. "When I went to Harvard-Westlake's theatre production," said one of our girls, "and I saw professional-quality lights, costumes, stages, I didn't feel jealous, I felt scorn, really. . . . I mean, who has the real learning experience?"

The civic struggles, the banners which said, "No to Archer," the petitions the neighbors signed for and against the school contributed to the solidarity the students felt. "They were mean," said Dominique, referring to Archer's opposition. "It made me glad I went to a school where people were tolerant of others."

Almie, who had come from a large, public school, was impressed with the sense of camaraderie she found here. "I couldn't fully grasp the idea of an entire school eating lunch together in a sunny courtyard. But lo and behold, there it was in front of me."

She adds with a glimmer of a grin, "Everyone at Archer seemed so happy that I expected them to join hands and break out into *Kumbayah*."

The sense of community comes from shared values, experiences, and beliefs and from an interdependence; Henrik Ibsen said it's like a ship—everyone ought to be prepared to take the helm (some girl-mates would add, *and the galley*). For girls, community is the context that gives meaning to competition.

I'm remembering being in the women's bathroom at the L.A. Forum, a tarantula-legged temple of spectacle, which is the site of a regional robotics competition, some fifty-plus high schools engaged in timed-trial robot games.

There are two all-girls' teams (the room is 90 percent male), and they recognize each other in the bathroom easily enough, since they herald their girlieness in the uniforms they've designed for themselves: one in baby-blue t-shirts with white letters, the other (Archer, calling themselves "The Muses") in baby pink. On the back of the pink t-shirts in black letters are the team players' names, followed by, "Isn't it a muse-ing?" My dad, who loved puns, would have thought so.

"You guys were great," says a baby-blue shirt, a pale-skinned blonde with bangs and a ponytail. "That was a close match."

"You guys deserved to win. I'm glad one of us is in the finals," says pink shirt, a curly-haired, big-eyed, animated girl who asks, "Did you have trouble with your drive or your chain?"

"Chain."

"Us, too. We finally just took it off." (I have no certain picture of what esoterica this vocabulary represents, but I love seeing two attractive geek girls sharing robot woes in the bathroom.) Then pink shirt adds, "Good luck in the next round."

"To you too," says her competitor, then, softly, "thanks for your support—it means a lot."

As cultural evidence, this exchange isn't startlingly dramatic. Although the underpinning of the discussion is twenty-first-century students designing and constructing robots to perform certain tasks, convey some moves, conduct certain strategies, the conversation is polite and respectful, almost old-fashioned. It's characterized by expressions of sympathy and support: *You were great; you deserved to win; good luck; thanks for your support.*

Whatever else I'm seeing and hearing, this is a community of learners in a culture of mutual respect and mutual responsibility, a short paragraph in an essay on single sex education. Between and within these girls' teams is a supportive environment, where attitudes about capabilities are formed without gender implications. This is, pretty much, what the experts say good education is.

After all the conferences and books, after the panels, lectures, interviews, and talks, opinions on brains and on boys (*But what do you do about boys? And what about the real world? What do you think of this famous educator from a famous university?*), after all this, there is the evidence. In the tiled, utilitarian women's bathroom at the L.A. Forum is a glimpse of that blessing the Irish call *Light Without and Light Within.* Or, as Wallace Stevens spoke of spring:

Not Ideas About the Thing but the Thing Itself.

Appendix A

School in a (down-filled) Box

How to do a How-to Guide to Founding a School? All how-to pieces, while informative, maybe even important, seem artificial, lifeless, and a little dull. I find myself distracted by geese.

Out my window there to the north, several hundred yards away, is a small pond with reeds and resident frogs and, from time to time, eighteen Canada geese.

Before we got here—it's now midsummer in Vermont—the geese evidently made their nests and hatched their young, for there are shallow clefts on the sides of the pond lined with twigs, dried fern, and fluffy white down like the insides of pillows. Now, moving in pairs or family groups of two adults and several youngsters, they return almost every day to the pond of their birth to feed.

After studying them for portions of every day as I sit at my desk, I see them as guides to this section of the book. There are certain principles to a community enterprise, Starting a School, that are not unlike what goes on at the pond. Here are some things my goose guides have reminded me.

1. *What are you?* In the bird world, knowing what you are is a matter of survival. Mates and family within the flock recognize each other by display, showing their colors, so to speak. One day there was a loud honking and a flutter of wings as the entire flock took to the air at once. Moments later I saw a small red fox trotting in the woods near the edge of the pond. Geese evidently know who they are and who the foxes are.

In the school world, *who you are* means what is your mission, what exactly are you about? The one thing that cannot sustain itself is a thing that doesn't know what it is. There was a school in Southern California that began as a ranch for unschooled locals, then morphed into a place for wealthy miscreants, then tried to be something else, eventually (around the time we were starting) going belly-up despite some expensive real estate holdings. It didn't know if it was a *this* or a *that*; the school did not have a clear mission.

Gather potential supporters, in living rooms, to define who you are and what they can do to help you start. Consider inviting entrepreneurs, who know how startups should behave, and developers or commercial realtors, who are accustomed to combining services and politics; invite teachers and administrators from existing schools who know kids and facilities, including possible sites; invite parents in the community who have experience with the kind of school you want or who have children who might attend.

We had excellent help, hours of volunteer work, from parents of children way too young to go to our school; there were three mothers of toddlers, refugees from the world of paid employment as a lawyer, an executive, and an opera singer; there was a restaurateur who fed us, confiding his hope of marrying and having a little daughter who'd go to our school (at the time he didn't even have a girlfriend, as far as we knew). All of them worked for fun and for free.

There must be people who can get things done—who have served on nonprofit boards, represented their fellows, run organizations. Avoid dilettantes and cranks. They make the meetings go on too long, and they'll take the best seats on the couch.

In those living rooms, ask yourselves whom you serve. All female children between certain ages in a certain district? That is the universe Chicago's YWLCS defines for itself. The definition requires some remedial work before basic goals can be met: teachers of algebra teach reading; science instructors start with writing, so students can understand what they're observing. This school works because everybody knows whom they serve and chooses to serve them.

2. *Is it needed?* The Canada geese I see in the early morning have other habitats in the area at different times of the day. Once they climb on the grassy verge near the pond I see outside my window, they commit a large goose as guard, standing upright and watchful, as the rest feed. They honk their way to the water if one of our dogs appear.

In your habitat, appoint someone to determine if there is a good reason to start a school there, by doing a needs assessment of your district. We looked at the yield figures of the independent schools in our area that we considered likely competition: of the four coed and one single sex secondary schools, three turned away two-thirds of their applicants and two rejected more than a third, so we figured there was room for us in that market. Now *we* turn away two-thirds of our applicants.

In Atlanta the founders kept saying, "No other metropolitan area of comparable size is without a girls' school" (so it would seem to be an unfilled need). In New York City, where there was a thriving culture of single sex sister schools, there was no public version, so making that education available for poor children became the raison d'être.

In Dallas it was more complicated. In 2002 the Dallas Independent School District (DISD) agreed to take some bond money and prepare an old brick building the district owned to become a girls' school. It would be a college preparatory (magnet) school with a mission to nurture the intellectual curiosity and creativity of young women. The problem was the girls didn't really want to go. With room for three hundred, only fifty signed on.

Enter the new principal, Vivian Taylor Samudio. Although her appointment to Irma Rangel School the spring before it was to open effectively delivered her to two jobs at once, canceled her summer vacation, and offered a host of new obstacles, she found the biggest problem to be the district's failure to attract students.

By extending the application deadline and holding Open Houses (*Casa Abiertas*, in the Spanish-language version) to recruit families, Taylor in only twenty months on the job raised the school's profile, its standards, and its number of students. She proved that there was a need for the school she'd been hired to lead.

3. *Who's on first?* The first geese in the pond test the waters and establish the suitability of the site for the flock's current needs.

Recruit the founding board carefully, people with talent and experience in diverse fields, people who agree to make this school their community work, who have a passion for the mission and time to devote to it. Those who support the endeavor but with a lesser commitment of time and resources can be advisory board members. When we discovered we were in a big civic struggle, we were glad for every kind of supporter we had.

When I joined the cause, Vicky had already assembled what would be our founding board. We were a couple of lawyers, an architect, a small-business person, a producer, a writer, and me, an academic. We really needed everybody, and everybody worked hours every week on the school in the first twenty-four months.

The board devised the mission, the plan, and the budget. We used living room gatherings to recruit ideas and additional talent (our godmothers). We invented a name and further developed our mission at these informal meetings. We found a lawyer among us who researched and registered the name and who advised board members about filing incorporation papers, all pro bono. We talked about sites and building plans and possible public facilities, such as libraries and parks.

Living room gatherings supplement board meetings at several stages: Knowing who you are, whom you're serving, and if there's a need for you (principles 1 and 2); committing an initial group of hardcore supporters by assigning tasks such as naming, incorporating, filing with the state office, raising funds, broadcasting intent (which is everything from local gossip to fancy websites), and beginning a search for a site.

4. *Secure a site.* When the geese are in the pond, one watches for predators. If Fiona, our Lab, enters the water, all the geese swim away, but one turns and faces the dog, leading the predator away from the others. When the two have swum for awhile and the dog is tiring, the goose flies to another part of the pond, and a different goose becomes the coy bait. Eventually they either fly off (especially if the Newfoundlands also enter the water), or the dog tires and pulls herself from the water, leaving the pond for the flock.

We spent most of our efforts in the first five years on securing a site. Initially we rented rooms in a dance studio and then in a church. Our architect and one of our lawyers worked on the negotiations for space in these two locales, which were a block from each other. Raising funds, getting tax exempt status, and determining our needs were related tasks in this stage.

Public schools cannot completely skip this stage, although they usually acquire their classrooms from their school districts. Chicago's YWLCS was in temporary quarters initially. When I visited them in 2006, they were in a beautiful building with factory-style windows and iron doors and staircases, but if that will be their permanent home, I'd wish them some state-of-the-art science labs to go with it.

Irma Rangel School in Texas had a building offered to them that had been a district administration building—a lovely setting, but again, no labs, no gym, no studios. Moreover, the construction crew hired to transform the building into a school for girls over the summer months had to go into overtime, an unexpected expense, to get the job done.

Most independent schools I visited had their time in rental space (Julia Morgan, Seattle) or the church basement (Atlanta) before finding a more permanent home. This is the costly stage, but as the geese demonstrate, if it's your space, it's worth defending.

5. *Show me the money.* Geese don't use money, but they do line their nests with down. I'm not sure how this fits but it's a lovely image and indicates an attitude of preparedness, I think.

Be fiscally responsible: develop a budget and a plan. We did a poor job of it, but we were lucky. You need to be lucky or smart to get past this stage.

The area in which we were least experienced, most naïve is finances. We really didn't understand how money works. One thing we did early on was get trustees, Mary McCarthy, then John Emerson, and then two brilliant entrepreneurs, Jeffrey

Sudikoff and Jess Ravich, to shepherd us through the maze. All I can say about them is *Bless you*.

Ideally, someone on the board leads on the finance piece, developing a budget that projects forward into the first year or two of operation and includes income, expenses, and what we thought of as *unmentionables*, the things that could go very, very wrong.

Robert, one of our board members, was always pressing us to get a bond as a way to finance our mortgage. For the first few years we were not strong enough to qualify for one, but once we were, our Head, Arlene Hogan, and Jeffrey jumped us through the hoops and rewarded us with black ink and a very pretty bond.

This phase of development necessarily follows from the early stages of determining the mission and the market, for it involves translating the concept of the school into numbers that represent costs and projections of future costs. The numbers, in turn, stand for hope, liability, security, and expected heartbreak, shared equally among all.

To make this new, somewhat unstable venture work, we needed more than anything a leader who could envision the future, govern the unruly, guide the young, and control the budget. More than the Finance Committee, more than United Allied Irish Bank (who had our bond) or First Republic (who had our mortgage), more than any of these the responsibility for our solvency lay with the Head of School.

The Head is the CEO and matriarch of a large, disorderly (sometimes dysfunctional) family who has, in addition to a job, real estate questions, marital problems, child care issues, and sometimes financial instability of her own. A good business manager can help with some of this. But most of the weight of that mantle that is professional on one side and personal on the other falls on the shoulders of the Head.

Until we found Arlene Hogan, we were failing, and our grade in financial security was an F. Now, according to the two professional associations who accredited us (Western Association of Schools and Colleges and California Association of Independent Schools) and the two financial institutions who underwrite us, we've earned an A. Credit to all the aforementioned, but more than anyone, credit Arlene Hogan.

6. *Share the leadership.* When the lead goose tires, he or she falls back in the formation, and another takes the lead position. Leading at any given time is a matter of strength and ability to fly. Those farther back in formation honk at the lead to keep up speed and call out bodies of water they're passing over.

When we began the living room meetings, they were hosted by Vicky initially, then me. Vicky did all of the early recruiting of board members (in consultation with Megan), and Vicky was the first board chair. Eventually, outside events forced Vicky to fall back, and at that time I became co-chair. Board leadership was shared for the next five years. In our tenth year, the Executive Committee became the leader, setting our direction for the long journey into the future.

In general, there are four types of leaders in a school founding: parents, educators, school trustees, and students. All of them help shape school policy, participate in activities which support the program, attend school events, and create a community with a shared culture. Their communication skills largely determine how shared the goals are, how binding the trust is, and how understanding the community is.

They share the lead but have different responsibilities and must agree in advance on their role: Parents are responsible for providing students who are healthy, fed, and motivated to learn. Educators are responsible for planning, executing, and evaluating student learning. Trustees set institutional goals and policy, as well as find the resources to accomplish the goals. Students are responsible for presenting themselves *program-ready* to the best of their ability.

7. *Lose the one who is a lone goose.* When a goose decides to fly her or his own way, the drag and resistance of flying alone may convince the loner to get back in formation. Geese will let him. You shouldn't.

We had board members who got weary after their stint in the V, but their honking encouragement from time to time told us they still honored our journey. Some there were, however, who diverged and dissented. When their honking distracted us too much, we continued without them. This is equivalent to the directive in Jim Collins's *Good to Great:* "As important as who is on the bus is who is not."

Other schools recently founded had their own versions of the lone goose, someone flying off course and taking the mission, the budget, the whole school south, if allowed. At one school it was two parents second-guessing the Head of School and the way seed capital was spent. At another, it was those other volunteers, the trustees, who caused trouble.

In any new school, parents have to be educated about their role. In charter or independent schools there are a lot of parent meetings, lots of volunteer hours, workshops. But sometimes parents cannot separate the needs of the institution from their own or their children's needs and wants, especially in emotionally laden issues like dress, discipline, and drugs. Sometimes parents are less objective than the students themselves, and their hours at the school (as volunteer or trustee) are more liability than asset.

Oddly enough, we had more wrong'uns among those we *hired* than those who worked for fun and for free. Perhaps because

their models were all established schools, many of the professionals wanted lots of people on the payroll, more than a startup
should need; many of those hired, from business managers to administrators, had some history or some personal quirks that made
them problematic. We'd lose them eventually, but in the process
they'd drag us back and stop our momentum in energy output, in
money, sometimes in court.

8. *Protect the fallen.* When a goose becomes sick or wounded,
two healthy geese drop out of formation and stay on the ground
with the injured bird until she or he dies or flies again. They protect and feed the vulnerable one and rejoin their flock or join another when the protection is no longer necessary.

When I got sick, when Arlene had heart surgery, when someone else lost a job and means of support, the group of women
and men and girls who formed the school community nurtured
us with food and flowers, prayers and poems. It makes you strong
and vital to be a group that cares for each other when one is
down as well as when all are flying high.

Too, it is part of the lesson that students absorb with the sense
of belonging. At Archer, Dinah, one of the girls on the robotics
team, talked about teammates supporting each other, overcoming the adversity of a match scheduled during midterms when
some had colds and other ailments:

> It was a difficult weekend; we had exams the following
> Monday. . . our robot competed with the wrong type of
> wheels and [a faulty] drive system. . . . At the end of the
> day there were still things that needed to be figured
> out, but we had worked together, helped each other,
> passed each other Kleenex and water and soup and
> tried to solve the problems.

In Chicago's YWLCS, a conversation in art class about supporting each other yielded this dramatic adolescent assertion: "I mean, we'd go into a burning building for each other." Nods all around.

9. *Work hard. Play when you arrive where you're going.* In formation, every wing flap of every goose creates an updraft for the one following, adding a 70 percent increase in the range a single goose could achieve. In this way the flock flying together reaches home.

As founders, expect to give up a goodly portion of your waking hours doing your part until you achieve your goal, which may be accreditation or financial security, or winning the academic decathlon. In the early days founders often have to do every job, from recruiting to marketing to mopping the floors. At one of our early drama productions, our newly hired Head of School, Arlene Hogan, arrived early. Discovering that the maintenance crew had failed us and with a young man standing nearby, she began to pick up trash and sweep the courtyard before parents appeared. To my mind, at least, she became our Founding Head of School at that moment.

If you do everything and give up the notion of spare time—no reading the paper, let alone reading a whole book—until the school is fully launched and flying under its own power, you will feel a deep satisfaction at your school's success. Get a cake and celebrate. Remember all who provided their support in the early days of the journey and be glad for those who've assumed the lead now. Probably you'll miss the old days just a little.

Appendix B

Mothers of Invention

Who is it that starts schools? What sort of person with what sort of securities and insecurities, abilities and instabilities, gift and grievances? Talents? Traits?

Traits for a founder to have: naïve optimism, stubborn perseverance, comic vision. We at Archer had all the requisite traits.

We were absurdly optimistic, always believing we'd succeed, first in attracting students, then in fulfilling our mission, and finally in securing Eastern Star on Sunset as our site. The second trait, perseverance, followed from the first; we didn't know enough to realize we might fail.

We did have a visionary purpose—to educate girls, diverse in background, to be leaders—accessing the research which hinted how best to do that. We were writers and therefore able to imagine things; we were products of single sex education and moderately successful in our outside fields of endeavor. But most important, we had daughters. Our motivation was less vision than need, the need to find a girl-affirming institution for our own girls.

At Archer we were slightly ahead of the pack (opening our doors a few months or a few years ahead of the dozens who came after), but we are hardly unique in who we are, what we were about, or why we did it.

Who we are: Vicky, Megan, and I are all firstborn, feminists, and optimists. As founders we are what are known in L.A., in the trade papers, as *non-pros*, which calls up our amateur status in the school business. We are three mothers, three writers, non-natives. As writers, none of us had schools as an item on our résumés. Vicky and Megan had recently arrived from outside the country; I'd come from graduate school, which is almost the same thing.

Being outside the epicenter in L.A. means being surrounded by but not within the entertainment industry. Los Angeles royalty are directors, producers, stars; our "debutantes" are the offspring of same; our Bel Air, Beverly Hills, and Brentwood mansions are notable only if Diane Keaton "flipped" the property or Sly Stallone built the fence.

Furthermore, we three are artists, however prosaic, and thus observers by profession: Vicky codifying her observations in short fiction; Megan turning hers into that starving cousin of entertainment, the documentary; and I studying and investigating, in an academic way, mass media. This combination of experiences and roles offers a perspective straddling different worlds.

There is the world of Westside L.A., to which none of us were integral or had long known, and the world of schools, with which we had only whispers of connection (and those from long ago and far away in our own girlhoods). Countering our unbelonging in the social center is a spiritual/political bond. Feminism and our outsider status gave us the courage to risk ourselves—to struggle against those who didn't want a school or who didn't like girls or who thought women activists were profoundly profane.

The sense of perspective that results from being interlopers challenging the staid assumptions of the local established practices and conventions helped us to answer the basic questions: Why a school? Why girls? Why here and now? And it helped us persevere when no one else wanted to hear those questions.

I think many, perhaps most, founders of schools have an outsider perspective, the art of seeing things invisible to the native-born. Their vision of what might be, coupled with the determination not to yield to complainers, feeds the fires of reform. They're interlopers altering, if not overturning, the existing order. (Think Teresa de Cepeda y Ahumada, Emma Willard, Mary McLeod Bethune.)

Pursuing that thought, I became intensely interested in other founders—the early pioneers of women's education (who, for my purposes, included Teresa, Emma, and Mary but also Mary Lyon, M. Carey Thomas, Clara Spence, and Ela Hockaday) and the Otherwise Intelligent Life Forms in this day and age who chose to add to their existence the aggravation, wrinkles, and stress of trying to open a girls' school. I was fortunate in meeting with those whose whereabouts were within a thousand-mile range of my own and in extensively emailing two who weren't. In this way I got to investigate six founding women besides Vicky, Megan, and me:

1. Ilana DeBare: cofounder, Oakland's Julia Morgan School; president, Julia Morgan School Board of Trustees; journalist, *San Francisco Chronicle*; mother, one daughter.
2. Emily Ellison: cofounder, Atlanta Girls' School; former journalist, *Atlanta Constitution*; novelist; mother, one daughter.
3. Joan Hall: cofounder, YWLCS in Chicago; chair, YWLCS board; former law partner in a Chicago firm, now retired;

mother, two sons; stepmother of five, three girls and two boys.

4. Sharon Hammel: cofounder, Seattle Girls' School; financial analyst, Russell Investment Group; mother, one daughter, one son.

5. Ann Rubenstein Tisch: cofounder, TYWLS in East Harlem; chair, board of trustees; former journalist, NBC News; mother, two daughters.

6. Brooke Trible Weinmann: cofounder, Atlanta Girls' School; former IBM executive; cofounder, Pacesetters, Richmond, Virginia; mother, two girls, two boys.

With the Archer three, that makes nine, with an average 2.1 children, a notable entry against the argument that life is all either-or. We're women of a certain age with highly helpful husbands and families and a camaraderie and comic vision that sustains us when we'd like to do something dangerous. Like quit.

All the founders I interviewed mentioned the experience of being outside the main event: personally, none were rooted in the tradition, custom, and heritage of the school's community but had originated somewhere else and moved to the community; professionally, none had started a school before or, as one said, "I wasn't a PTA mom. I'm not an education specialist. I had never written a business plan." They were naïve and not native, just like us.

They talked about a sense of being outsiders in adolescence: "I was one of two day students in my class. . . not by any stretch of the imagination an IN member of a particular group."

Another wrote me: "I have always been on the fringe when it comes to the popular groups or the crowd that joins things."

Despite the sense, as one put it, that she was "an outsider in my high school where the dominant culture was very snooty, shallow, and materialistic," each of these women decided to create an adolescent society, presumably one accepting of oddballs on the fringe. Moreover, they expected to succeed.

They were optimistic. "I am optimistic by nature," offered one founder, "and do not give in to momentary fears (at least for long)." Another justified her stamina and belief in the project by saying, "I just knew it was right . . . with the right allies it had to happen."

Everyone had read the studies: *Reviving Ophelia* by Mary Pipher and Carol Gilligan's *In a Different Voice*; some had also found *Failing at Fairness* by the Sadkers. The research was the stimulus, intensified often by their own daughters' development and upcoming adolescence.

Despite the evident lack of expertise in education, fundraising, and finding a site, they boldly announced they were opening a school and asked people for money. Sometimes their optimism was rewarded, literally, as when Emily Ellison, Candace Springer, and Brooke Weinmann of the future Atlanta Girls' School pitched their cause before the all-male board of the Livingston Foundation and got $20,000 in seed money.

IT'S THE VISION, STUPIDHEAD

They were visionary, all of them, dipping into a future that seemed unlikely at best and unreasonable in some instances, such as Ann Rubenstein Tisch's promotion of an idea (a public girls' school in Harlem) that challenged all the contentious Powers That Be in the Big Apple, including City Hall, the ACLU, NOW, and the largest, "most tumultuous" school system in the country. But then Ann had been a journalist (as had Emily Ellison and Ilana DeBare), and that may have helped with the vision thing.

Ann Tisch could not erase the memory of the despair she'd seen on the face of a girl she'd interviewed in a public high school in Milwaukee. That image fueled the quest: a girls' school for inner-city kids. "It was a clear mission," she felt.

The mission was enlivened ("Add a college counselor," counseled Spence's Arlene Gibson) and enhanced ("Make it replicable," urged Rudy Crew, NYC's then-new superintendent of public education). Tisch did both, creating by collaboration an extraordinary school instead of just a very good one.

The girls' school mission was rooted in active feminism—what Joan Hall of Chicago's YWLCS called "a strong sense of social justice"—but not necessarily a personal experience with single sex schools. Of the six additional founders, only one, Brooke Weinmann, attended a girls' school.

The founders were not all firstborn but were middle children in three cases. They were Methodist or Jewish or not. They were born in Manhattan or the Midwest, the South or the West in the 1950s and had their daughters (and sons in four cases) late in life.

They came of age in the bloom of the Second Stage of American feminist activism and identified as feminists and community activists: Explaining her activism, Joan Hall, who was the only one besides me not born in the 1950s, said, "When I came into the law profession . . . only 4 percent of the lawyers were women. . . . I never saw another woman."

Joan Hall was a trial lawyer, now retired partner at the firm of Jenner and Block, IBM Plaza, in Chicago—a big, overtly successful establishment in a glass building with granite floors, limestone walls, uniformed guards with sci-fi electronic equipment, and constant sweeping of the lobby by people dressed as custodial staff, buffing floors and mining phantom debris.

Hall is about 5'4", blonde, black-suited (attorney clothes), with a measured, succinct manner and, unexpectedly, an occasional teardrop, followed by a 1,000-watt smile. Here in this upscale, hard-edged building at the IBM Plaza, she talks about kids at a public school on Chicago's South Side, home to immigrants from Africa and the Caribbean, the DuSable Museum of Black History, and birthplace of Chicago blues. She talks about girls surviving, thriving, and overcoming family deaths, poverty, monstrous inequality. And she's unexpectedly soft-edged.

Her roots are in Nebraska, a town of eight hundred people, where she attended a small church school. She went to Yale. She had never started a school before, but even as an outsider, she had a strong conviction that it was necessary that "all adults in the building really believe every child can learn."

TWO FEMINISTS WALK INTO A BAR

Founders had a wry assessment of how they came to be in this place.

Ilana DeBare considered an early life experience that trained her for the job at Julia Morgan:

> As a teenager I found a home for myself in a socialist Zionist youth group that grew out of the kibbutz movement . . . a lot of time talking about the Vietnam War, the coup in Chile, Watergate, labor unions, red diaper families, etc. . . . feminism is what led me to the girls' school idea; [but] my left-wing activist perspective is what made me willing to go to all those meetings.

Emily Ellison's teen preparation for the requirements of school founding was to be elected "friendliest" in high school, a characteristic that was handy in the three years of pitches, proposals, and programs that preceded AGS's opening day. There in the rented church space, she received loud, emotional applause from adults and students, five hundred strong, leading to her droll observation:

> I never thought that I'd be in a church filled with this many friends and not be dead.

Vicky's perspective on our own obstacles was always funny, slightly skewed: When we attended a Brentwood Homeowners Association board meeting in 1996, she wrote about this first encounter:

> All-in-all, we felt that some of the board members were reasonable, most were not necessarily in active opposition, and that, with all the luck in the world, and under the aegis of Artemis (did she have an aegis?) and Athena, God the Father, and everyone else out there, we might, touch wood, do all right on this.

PREPARING TO START A SCHOOL

Perhaps there is something inherently activist in the families who choose a new, untried school. Maybe at heart they are idealists, trying to make the world somehow safer, saner, sweeter. That seems to be the trait that Mothers of Invention, from founding trustees to founding heads, have in common and the preparation they had for their founding roles.

The founding trustees at other schools (some of whom, it should be noted, were Fathers of Invention, although because they were atypical, they were not included in the study) were, at this moment of their lives, activist. They weren't, however, particularly prepared. We exemplified the not-ready-for-active-role condition.

There is only one thing to say about our preparedness at Archer to be founding trustees. We weren't. We had no experience to call upon other than life experience, being firstborn and a little bossy (me), being multicultural and multilingual (Vicky), being a producer, as in organized and very directed (Megan).

The only good thing about our lack of knowing what we were doing is it should give heart to anyone who thinks it might be a good idea to start a girls' school: Do it. You can't be less experienced than we were.

Appendix C

Every Which Way but Here

STRATEGIES FOR FINDING GIRL-NURTURING SOCIETIES IF YOU CAN'T MAKE A SCHOOL

The idea of creating all-girl groups dedicated to girls' well-being is nothing new. The story which inspired us to name our school Archer is an ancient tale of young girls under a goddess's protection going into the forest for a period of time to practice skills in science and the arts which would help them become the kind of adults who are strong and able members of society. A version of this custom has been observed on every continent but Antarctica and recently has evolved to include not only girls' schools, but Girl Guides, Girl Scouts, Girls Inc., and a host of virtual groups of girls on websites.

There are obvious merits to gathering girls together for what today would be termed female empowerment: role modeling, girl valuing, and leadership training are attributes of what a good girls' community can provide. Look for those qualities in the programs you find. Imagine the young girl of your heart (or your family or your neighborhood) going off into the forest with others like her, in pursuit of an Ideal Her.

Ancient societies emphasized different aspects of the ideal with different goddesses. Most of us are familiar with Greek goddesses Aphrodite, representing beauty and sexuality, and Hera, representing domestic virtues. For an eclectic ideal, embracing other images of strong and able women, we might go further afield for inspiration. To Isis, Inanna, and Artemis.

ISIS

Isis, an Egyptian goddess revered as wise and just. She is said to be the one who invented agriculture, established law, and, as Star of the Sea, created navigation. In her honor we might seek to enlighten girls in science, math, astronomy, and politics.

Star of the Sea

There are all-girl camps of virtually every description. Among the special programs some offer are science, math, and technology expertise. My favorite is a new program called Coastal Studies for Girls in Maine, which is a semester-long academic and experiential program for sophomores in high school.
www.coastalstudiesforgirls.org

Many single sex schools offer summer programs in subject areas like archeology, astronomy, and the arts. See a list of member schools from the National Coalition of Girls' Schools and check out special programs offered by a school near you.
www.ncgs.org

Sally Ride, the first woman astronaut in space, spoke at Archer's graduation in 2006. She is the only engineer I've ever met who is also an inspiring speaker. She is also a very good role model.

There are Sally Ride Camps for girls entering grades six through nine at several California college campuses: the University of California campuses at Berkeley, Los Angeles, and San Diego and at Stanford University. The camps address primarily three subjects—astronomy, marine science, and robotics; there is need-based financial assistance available for those who qualify. Ride has a website encouraging girls in science and offering ideas and programs to help make it likely that more girls will study science.

www.sallyridescience.com

Classes or programs for high school girls are offered in a variety of subjects at colleges around the country. The following have been recommended by former Archer students:

Barnard
Smith—Robotics, Engineering
University of Nebraska—All Girls/All Math
Vassar

Many all girls' boarding schools in the United States offer summer programs.

www.boardingschoolreview.com.

There are coeducational classes designed for girls, often in math or science. There is some evidence that math classes that are single sex are more effective for girls than the traditionally male-dominated mixed sex math classrooms. Contact parents who are likely to harbor similar hopes for a girls'-only class in math or science.

www.familyeducation.com

Daughters is a publication that provides parents of girls with information on topics from science homework to sexual harassment and guidance on how parents can help. The magazine is not free, but the community forum online apparently is.

www.daughters.com

INANNA

Inanna, a Sumerian goddess who, among other things, represents creativity, language development, and financial acumen. There are many all girl settings which address the gifts of this goddess. There are art programs, language courses (one in Los Angeles some years ago combined French cuisine and French language for eleven-year-olds), and a variety of creative activities.

Girls Inc. is one of the oldest community organizations serving girls. Its motto is *Inspiring all girls to be strong, smart, and bold*. It is a nonprofit organization with more than 800,000 girls in its membership and hundreds of centers in the United States and Canada. It has many programs suitable to honoring Inanna's aspects.

There are other characteristics of Girls Inc. which appeal: The Girls' Bill of Rights is a platform offering a framework for girls to remain strong, smart, and bold despite societal pressures to be other; the centers provide caring adults as guides and role models; in some cases, there is financial aid.

Like the very best schools, Girls Inc. grows and adapts to societal changes by conducting research on girls' experiences. Results from the latest Girls Inc. research, *The Supergirl Dilemma: Girls Grapple with the Mounting Pressure of Expectations* (2006), and program offerings are available on the website.

www.girlsinc.org

Boys and Girls Clubs of America have curricular offerings that are similar to Girls Inc., including SMART Girls, designed for girls ages ten to fifteen. The program focuses on enhancing girls' skills and self-esteem.

www.bgca.org

Traditional and Untraditional

There is a virtual community of girls on the Internet. GirlSite is the brainchild of former Archer parent Holly Holmberg Brooks and provides a vehicle for girls to explore questions about themselves, share ideas, and seek advice. And make virtual friends, similar to the pen pals of other times.

www.girlsite.org

The traditional path is Girl Scouts, and they do a lot more than sell cookies. Its programs have grown to include international travel opportunities, as well as an extensive online component. Each Council is unique to its community, so check the one in your area to investigate their offerings and ways to be involved.

www.girlscouts.org

World Association of Girl Guides and Girl Scouts focuses on a global perspective, connecting troops from one hundred forty-four countries.

www.waggsworld.org

Since business skills like budgeting and accounting are important elements of financial security, and since women, more than men, are likely to live long and suffer economic hardship, these skills can be vital. There are excellent programs combating economic ignorance among young, potential female entrepreneurs.

An Income of Her Own specializes in finance-related material; its website has a wide range of useful information.
www.anincomeofherown.com

Mentors come from many walks of life and provide guides who are successful women in business, finance, medicine, and other career paths. One of the most successful programs in this area for girls has been the Take Your Daughters to Work campaign, founded by Marie Wilson of the Ms. Foundation.
www.ms.foundation.org

Marie Wilson also created the nonprofit, nonpartisan The White House Project, dedicated to finding and supporting women as political leaders at all levels of government. Giving a feminist slant to the standard business term *research and development,* the project provides a Girls Leadership Resource List, among other training tools.

There are networks seeking successful women who can inspire girls and informal ways to "adopt" role models. Try researching mentoring programs via websites such as Career Launch of the Boys and Girls Club of America for tools and ideas about organizing mentor programs.
www.bgca.org

Another source of possible mentors is the Role Model Project for Girls.
www.womenswork.org

ARTEMIS

Artemis, Amazonian moon goddess, dog whisperer, hunter, and athlete. To her we can assign physical pursuits like sport, fitness, and outdoor adventure, as well as the psychological fitness that builds resilience, confidence, and strength of character.

A haven in the Jungle. . . . A place of great women, stories, knowledge, resources, oh the resources: One of the girl clients of Hardy Girls Healthy Women described it thus. This nonprofit is organized around leadership, social action, and social relevance for girls. It sponsors conferences for girls in grades five to eight and has a girls' speakers bureau and an advisory board of girls.

This advocacy group is worth investigating. It was co-created by Lyn Mikel Brown, professor of Education and Human Development, coauthor with Carol Gilligan of *Meeting at the Cross-roads*, and coauthor with Sharon Lamb of a new book on media literacy, *Packaging Girlhood* (2006). Hardy Girls's physical location is in Maine, but you can find them on the web.

www.hardygirlshealthywomen.org

Sweat It: Girls' Sports Teams

Participation in sports provides an opportunity to be in an all-girls community; learn teamwork, discipline, and leadership; and become physically fit and body-aware. If your daughter doesn't have a natural attraction to the grit and grime of the soccer field or the aggression of the volleyball game, experiment with nontraditional "sports" like yoga and fencing. A magazine designed to promote healthy activities for women can be found at the following website.

www.hersports.com

Tennis star and role model Billie Jean King founded a non-profit organization to promote vitality through physical fitness.
www.womenssportsfoundation.org

All Girls' Camps

Many, many women who did not attend single sex institutions of learning spoke to me of warm memories and important life-changing or life-affirming experiences they had in some summer camp for girls somewhere in the United States or Canada.

There are hundreds of all-girls camps in the United States; many are partnered with "brother" camps, which present coeducational opportunities. Camp is a wonderful opportunity to explore a female-empowering environment.

The American Camp Association
www.find.acacamps.org
For a large and detailed directory of camps, see
www.campchannel.com

Go Worldwide

Archer students have also urged everyone—girls, adults, teachers, parents, philanthropists—to become involved with Educating Girls Globally (EGG), a grassroots organization that promotes girls' schools, provides scholarships, and encourages communities all over the world to address the gender gap in education between boys and girls. Our students have twice gone to India to see EGG projects being implemented there.
www.educategirls.org

On another website for a similar group, Girls' Global Education, the stories of individual girls are a glimpse into the challenging circumstances of some of the lives of poor children in other parts of the globe.

www.ggef.org

You can find advice for adults and wonderful worlds for girls on the world wide web. You can find communities of girls and mentors engaged in outreach, activism, and community service. If you don't have a computer, call the nearest Girls Inc. center. They might let you use theirs. And once you get there, you won't need to go any further to find a good program dedicated to girls' well-being anyway.

Appendix D

Who Was Who (in Order of Appearance)

Gary Brooklyn-born, father of two daughters, comedy writer, husband, hero.

Vicky Shorr first board chair of the Archer School for Girls, fluent in Portuguese and Joan of Arc, mother of three.

Megan Callaway translates the odd, ill-mannered world of unsavory individuals like the Unabomber for the documentary film audience; mother of two girls; cofounder (with Vicky and me) of the Archer School.

Jim McManus kindly consultant in tweed jacket, nineteen years' experience with girls' education, former Head of Castilleja School in Palo Alto.

Godmothers 1994 June Baldwin, Keven Bellows, Julie Bergman, Diane Cooke, Deirdre Gainor, Kathy Garmezy, Susan Grode, Cindy Harrell Horn, Wendy Lazarus, Leslie Lurie, Patti Meyers, Gail Devlin Moradi, Marge Tabankin.

Godmothers 1995–1996   Cecelia Andrews, Marilyn Bergman, Barbara Boxer, Tricia Brock, Kate Capshaw, Rita Cohen, Frances Lear, Jennifer Perry, Nancy Daly Riordan, Ann Richards, Pat Schroeder, Susan Shilliday.

Pythia Lazarre   a composite of several pugilistic authorities and bad fairies.

Ruth Jenson   buxom, maternal Admissions Director, initially shared between Archer and Arizona.

Board members 1994   Charles Dolginer, attorney; David Higgins, attorney; Scott Carde, architect; Betsy Bridges, businesswoman; Vicky, Megan, and me.

Board members 1996   All of the above, plus Deborah Bass, attorney; Ann Hollister, political consultant; Kathy Kennedy, producer; Mary McCarthy, entrepreneur; Jeffrey Wasson, M.D.

Among the students   Katie, Neilah, Dominique, Helen, Cailey, Kyla, Romy, Fofy, Lizzie, Natalia, Andrea, Rebecca, Minka, Susan, Sophie, Shireen, Liz, Lauren, and Cailin.

Arlene Hogan   light, quick, smart, with long lashes and a lovely résumé, this mythical being is who we want as Head of School.

Lucy   zany misadventuress brought in as the initial Head of School; not her real name.

George III   not his name either—why cause trouble—but he made Lucy look like Catherine the Great.

Joanne Schuber   first-year middle school director (we didn't need one, but she'd have been a good choice if we had).

Jon Byk   vociferous, relentless opponent of our existence in his neighborhood; head of Concerned Brentwood Citizens, disgruntled offshoot of Brentwood Homeowners Association.

Ann Hollister   the Byk antidote, political advisor, tireless trainer of teams of activist teens.

Miss Sunshine   another bad fairy, owner of Sunshine Pre-School on Sunset Boulevard.

Lisa Specht   the glamorous attorney, our side.

Cindy Miscikowski   councilwoman for Brentwood area, supports democracy *and* schools.

Daniel Green   associate zoning administrator for the City of Los Angeles.

Dogs of Archer   Dreamer, Chelsea, Sunny, Teddy, Grace, Corduroy, and Cooper.

Ten Important Teachers   Raisa Adolphe, athletic director; Jean Bennett, history; Shelby Brown, Latin; Jennifer Chalsma, science; Pam Crawford, Spanish; Rob Everett, history; Harris Hartsfield, photography; Patti Meyers, art; Genevieve Sanchis-Morgan, English; Amy Willerson, theater.

Wise Women of Other Shires   Ilana DeBare and Ann Clarke of Julia Morgan School in Oakland, California; Emily Ellison, Brooke Trible Weinmann, and Sue Thompson of Atlanta Girls' School; Joan Hall, Michele Russell, and Margaret Small of Young Women's Leadership Charter School in Chicago; Sharon Hammel and Marja Brandon of Seattle Girls' School; Ann Rubenstein Tisch and Kathleen Ponze in New York City's The Young Women's Leadership School; Vivian Taylor Samudio of Irma Rangel School in Dallas. Arlene Gibson, Spence's (then) Head of School, Fran Scoble of Westridge in Pasadena, and David Trower were guides to the established independent school world.

Notes

PREFACE

p xi   *It was at a screening of. . .* The Rocketeer was a movie from Disney Studios, released in 1991. The lead actor was Bill Campbell.

p xii   *Inanna, Athena, Caileach, and Spider Woman. . .* Inanna, Sumerian goddess of Heaven and Earth; the Greek goddess Athena, born fully formed, fully armed from Zeus' head; Caileach, Celtic creator-destroyer goddess; and Pandora, Echo, Delilah, and the Furies are described in Barbara Walker's acclaimed *Woman's Encyclopedia of Myths and Secrets* (Castle Books, 1996). Spider Woman, a creator deity among the pueblo peoples such as the Hopi, and cannibal kachinas used to frighten and discipline Zuni and Hopi children in the mythic past are described in *The Feminist Companion to Mythology*, edited by Carolyne Larrington (Pandora Press, 1992). Deirdre of the Sorrows is described in Mary Murray Delaney's *Of Irish Ways* (Dillon Press, 1973).

p xii   *Persephone, dancing around. . .* is described in Larrington's book.

p xiii   *Mary Pipher, a Nebraska therapist, wrote an important book. . .* *Reviving Ophelia: Saving the Selves of Adolescent Girls* (Ballantine, 1994), p. 22. See also Peggy Orenstein, *School Girls* (Doubleday, 1994); and Judy Mann, *The Difference* (Warner, 1994).

p xiii   *from Carol Gilligan challenging. . .* See Gilligan, *In a Different Voice: Psychological Theory and Women's Development* (Harvard

University Press, 1982); Gilligan, with Nora P. Lyons and Trudy Hammer, *Making Connections* (Harvard, 1990); and Gilligan, with Lyn Mikel Brown, *Meeting at the Crossroads* (Ballantine, 1992).

p xiii   ***Myra and David Sadker observing our public schools.*** . . See *Failing at Fairness: How America's Schools Cheat Girls* (Touchstone, 1995). For American Association of University Women (AAUW) studies, see *Shortchanging Girls, Shortchanging America* (1991); *How Schools Shortchange Girls* (1992); *Hostile Hallways* (1993); *Girls in the Middle* (1996).

p xiv   ***A strong argument for single sex schooling.*** . . Social scientists researching school differences and finding advantage to single sex schooling include Valerie Lee and Anthony Bryk, "Effects of Single-Sex Secondary Schools on Student Achievement and Attitudes," *Journal of Educational Psychology*, 78 (1986), pp. 381–395, and "Effects of Single-Sex Schools: Response to March," *Journal of Educational Psychology*, 81 (1989), pp. 647–650; Lee, with Helen M. Marks, "Sustained Effects of the Single-Sex Secondary School Experience on Student Achievement and Attitudes," *Journal of Educational Psychology*, 82 (1990), pp. 378–392; Cornelius Riordan, *Girls and Boys in School: Together or Separate?* (Teachers College Press, 1990); Fred A. Mael, "Single-Sex and Coeducational Schooling: Relationships to Socioemotional and Academic Development," *Review of Educational Research*, 68 (1998), pp. 101–129. Advantages to women's colleges were found in Riordan's 1990 study (see above), as well as in Leslie Miller-Bernal, *Separate by Degree: Women Students' Experiences in Single and Coeducational College* (Peter Lang, 2000). In 1995, according to the National Coalition of Girls' Schools, 9 percent of the school-age population could attend a girls' school.

p xiv   ***Researchers for the U.S. Department of Education.*** . . Three researchers, Mary Moore, Valerie Piper, and Elizabeth Schaefer, did a thorough review of research on single sex schooling published in 1992 ("Single Sex Schooling and Education Effectiveness: A Research Overview," in *Single Sex Schooling: Perspectives from Practice and Research* (U.S. Department of Education). The list above includes sociologists, psychologists, historians, and education policy-makers (such as Diane Ravitch, who fits into two categories, being both a historian and an assistant U.S. secretary of education).

p xiv   ***What's good about them.*** . . . Research about a place girls can own was probably first discussed by Rachel Belash, former head of Miss Porter's School and education researcher. See her article, "Girls Schools: Separate Means Equal," in *Independent Schools, Independent Thinkers*, edited by P. Kane (Jossey Bass, 1992), pp. 73–90. Values and ways of knowing were discussed thoroughly and thoughtfully by Mary Belenky, Blythe Clinchy, Nancy Goldberger, and Jill Tarule in *Women's Ways of Knowing* (Basic Books, 1986) and before that by Nancy Chodorow in *The Reproductions of Mothering* (University of California Press, 1978). Documentation for each of these advantages is examined and will be provided in later chapters.

p xiv   ***The research about how girls learn.*** . . . will be presented in subsequent chapters.

p xiv   ***This kind of school provides an antidote.*** . . . Riordan argued that unlike what has been observed in coed schools, "single-sex schools are places where students go to learn; not to play, not to hassle teachers and other students, and not primarily to meet their friends and have fun." See "What Do We Know About the Effects of Single-Sex Schools in the Private Sector? Implications for Public Schools," in *Gender in Policy and Practice*, edited by Amanda Datnow and Lea Hubbard (Routledge-Falmer, 2002), p. 19.

CHAPTER ONE

p 3   ***I've read Carol Gilligan.*** . . . whose relevant works (1982, 1990, 1992) have already been cited. Although she has been criticized by those who find inconsistencies in her thinking or question her methodology, there can be no quarrel with the impact of Gilligan's work: widely translated and distributed in this and other countries, it is heuristic, stimulating new theoretic viewpoints, and practical. Although it was apparently not her intention, her work inspired many parents and educators, like us, to seek single sex schools.

p 3   ***Adolescent girls in the classroom.*** . . . behave differently from same-age boys. See Barrie Thorne and Nancy Henley's *Language and* Sex (Newbury House, 1975) and Jesse Bernard's earlier work on differences in discourse between the sexes, *The Sex Game* (Atheneum, 1972). Deborah Tannen found males and females using language differently in *You Just Don't Understand* (William Morrow, 1990).

Female students, according to authors Mary F. Belenky et al. in *Women's Ways of Knowing*, are socialized to be cooperative and interconnected, but the classroom discourse discourages their way of knowing and ultimately angers, frustrates, and silences them. Reading *Women's Ways of Knowing* twenty years after I first read it was edifying and delightful; this is a classic that holds its own long after the writing is done.

p 4   ***The girl pause is not . . . a bad thing. . .*** The Sadkers' *Failing at Fairness* documented the observation of girls pausing or hesitating to participate in classroom interactions in coeducational schools. It is apparently widespread; even in elite law school classrooms, women silence themselves, according to Lani Guinier in "Becoming Gentlemen: Women's Experiences at One Ivy League Law School," *University of Pennsylvania Law Review*, 143 (1994), pp. 1–110. Deborah Tannen reported that girls regard the active participation of boys as "selfish and hoggish": "Teachers' Classroom Strategies Should Recognize That Men and Women Use Language Differently," *Chronicle of Higher Education*, 19 (June 1991), pp. B1–B3.

p 4   ***A friend describes. . .*** Interview with Ann Clarke, Oakland, California, May 27, 2005.

p 5   ***Girls have the advantage in grade school. . .*** See Carol Dwyer and Linda Johnson's article, "Grades, Accomplishments, and Correlates," in *Gender and Fair Assessment*, edited by Warren Willingham and Nancy Cole (Erlbaum, 1997).

Boys' problems with writing, in which they are several years behind girls, are documented in a U.S. Department of Education report, *Educational Equity for Girls and Women* (U.S. Printing Office, 2000), p. 18. See also the discussion in this book in Chapter 22 on boys and research on development differences.

p 5   ***Society intervened. . .*** For a good discussion of gender bias in teaching and in teaching material, see Janice Streitmatter, *For Girls Only* (State University of New York, 1999), pp. 53–56. Pipher (1994) writes about social messages in schools and in mediated contexts such as television, film, and radio. *Born to Buy* by Juliet Shorr (Scribner, 2005) presents considerable evidence that the messages from those media and the Internet have only become worse for our children in the thirteen years since Pipher's book was published.

p 6   ***The Research is. . .*** In 1995 the social science research on girls in coed schools was definitive: thousands of studies, from the observations of the Sadkers to the reviews by the AAUW to studies by researchers commissioned by the U.S. Department of Education, agreed with the statement about competence.

p 6   ***One educator puts it. . .*** Arlene Hogan, in a speech before parents of the Archer School, spring 1996, perhaps quoting Ruth D. Tschumy who said much the same thing in "What do we know about girls?" *NASSP Bulletin* (National Association of Secondary School Principals, November 1995).

p 6   ***David and Myra Sadker. . .*** Myra and David Sadker, *Failing at Fairness: How America's Schools Cheat Girls* (Touchstone, 1995).

p 6   ***How Schools Shortchange Girls. . .*** The AAUW Report by that title was published in 1995. Alice Ann Leidel's comments appeared in the Foreword.

p 7   ***Gilligan has warned. . .*** *Meeting at the Crossroads*.

p 7   ***Boys and boyhood are . . . "feminized". . .*** according to Michael Gurian, *The Wonder of Boys* (Tarcher/Putnam, 1997).

p 7   ***Two books. . .*** For two of the better books about boys and gender see *Raising Cain: Protecting the Emotional Life of Boys* by Dan Kindlon and Michael Thompson (Ballantine, 1999) and William Pollack's *Real Boys: Rescuing Our Sons From the Myths of Boyhood* (Random House, 1998).

p 7–8   ***They take turns in discussions. . .*** One of the most readable reports of female and male communication styles is Deborah Tannen's *You Just Don't Understand* (1990, cited earlier); female classroom behavior is observed in Tannen's "Teachers' Classroom Strategies" (1991), cited earlier. Most recently Tannen has authored *You're Wearing That? Understanding Mothers and Daughters in Conversation* (Random House, 2006). Also interesting are studies by Nancy Henley and Barrie Thorne, "Women Speak and Men Speak: Sex Differences and Sexism in Communications, Verbal and Nonverbal," in *Beyond Sex Roles*, edited by A. Sargent (West, 1977); and Robin Lakoff in *Language and Women's Place* (Harper Colophon, 1976).

p 8   ***They have different motivations***. . . The different motivations of boys and girls in striving for success, especially academic success, are addressed by Eva Pomerantz, Ellen Altermatt, and Jill Saxon in "Making the Grade but Feeling Distressed: Gender Differences in Academic Performance and Internal Distress," *Journal of Educational Psychology* 94 (2002), pp. 396–404, and "Conceptions of Ability as Stable and Self Evaluative Processes: A Longitudinal Examination," *Child Development*, 72 (2001), pp. 152–173.

p 8   ***Arlene Hogan***. . . The frog dissection anecdote is part of her open house presentations from time to time. Not only does it show the emotional basis for learning in middle school girls, it suggests they're very, very gullible.

p 8   ***The importance that empathy***. . . Gilligan (1993, pp. 7–10) discusses Nancy Chodorow's theoretic framework in *The Reproductions of Mothering* (1978) for this sex difference in psychological development, evident in middle childhood. Gilligan adds her observations as evidence. The authors of *Women's Ways of Knowing* present further evidence.

p 8   ***The River Project***. . . a project at Chicago's Young Women's Leadership Charter School, 2003.

p 8   ***their [girls'] sense of color***. . . Originally I wrote this as a humorous aside, referencing a folk belief that females see colors more keenly. There may be some evidence for it; Leonard Sax (2001, p. 25) cites a study by four researchers reporting in *Hormones and Behavior* (2001) that female children prefer to use many colors, choosing reds, greens, beiges, and browns typically, whereas male children used fewer colors, choosing greys and blues and noncolors such as silver and black.

p 9   ***Title IX's hot breath***. . . This, of course, refers to the 1972 Education Amendments (to the Civil Rights Act of 1964) barring sex discrimination in education. Title IX had the effect of totally redefining and invigorating girls' athletic programs: in 1972 only 7.5 percent of high school athletes were female, but twenty-five years later, nearly 40 percent of all of them were. (See U.S. Department of Education, *Title IX: 25 Years of Progress—June 1997*.)

p 12   ***The fifth freedom.*** . . . Norman Rockwell's series of paintings celebrating American ideals is titled "The Four Freedoms," for the freedom of assembly, freedom of religion, freedom of speech and the press, and freedom from fear. One he might have painted is freedom of education, celebrating free and universal education.

p 12   ***The way brains work.*** . . . See the findings of Rachel and Ruben Gur, discussed in Deborah Blum's *Sex on the Brain* (Penguin, 1998) and Dianne Hale's *Just Like a Woman* (Bantam, 1999). Sally and Bennett Shaywitz's article, "Sex Differences in the Functional Organization of the Brain for Language," is found in *Nature* 373 (1995), pp. 607–609.

CHAPTER TWO

p 15   ***in upstate New York, in the town of Troy.*** . . . The "Uncle Sam" who made his home in Troy was Samuel Wilson, who did not resemble the tall, skinny, white-haired patriarch cartoon but looked more like a meatpacker, which he was, supplying the army with beef during the War of 1812. The label on his product, "U.S. Beef," caused some to believe that it stood for *Uncle Sam's Beef.*

p 16   ***A legacy of leadership.*** . . . See Ann Firor Scott, *Making the Invisible Woman Visible* (University of Illinois Press, 1984); Nancy Cott, *The Bonds of Womanhood* (Yale University Press, 1977). *Emma Willard and Her Pupils* by Slocum Sage (Mrs. Russell Sage), an alumna, is fascinating, delineating fifty years of influence (Sage, 1898). Emma Willard School has remembered its radical roots, honoring, at various times, two of its famous alumnae, suffragist Elizabeth Cady Stanton and antiwar activist Jane Fonda. In her book, *Where Girls Come First* (Tarcher, 2004), Ilana DeBare also discusses Emma Willard School instituting women's studies in the high school in 1972 (probably the first in the country to do so).

p 16   ***infertile, feverish, or insane.*** . . . Harvard professor Edward H. Clarke, cited in DeBare; noted psychologist G. Stanley Hall, according to Ann Firor Scott (1984, p. 303) "held somewhat similar views."

p 16   ***the city of Troy granted.*** . . . As is perhaps typical of such public entities, it took many years for the school to actually get money. Promises were made in 1821 when Willard moved the school to Troy, but by

1833, when the lease was to be renewed, no grant money had yet been given. Finally in 1837 Troy signed the long-awaited charter and granted the money, according to historian Ann Firor Scott (1984, pp. 45–52).

p 16   *[EWS] today leads by teaching itself...* The study at Emma Willard was published as *Making Connections* (Harvard, 1990).

p 17   *small, daring, and safe...* My friend Marc Tucker, who in 1992 cowrote *Thinking for a Living* (because that's what he does), has suggested a maximum size of four hundred students for a school that's a genuine community. Personal communication, fall—winter 1994.

p 18   *sound mind in a sound body...* The Winsor website (www.winsor.edu) details a school philosophy that has a New England feel, emphasizing both independence and interdependence, intellectually and individually. The curriculum, too, embraces the tension between the individual's creative, independent thinking and the school's integration of disciplines, sort of a be-unique and be-on-the-same-page program. Which may be why I saw both vigor and rigor there.

p 21   *Castilleja ... on the website...* See www.castilleja.org.

CHAPTER THREE

p 27   *FeelingCaring school...* I must confess to being impressed with our daughter's class of twenty-four sixth graders who have attained remarkable success: four professional writers and two actors, one on Saturday Night Live, one a movie star known widely by her first name. They have several Golden Globes, Emmys, Oscar nominations. Our own daughter's contributing credit is at least three television shows, all successful comedies. Maybe FeelingCaring works—at least in grade school, at least in the arts.

p 28   *The schools we like...* Quotes about research and global community are from the mission statements of the schools.

p 28   *small, daring, and safe...* *Smallness* has been a characteristic of successful schools, according to John Goodlad in *A Place Called School* (McGraw-Hill, 1984) and Marc Tucker (cited earlier). *Daring* implies innovation (responsiveness to research) and commitment to academic rather than entertainment curricula, as shown by Cornelius Riordan in *Girls and Boys in School* (Teachers College, 1990) and James Coleman in *The Adolescent Society* (Free Press, 1961). *Safe* means physically, socially, and emotionally secure, according to Janice Streitmatter in *For Girls Only* (New York University, 1999) and Carole B. Shmurak in *Voices of Hope* (Peter Lang, 1998). Girls' schools typically score higher than coed schools on the first and last of these criteria, as we shall discover.

p 28   *I'm thinking of Mary McLeod Bethune*. . . See the following for biographical data: Florence Hicks, ed., *Mary McLeod Bethune: Her Own Words of Inspiration*, (DARE Books, 1975); Rockham Holt, *Mary McLeod Bethune: A Biography* (Doubleday, 1964); Emma Gelders Sterne, *Mary McLeod Bethune* (New York, 1957).

        Bethune's experience starting a school is also described in *Mary McLeod Bethune: Building a Better World*, edited by Audrey Thomas McCluskey and Elaine M. Smith (Indiana University Press, 1991), and in Gerda Lerner's *Black Women in White America* (Vintage, 1992).

p 29   *Emma Hart . . . lived up in New England*. . . Emma Hart Willard's influence was considerable, both through her own words ("An Address to the Public" in 1819 and "Advancement of Female Education"), the impact of her students, and as many as 200 schools modeled on the Troy Seminary. "Biographical Overview: Emma Hart Willard," *The Conservationist* (March–April, 1979), http://emmawillard.org. Also see Willystine Goodsell, Emma Willard, and Catharine Esther Beecher, *Pioneers of Women's Education in the United States: Emma Willard, Catherine Beecher, Mary Lyon* (AMS Press, 1931); and Alma Lutz, *Emma Willard: Pioneer Educator of American Women* (Greenwood Press, 1984).

p 29   *letting her open a girls' school in their house*. . . Emma Hart Willard's educational philosophy is described in numerous publications, including Ann Firor Scott's "Ever-Widening Circle: The Diffusion of Feminist Values from the Troy Female Seminary, 1822–72," in *Making the Invisible Woman Visible* (University of Illinois Press, 1984); see also John Lord, *The Life of Emma Willard* (Appleton, 1873); and Mary Fairbanks, ed., *Mrs. Emma Willard and Her Pupils* (Slocum Sage, 1898), cited earlier.

p 30   *Teresa de Cepeda y Ahumada was something of a lady.* . . . A terrific book on this sixteenth-century pioneer is Cathleen Medwick's *Teresa of Avila: The Progress of a Soul* (Image Books, 2001). Also instructive: J. M. Cohen, *The Life of Saint Teresa of Avila: By Herself* (Penguin Books, 1988); and William Walsh, *Saint Teresa of Avila: A Biography* (Tan Books, 1987).

p 30   *Teresa had powerful enemies.* . . . but sometimes her friends were the problem, as when her religious superior appointed Teresa the official head of her former convent because it was in financial ruin and social chaos. Her arrival there was greeted with a rebellion which degenerated from shouting into physical insult, obscenity, and demands for a vote. Teresa serenely waited for calm to descend, acknowledged the concerns of the congregation, and won their alliance with humility and tact.

CHAPTER FOUR

p 37   *Pythia Lazarre.* . . . is no name of anyone I know but a composite. See "Who Was Who" in Appendix D for other name changes.

p 37   *Westside Affiliation of Seminaries and Preparatory Schools.* . . . is not a real name and any similarity to organizations with similar purposes is purely accidental.

CHAPTER FIVE

p 47   *comedian Mary Sue Terry.* . . . is quoted in *Women Who Joke Too Much* (Perigee Trade, 1995).

p 50   *In adolescence kids explore.* . . . There is a rich body of theory and observation about identity development, starting with Erik Erikson's *Identity, Youth, and Crisis* (Norton, 1968). Although it is a theory about moral development, Carol Gilligan's *In a Different Voice* addresses cultural and individual definitions of self, especially gender differences.

p 50   *a sociologist named James Coleman.* . . . See *The Adolescent Society* (Free Press, 1961).

p 50   ***Rosemary Salomone***. . . quoting from *Same, Different, Equal*, cited earlier, began by saying, "Much of what Coleman found in values, climate and status ascription rings true of contemporary high school and even middle school" (p. 199).

p 50   ***As Peggy Orenstein demonstrates***. . . in her study of two coed middle schools, *School Girls* (Doubleday, 1994), p. xvi.

p 51   ***But maybe not in girls' schools***. . . From Coleman's conclusion in 1961 that coed schools encourage the adolescent subculture, to studies in the 1980s and 1990s that conclude single sex schools provide a better environment for pursuing academic goals, there is almost unanimous agreement: girls' schools are pro-academic and encourage academic achievement. See, for example, Valerie Lee and Anthony S. Bryk, "Effects of Single Sex Secondary Schools on Student Achievement and Attitudes," *Journal of Education Psychology* 4, 78 (1986), pp. 381–395. See Cornelius Riordan, *Girls and Boys in School: Together or Separate?* (Teachers College, 1990) for a discussion of issues and effects. The only study I found which provides an exception to the common finding was one in 1994 by Lee, Helen, Marks, and Tina Byrd, "Sexism in Single Sex and Coeducational Independent Secondary School Classrooms," *Sociology of Education* 67 (1994), pp. 92–120, which saw a tendency in girls' schools as opposed to boys' schools or coed schools to coddle students, what the authors called a "pernicious" form of sexism, p. 1.

p 51   ***justified by the research***. . . "Girls still receive an unequal education in our nation's schools," wrote Jackie DeFazio, president of the American Association of University Women in the Afterword of *School Girls* (1994, pp. 276–277). She referred to research documented in *Shortchanging Girls, Shortchanging America*, AAUW's 1990 survey, as well as Orenstein's work. She concluded, "Girls today deserve better. . . . True educational reform will happen when girls, as well as boys, become all they can be."

CHAPTER SIX

p 55   ***scholar Carolyn Heilbrun***. . . wrote *Reinventing Womanhood* (Norton, 1993). The quote is on p. 30.

p 55   *at the first board meeting I attend.* . . . See "Who Was Who" at back of book for list of members.

p 59   *In my readings I find a quote.* . . . the quote was originally found in Amelia Earhart's *Last Flight* (Harcourt Bruce, 1937), p. 10. Our version is somewhat altered from the original of: "Who would refuse an invitation to such a shining adventure?" The National Woman's Hall of Fame website (www.greatwomen.org) has it closer to our version: "How could I refuse such a shining adventure?" I think ours is the most powerful.

CHAPTER EIGHT

p 72   **Los Angeles *magazine* open.** . . . article was by Maureen Sajbel, "Boys and Girls Together," *Los Angeles* magazine (March 1995), pp. 88–98.

p 73   **M. Elizabeth Tidball.** . . . did a study in 1973 entitled "Perspective on Academic Women and Affirmative Action," *Educational Record*, 54, pp. 130–135, and a follow-up article in 1980, "Women's Colleges and Women Achievers Revisited," *Signs: Journal of Women in Culture and Society*, 5, pp. 504–517. Tidball's work over the last thirty-five years is considered significant to the question of the effects of single sex schooling, especially at the postsecondary level. See also Streitmatter's *For Girls Only* and Salomone's *Same, Different, Equal* for discussion of Tidball's research and criticism.

p 73   *One of the most referenced studies.* . . . Rosemary Salomone notes in her 2003 book that Tidball's 1973 article has been awarded the distinction of being a "Citation Classic" by the Institute for Scientific Information for the number of times other researchers have referenced or cited it (p. 195).

p 74   *Tidball studied a random selection.* . . . 1973, already cited. Tidball, Daryl Smith, Charles Tidball, and Lisa Wolf-Wendel wrote *Taking Women Seriously: Lessons and Legacies for Educating the Majority* (Oryx, 1999), pp. 49–53, 140–141.

p 74   *What's important.* . . . See Tidball et al., 1999, pp. 49–53, 140–141. Tidball's 1980 study found a high correlation between role models in single sex colleges and success.

p 74   ***Tidball has been criticized, supported, and validated***. . . Tidball's critics suggested that academic selectivity and the socioeconomic status of the applicants to certain women's colleges are what produced positive results. In *Girls and Boys in School*, for example, Cornelius Riordan critiques studies by Tidball and others for failing to control for initial capability and "home background" (1990, p. 116). Riordan's study of high school seniors (1990) does control for these factors, showing another example of the heuristic benefit of Tidball's work. Riordan concluded, furthermore, that women's colleges produced the effects Tidball found, after he'd controlled for the variables she did not. See also Streitmatter's *For Girls Only* and Salomone's *Same, Different, Equal* for discussion of Tidball's research and criticism.

p 74   ***Girls' schools . . . create a world***. Again and again social scientists have found that simply separating the sexes is not enough to promote equality, for traditional structures and ways of teaching are male-oriented and alien to female students. For confirmation see Belensky et al. (1986), as well as observations by Judy Mann in *The Difference* (1996) and Peggy Orenstein in *School Girls* (Doubleday, 1994). See C. Riordan in *Gender in Policy and Practice* (2000).

p 74   ***Since Tidball's thesis. . .*** Other researchers in the order in which they appear in text are Belash (1992), Shmurak (1998), and Riordan (1990), all cited earlier.

p 75   ***Academic culture . . . "cannot be produced". . .*** See Riordan (2002), p. 13.

CHAPTER NINE

p 82   ***In print publications.***. . . Arlene Gibson, head of Spence School in New York City, told me in spring 2005 that when the New York papers reported something Spence did that was potentially sensitive to race issues, the reporters added parenthetically, "Who'd have expected Spence to be so sensitive!?" Gibson noted, "We can't escape our [exclusive] address."

p 83   ***Exclusivity . . . versus cultural elitism.***. . . See Arthur Powell, *Lessons from Privilege* (Harvard, 1998), and DeBare, *Where Girls Come First*.

p 84   ***"the unremarkable Fresno State".***. . . kindly made me a Distinguished Alumnus in 2007, making me, and it, feel remarkable indeed.

Suskind's remark on Paul O'Neill from his book, *The Price of Loyalty* (Pocket, 2005).

p 84   ***To create an inclusive culture***. . . read Deborah Meier, *The Power of Their Ideas* (Beacon Press, 1995), quote from p. 38. See also Lisa Delpit, *Other People's Children: Cultural Conflict in the Classroom* (New Press, 1994).

p 89   ***What Patti Meyers does in her classes***. . . exemplifies an epistemological orientation discussed and developed in Belenky et al., *Women's Ways of Knowing* (1986, 1987). As it is based on the relationship between the knower and the known (a subject of inquiry), *connected learning* is presented as a contrast to *separate learning*, which is impersonal and authoritative, received more than experienced. Both sexes use both, but women typically access connected knowing, favoring it, according to Belenky et al.'s findings (pp. 102–121).

p 90   ***Connected learning is intended***. . . In middle school, boys who are put in cooperative learning groups with girls do not cooperate, according to several studies. See Weisfield et al., "The Spelling Bee: A Naturalistic Study of Female Inhibitions in Mixed Sex Competitions," *Adolescence* 18 (1983): 695–708; A. Ahlgren and D. Johnson, "Sex Difference in Cooperative and Competitive Attitudes from 2nd Through the 12th Grades," *Developmental Psychology* 15 (1979): 45–49; M. Lockheed and A. Harris, "Classroom Interaction and Opportunity for Cross-Sex Peer Learning in Science," *Journal of Early Adolescence* (1982): 135–143. All are cited in AAUW, *How Schools Shortchange Girls*. Other studies show a decrease in female achievement in adolescent mixed sex groups. See *How Schools Shortchange Girls*, pp. 118–130.

CHAPTER TEN

p 94   ***In both the animal world***. . . See Hales, pp. 27–28 (quote is on p. 28), 123–124, 268–270. See also Louann Brizendine's discussion about stress, fearlessness, and mating behavior in *The Female Brain* (Morgan Road, 2006), pp. 71–74.

p 95   ***Competition creates ambivalence***. . . Brain research would eventually show that girls at this age feel physically sick in aggressive competition. "Games and sports are," according to Leonard Sax, M.D., Ph.D., "an excuse to get together" for most girls, whereas for boys they are more central to their relationship, . . . more about hierarchy and domination, *Why Gender Matters* (Random House, 2005), p. 84. See also Brizendine's *Female Brain*.

p 95   ***Gilligan's book***. . . Although Gilligan addressed moral development initially, she and others worked with adolescent girls and reported findings in *Making Connections* (Harvard, 1990).

p 100   ***By the time girls are past early adolescence***. . . See Peggy Orenstein's *School Girls* for a fascinating look at coed middle school classrooms.

p 100   ***as networks of relationships***. . . Gilligan et al. (1990), Streitmatter (1999), and Shmurak (1998) all offer evidence of this female impulse to bond. As Rosemary Salomone (2003) has written: "There is some evidence that girls perform better in cooperative rather than competitive groups" (p. 97).

p 101   ***In 1999, Julia Morgan School***. . . whose co-founder Ilana DeBare and Head of School Ann Clarke hosted Arlene Hogan and me in May 2005.

CHAPTER ELEVEN

p 107   ***At about the same time***. . . Ilana DeBare, p. 154.

p 108   ***Seattle Girls' School***. . . interviews with Marja Brandon, September 16, 2005. Phone interview with Julita Elewald, October 23, 2005.

p 108   ***Atlanta Girls' School***. . . founding experiences are described in "School of Dreams," *Atlanta Journal*, August 28, 2000.

p 109   ***the search for the right site***. . . AGS ended up in Buckhead, an Atlanta neighborhood not unlike Brentwood. It's a land of mansions, long drives, big gates—very Tara in some instances. Yet they occupy a former school, so perhaps that made them more welcome than we were in Brentwood.

CHAPTER TWELVE

p 116   ***(TYWLS)*** . . . ***past threatening moves***. . . "Single-sex schools are politically incorrect; they are downright politically threatening to many people, and many of these people are in fact educational researchers, policymakers, and special-interest stakeholder groups such as the AAUW Educational Foundation. This is not a very inspiring thought, but it is important to realize that this is the nature of what we are working with." Thus concludes Cornelius Riordan, professor of sociology, Providence College, TYWLS consultant for Ann Rubenstein Tisch.

p 119   *Joel Garreau*... in *Nine Nations of North America* (Doubleday, 1988, p. 187), describes the "shadow governments" that create their own NIMBY culture. It's a little Faustian Covenant to hear it thus boldly sketched.

p 121   **As attorney Mark Warda**... Although Mark Warda says some people consider children to be a nuisance, he adds that "only in extreme cases" do courts rule against their existence (*Neighbor vs. Neighbor*, Sphinx Publishing, 2nd edition, 1999, p. 96). Evidently Warda is not from Brentwood. Also fun reading is Cora Jordan's *Neighbor Law* (Nolo Press, 1998).

CHAPTER THIRTEEN

p 127   *electromagnetic activity in brains*... Although I was way out of my ken, I believe what I witnessed was functional magnetic resonance (FMRI), a technique that detects different processes in brains. See Dianne Hales, *Just Like a Woman* (Bantam, 1999), for an explanation.

p 127   **Rachel Gur**... Her quote is found on p. 242 of Hale's book. Ruben Gur came to Archer in the late 1990s and talked about the Gurs' research. He wasn't sure what the pedagogical implications were, but as a father of a girl, he said he was pleased we were interested in the subject.

p 127   **When a woman uses her brain**... As Leonard Sax says repeatedly in *Why Gender Matters* (Random House, 2005): "I'm not saying that all boys are the same or that all girls are the same... but that differences in the brain associated with biological sex" are significant (pp. 35–36). Also see the Gurs' study, "Sex and Handedness Differences in Cerebral Blood Flow During Rest and Cognitive Activity," *Science*, August 13, 1982, p.659.

p 128   **She activates more neurons**... according to Mark George of the Medical University of South Carolina, cited in Hales, p. 244. See also Deborah Blum, *Sex on the Brain* (Viking, 1997).

CHAPTER FOURTEEN

p 147   *most teenage girls neglect intellectual pursuits*. . . Based on both clinical and empirical studies and broad-based surveys, the 1992 AAUW report *How Schools Shortchange Girls* concludes that girls in sixth and seventh grades care more about popularity than competence or independence; that high school girls, especially white and Hispanic, have low self-esteem; and that same-sex groups seem to be more effective for girls learning and performing academically (pp. 16–22, 130).

p 147   *Girls need role models*. . . It has been an article of faith at least since the 1950s, when sociologist Erving Goffman wrote about roles in *Presentation of the Self* (Doubleday, 1956). More recently, Dianne Hales wrote in *Just Like a Woman:* "Girls also need to see real-life role models — if only to counter the images of brain-dead bimbos that still monopolize the media" (p. 147).

p 147   *Sociologist Janet Chafetz described it simply*. . . See *Masculine, Feminine, or Human?* (Peacock, 1994), pp. 137–138.

p 149   *On a January day in Dallas*. . . The Hockaday School hosted me kindly and with little advance notice on January 9, 2006.

CHAPTER FIFTEEN

p 153   *Environmental Impact Report*. . . was filed in May 1997 as EIR No. 96-0147-(UZ)(ZV)(YV), State Clearinghouse No. 96071106.

p 162   *I live in the midst of comedy writers*. . . Our eleven-year-old, dryly noting my dedication to seeing this idea through, referred to it early on as the Mommy School. Our older daughter, after the worst of the battles, presented me with a cup she'd made with favorite family sayings, mine being, "There was a study at Dartmouth" and "I'll just make fettuccini alfredo," both of which referred more to coping mechanisms than actual events. Years after our battle with the neighbors (2003), there was a comprehensive study at Dartmouth supporting theoretical brain differences between males and females. So maybe my eldest daughter and I were only predicting the future. All three (two daughters and one husband) currently make their living writing comedy scripts. So I'm not kidding about *their* comic visions.

Vicky and Megan had budding comics and clowns of their own at home, and their comedy is discussed in Mothers of Invention (see the Afterword).

CHAPTER SIXTEEN

p 171   *these girls. . . have become a community*. . . Students who experience their school as a caring community are more likely to want to learn there; they find the classroom "an energizing and effective" place, according to Alfie Kohn in *The Schools Our Children Deserve* (1999). Kohn reports on the research that supports this observation, as well as evidence that such connection affects learning (p. 282). Deborah Meier's book, *The Power of Their Ideas*, makes a strong case for the relationship between community and learning.

p 172   *Women's Ways of Knowing*. . . by Belenky et al. was a significant breakthrough in thinking about female persons and their processes of acquiring knowledge. Goldberger made the remarks about their (the authors') processes in the tenth anniversary edition in 1997. In this book, the authors discuss how the school environment promotes or hinders the development of its female students.

p 172   *in a school that feels like "a caring community"*. . . See Developmental Studies Center, *At Home in Our Schools, Among Friends: Classrooms Where Caring and Learning Prevail*. See also Battistich et al. (1995, 1997).

p 178   *Tidball's "wholeness of the environment"*. . . See Tidball, Daryl G. Smith, Charles Tidball, and Lisa Wolf Wendel, *Taking Women Seriously* (Oryx, 1999), p. 140.

p 183   *At Chicago's Young Women's Leadership Charter School*. . . which I visited on October 19, 2005.

CHAPTER EIGHTEEN

p 187   *Girls this age are typically*. . . Studies from the late 1990s show that girls are critical of their own performance and lack confidence in themselves, especially in certain subjects, such as mathematics: L. Tartre and E. Fennema, "Mathematics Achievement and Gender: A Longitudinal Study of Selected Cognitive and Affective Variables

(Grades 6–12)," *Educational Studies in Mathematics* (1995): 199–217; Richard Durost, "Single-Sex Math Classes: What and For Whom? One School's Experience." *NASSP Bulletin* (February 1996): 27–31.

p 190   *Getting girls to risk. . .* There is a 2002 study that shows that girls generally lack the confidence to take academic risks: Eva Pomerantz, Ellen Altermatt, and Jill Saxon, "Making the Grade but Feeling Distressed: Gender Difference in Academic Performance and Internal Distress," *Journal of Ed Psych* 94(2): 394–404.

p 196   *French philosopher La Rochefoucauld. . .* wrote *Maxims*, published in 1665.

CHAPTER NINETEEN

p 201   *His education, too, was ongoing. . .* Maybe he's why I became a teacher. And my brothers became professional how-does-it-work guys: one using computers and chemicals and the other working with space and rockets, like Dad.

p 203   *And Barbie, at least for this generation . . . has been marketed. . .* When her reign as commodities queen is over, Barbie will be replaced by some other product of consumer culture, Bratz dolls, for example, another lure for kids' attentions and affections, some other marketed possession promising delight if parents purchase it. Unless and if we parents and these future parents and teachers of this classroom and other classrooms are wary and mindful of the meanings underneath a product like Barbie, we will repeat the messages with another messenger. See *Packaging Girlhood* by Sharon Lamb and Lyn Mikel Brown (St. Martin's, 2006) for strategies to fight the marketers.

p 203   *sociologist Juliet Schor. . .* *Born to Buy* (Scribner, 2005).

p 204   *Consumerism is a culture inimical to learning. . .* See Coleman, 1961, p. 15; Powell, 1994; Riordan, 1990.

p 205   *Girls' schools counter the materialism. . .* Educators who have noted academic advantages to single sex schooling (Coleman, Riordan, Salomone, Streitmatter, etc.) have linked the pro-academic climate in single sex schools for girls with the diminishment of materialism and youth culture values centered around teen popularity, less evident in girls' schools.

CHAPTER TWENTY

p 212   *The cumbersome and cutthroat conditions...* "Single-sex schools are politically incorrect; they are downright politically threatening to many people, and many of these people are in fact educational researchers, policymakers, and special-interest state holder groups such as the AAUW Educational Foundation. This is not a very inspiring thought, but it is important to realize that this is the nature of what we are working with." Cornelius Riordan, professor of sociology, Providence College, TYWLS consultant for Ann Rubenstein Tisch.

p 213   *The schools are small...* Other educators and observers, such as Oakland's Ilana DeBare, conclude that the size of the groups cannot be separated from who comprises the groups (only girls) and the subject matter they consider vigorously. "It's hard to separate any single part of the school's culture," writes DeBare. "But, as both the girls and the teachers attest, there is also something special about the all-girls environment and the focus on woman's achievement."

p 217   *Students at YWLCS are racially diverse and mostly poor...* The student body is 72 percent African American, 14 percent Latina, 13 percent Caucasian, and 1 percent Asian. 70 percent qualify for U.S. Department of Agriculture free lunch programs.

p 219   *Again and again...* Back in 1990, Cornelius Riordan concluded, "The first case for single-sex schooling is that it provides boys and girls more successful role models of their own sex" (p. 49). In 2002, writing in a volume on single-sex educational research, Riordan found many advantages to girls' schools, especially for "poor disadvantaged students"; successful role models was number three. See Riordan (2002), p. 19.

p 220   *This is a good ruling...* There have been fewer attempts to offer single-sex public schooling for boys. Both Milwaukee and Detroit experimented with schools essentially designed for African-American boys, but both attempts failed to survive legal challenges. Dade County in Florida tried an early elementary program for boys, but although it had good results, the county dropped it after a year. In the public sector, in most communities, there aren't any choices for families with boys, and in the private sector, the choices are diminishing.

p 221   **W. B. Yeats.** . . "I, being poor, have only my dreams." *Wind Among the Reeds* (1899).

CHAPTER TWENTY-ONE

p 229   *Seattle Girls School.* . . I visited September 16, 2005.

p 231   *Atlanta Girls School.* . . was the site I visited with our younger daughter while interviewing faculty, staff, students, and Head of School on December 6, 2005.

CHAPTER TWENTY-TWO

p 233   *Boys' schools . . . numbers have dwindled.* . . There were 961 private schools for boys in the United States in 1965; by 1978 there were 499. Both Ilana DeBare (2004) and Cornelius Riordan in *Girls and Boys in School* discuss the backstory of boys' schools. The figures are from U.S. Department of Education, National Center for Education Statistics, "Private Schools in American Education" (1976–1978).

p 233   *citadels of certitude and privilege.* . . include the Virginia Military Institute up until 1996, when the U.S. Supreme Court ruled against its all-male policy of admission, and the Citadel in South Carolina, both of which are reviewed by Rosemary Salomone (Yale University Press, 2003, cited earlier). Besides the culture that military schools embody, they are typically boarding schools, not only "bastions of male privilege and exclusion," in Rosemary Salomone's words, but bastions 24/7.

p 234   *Still, it is generally assumed.* . . Riordan's 1990 study found that white girls and minority students of both sexes were better off in single sex schools but "co-education seems to benefit white boys" (p. 79). He measured cognitive achievement, self-esteem, self-discipline, and egalitarian attitudes toward women and found for Caucasian male students that those in boys' schools fared slightly less well.

p 234   *At the end of the 1990s.* . . Riordan amended his conclusions in 1997, indicating single sex school benefits for minority (African-

American and Hispanic) girls and, to a lesser extent, all boys. "The Silent Gender Gap," *Education Week* (November 1999), pp. 46–49, was subtitled "Reading, Writing, and Other Problems for Boys."

p 234   ***Boys and girls . . . are developmentally diverse. . .*** See Sax (2005) and Salomone (2003) on developmental differences. See also *Raising Cain* by Kindler and Thompson (1999).

p 235   ***Diane Hulse, studying middle school boys. . .*** found that the school boys in her sample also felt more comfortable in their relationships with girls. The sample was small, and not all effects were great enough to be significant, but the study represented an intriguing possibility: boys' schools, unlike what they'd been just a decade before when Riordan (1990) had found them to be sexist, were new models of enlightenment regarding gender.
Diane J. Hulse writes in *Brad and Cory: A Study of Middle School Boys*, that after a review of the literature, "it is impossible to read the research and conclude that there are no academic advantages to single sex schools for both boys and girls" (University School Press, 1997), p. 37. Some positive effects in Hulse's own study concerning attitudes for boys' school students versus male coed students include being less susceptible to social pressure, less defensive, and less conflicted about school's academic demands and more interested in school, ability being equal (pp. 30, 31).

p 235   ***Five years later. . .*** Hulse wrote "A Look at Boys' Schools," published in the 2002 edition of the *Parents League Review*, New York.

p 235   ***Rosemary Salomone. . .*** (2003) quote, p. 242.

p 236   ***Eleven-year-old boys. . .*** Gilligan's *In a Different Voice* discusses sex differences in fantasies and fears: males fear intimacy, rejection, and deceit; females fear isolation and being set apart (pp. 42–45). In Riordan's (1990) book on boys and girls in school, he directs us to studies about sex differences in interactions with teachers and with each other.

p 237   ***Boys at this age don't hear. . .*** This finding that girls and boys, women and men literally hear differently explains the disparate experiences of some male coaches and girl players, male teachers and girl students, fathers and daughters: "He yelled at me," says the girl in tears. "I didn't yell!" says the man, raising his voice for emphasis. It would seem they are both correct from their different perspectives; they hear the sound at different decibel intensities. Leonard Sax wrote that a seventeen-year-old girl "is going to experience her father's voice as being more than 100 times louder in amplitude than what the father himself is experiencing" (p. 18). That's a big difference.

p 238   **At another boys' school**. . . that would be Woodberry Forest School, with Dennis Campbell as head (see *Why Single Sex?* 2004). See Riordan's discussion of sex roles in his 1990 work. See also Lockheed and Klein (1985), Hughes and Sandler (1988), and Hanes, Prawat, and Grissom (1979), cited in *Hostile Hallways* (1993).

p 238   **Studies confirm**. . . Rosemary Salomone (2003), cited earlier, see p. 242 for discussion.

p 239   **David Trower . . . cites**. . . Recently married, David Trower was startled to be asked by a young student, age six, if he had a good honeymoon night. "I think he meant Happy Tidings," Trower notes drolly. Interview, New York City, October 25, 2006.

p 240   **Can they learn**. . . Hulse's study in 1997 found, among other things, that stereotypes may actually be reinforced when boys and girls are taught together.

p 241   **Two different researchers**. . . Hulse (1997), pp. 15–16; Riordan (1990), pp. 49–50.

p 241   **The third factor**. . . Jean McCauley, my guide at A-S, described her son before he quit coed dances: a short string bean with pimples and a sensitive soul. "Mom," he told her, "a cute girl would look at me and not want to dance with me. If I ask a girl who isn't cute, the other guys would say, 'you got a dawg.'" This boy, now a handsome 6'4" college man, his mother tells me proudly, in earlier years opted to avoid dances and instead meet female debaters and scientists, with whom it was more a battle of wits than a beauty contest on either side.

AFTERWORD

p 243   **The students. . . are . . . at a beginning**. . . Graduation 2006 featured thirty-nine young women, all off to collegiate destinations from Rhode Island to Berkeley, Santa Cruz to Switzerland, with more than a million dollars in scholarships. Amazingly, in this year of failed hopes and expectations (the subject of numerous news articles and cover stories), the girls from this Archer class all got the colleges they wanted.

p 243　**Archer's student speaker.** . . . Sofi's speech fit nicely with commencement speaker and astronaut Sally Ride, who urged the girls to reach for the stars and reminded them that she, too, was a single sex graduate from an L.A. school, the former Westlake School for Girls.

p 244　**The journey . . . in lurches and stops.** . . . I once was that twelve-year-old whose parents, gone for the day, left my dad's MG in the garage, beckoning.

p 245　**Harvard professor.** . . . Eleanor Duckworth's book is actually titled *The Having of Wonderful Ideas* (Teacher's College Press, 1987).

p 247　**Cornelius Riordan . . . remarked.** . . . Riordan, 1998 conference, cited in Salomone, p. 276.

p 248　**Ibsen said it's like a ship.** . . . Henrik Ibsen, *An Enemy of the People*, Act I, trans. William Archer.

p 248　**A regional robotics competition.** . . . The games, sponsored by NASA and an organization called FIRST, are field trials in which pairs of high school teams pit their robots, student-designed-and-built, against other pairs in a timed competition.

p 249　**What the experts say.** . . . See Deborah Meier, *The Power of Their Ideas* (2002); Eleanor Duckworth, *The Having of Wonderful Ideas* (1987); Janice Streitmatter, *For Girls Only* (1999).

p 249　**Not Ideas About the Thing but the Thing Itself.** . . . Title of a poem about spring by Wallace Stevens.

APPENDIX A

p 259　**Jim Collins's.** . . . *Good to Great* (Random House, 2001).

APPENDIX B

p 264   *At Archer we were slightly ahead*. . . According to the National Coalition of Girls' Schools, at least thirty-five girls' schools have opened since 1996. We opened in 1995.

p 264   *Who we are*. . . Our founding Head of School, Arlene Hogan, shares these traits: firstborn, feminist, optimist. In addition, she is originally from Brooklyn, so she is not only an outsider but has the comic vision that seems native to that borough.

p 264   *If Diane Keaton "flipped"*. . . See *New York Times*, March 2, 2006, D1, D6, for the "flipping" of houses (buying, restoring, or remodeling and reselling soon after) by Diane Keaton, Cher, and others. Obviously the house has more "interest" if Diane or Cher has flipped it.

p 264   *Artists. . . observers by profession*. . . Marcel Proust observed, "Only through art can we get outside of ourselves and know another's view of the universe which is not the same as ours and our landscapes which would otherwise have remained unknown to us like the landscape of the moon." *The Maxims of Marcel Proust*, trans. Justin O'Brien (1984).

p 264   *Feminism and our outsider status*. . . Because we were fortunate to be adolescents and young women during a time of intense feminist activity, as Carolyn Heilbrun calls it (*Reinventing Womenhood*, 1979, p. 26), we benefited from a political climate of solidarity with those of our gender. All the earlier founders (Willard, Bethune, etc.) believed that female persons were at least academically the equals of men. In their day that was feminist enough to invite negative sanction. I don't know what sustained Emma Willard, although first her father and then her husband encouraged her, but I know she had a sister who also started a school. That must have made a difference.

p 265   *The art of seeing things*. . . Jonathan Swift, with his pointed pen, observed in 1726, "Vision is the art of seeing things invisible."

p 265   *Six founding women*. . . Plus I interviewed the founding heads and first principals of all seven SIGNS schools (small, innovative, girl-nurturing societies). That would be Marja Brandon (Seattle), Ann Clarke (Oakland), Kathleen Ponze (TWYLS, East Harlem), Margaret Small and Michelle Russell (YWLCS, Chicago), Vivian Taylor Samudio (Dallas), and Sue Thompson (Atlanta).

SIGNS schools included in my investigation were as follows: Archer, of course; Atlanta Girls' School; Irma Rangel Young Women's Leadership School; Julia Morgan School; The Young Women's Leadership School (TYWLS) of East Harlem; Seattle Girls' School; and the Young Women's Leadership Charter School (YWLCS) of Chicago. For comparison purposes, I interviewed administrators and students at the following: Allen-Stevenson School for Boys in New York City; Emma Willard School, Troy, New York; the Hockaday School, Dallas; Spence School, New York City; and Westridge School, Pasadena, California.

p 266   *I wasn't a PTA mom.* . . . Emily Ellison quoted in Miriam Longino, "School of Dreams," *Atlanta Constitution*, August 28, 2000, C1.

p 266   *I was one of two day students.* . . . Brooke Weinmann's 2000 address to St. Margaret's, http://www.sms.org/comspeak.htm.

p 266   *I have always been on the fringe.* . . . Sharon Hammel, email from Barcelona, February 10, 2006.

p 266   *An outsider in my high school.* . . . Ilana DeBare, personal communication.

p 267   *I am optimistic.* . . . Sharon Hammel, email from Barcelona, February 10, 2006.

p 267   *I just knew it was right.* . . . Ann Rubenstein Tisch, interview, Regency Hotel, New York City, October 25, 2005.

p 267   *Their optimism was rewarded.* . . . AGS ended up in Buckhead, an Atlanta neighborhood not unlike Brentwood, where there may not have been a warm welcome for their student body, 23 percent of whom are children of color. It is a land of mansions, long drives, big gates—very Tara in some instances. Yet they occupy a former school, so perhaps that helps.

p 267   *Public girls' school in Harlem.* . . . "Tumultuous" is Joe Dolce's word: See "The Power of One," *O: The Oprah Magazine*, October 2001. "Dipping into the future" is from Tennyson's "Locksley Hall."

p 268   *Joan Hall of Chicago's YWLCS*. . . Joan Hall, interview at Jenner and Block, Chicago, October 19, 2005.

p 268   *Explaining her activism*. . . Hall wouldn't be cast in the Hollywood movie as founder of a public school in a black community; neither is she typical of the other founders. She's older, born just before baby boomers, without an age-appropriate daughter sensitizing her to the need; furthermore, she's not moderately successful but highly successful—making partner at a time women just didn't. But like the others she's a feminist, an optimist, a non-pro.

p 269   *Ilana DeBare*. . . Personal communication, spring 2006.

p 270   *Ellison's droll observation*. . . appeared in Miriam Longino's "School of Dreams," *Atlanta Constitution*, August 28, 2000, C1–2.

Index

PublicAffairs is a publishing house founded in 1997. It is a tribute to the standards, values, and flair of three persons who have served as mentors to countless reporters, writers, editors, and book people of all kinds, including me.

I.F. STONE, proprietor of *I. F. Stone's Weekly*, combined a commitment to the First Amendment with entrepreneurial zeal and reporting skill and became one of the great independent journalists in American history. At the age of eighty, Izzy published *The Trial of Socrates*, which was a national bestseller. He wrote the book after he taught himself ancient Greek.

BENJAMIN C. BRADLEE was for nearly thirty years the charismatic editorial leader of *The Washington Post*. It was Ben who gave the *Post* the range and courage to pursue such historic issues as Watergate. He supported his reporters with a tenacity that made them fearless and it is no accident that so many became authors of influential, best-selling books.

ROBERT L. BERNSTEIN, the chief executive of Random House for more than a quarter century, guided one of the nation's premier publishing houses. Bob was personally responsible for many books of political dissent and argument that challenged tyranny around the globe. He is also the founder and longtime chair of Human Rights Watch, one of the most respected human rights organizations in the world.

For fifty years, the banner of PublicAffairs Press was carried by its owner Morris B. Schnapper, who published Gandhi, Nasser, Toynbee, Truman, and about 1,500 other authors. In 1983, Schnapper was described by *The Washington Post* as "a redoubtable gadfly." His legacy will endure in the books to come.

Peter Osnos, *Founder and Editor-at-Large*